—— MARKET —— MICROSTRUCTURE THEORY

For David, Megan and Casey

——MARKET—— MICROSTRUCTURE THEORY

Maureen O'Hara

BLACKWELL
Business

Copyright © Maureen O'Hara, 1995, 1997

The right of Maureen O'Hara to be identified as author of this work has been
asserted in accordance with the Copyright, Designs and Patents Act 1988.

First published 1995
Reprinted 1995, 1996 (twice)
First published in paperback 1997

Blackwell Publishers Inc
350 Main Street
Malden, Massachusetts 02148, USA

Blackwell Publishers Ltd
108 Cowley Road
Oxford OX4 1JF, UK

Library of Congress Cataloging in Publication Data
O'Hara, Maureen
Market microstructure theory/Maureen O'Hara
p. cm.
Includes bibliographical references and index.
ISBN 1–55786–443–8 — ISBN 0–631–20761–9 (pbk)
1. Securities—Mathematical models. 2. Stock-exchange—Mathematical models.
I. Title.
HD4515.2.020 1994
332.9'92—dc20
94–28078

British Library Cataloguing in Publication Data
A CIP catalogue record for this book is available from the British Library

Typeset in Bembo on 10.5pt
by ATLIS Publishing Services
Printed and bound in the United States of America

This book is printed on acid-free paper

About the Author

Maureen O'Hara is the Robert W. Purcell Professor of Finance at the Johnson Graduate School of Management at Cornell University. She holds a Ph.D. in Finance from Northwestern University. Professor O'Hara has also taught at the London Business School and the University of California at Los Angeles. She received the Young Scholar Recognition Award from the American Association of University Women in 1986. She is a director of both the American Finance Association and the Western Finance Association. Professor O'Hara is the co-editor of the *Journal of Financial Intermediation* and is an associate editor at numerous finance journals. Maureen O'Hara resides in Ithaca, NY with her husband and two children.

Contents

Foreword

This book began as the basis for a Ph.D. course in Market Microstructure that I taught at Cornell University. My motivation then, as it is now, was to provide a unified exposition and examination of the major models and theories used in market microstructure. These modeling issues are extensive, as microstructure has evolved from focusing primarily on inventory-based problems to being focused more recently on issues typically associated with information economics. The literature has now developed to the point that there are several widely used paradigms, but the generality of their results, and hence their applicability, is not well understood. Moreover, the complexity of the models requires a familiarity with rational expectations models, Bayesian learning, and game theory to appreciate their behavior. For both theorists and empirical researchers, there appeared a need for a unified treatment of market microstructure theory, whence the origins of this book.

This book analyzes the development of microstructure theory from the initial inventory models through the information-based and game-theoretic paradigms of more recent research. In this development, I explain how the main theoretical models work, the evolution of the literature to that point, the strengths and weaknesses of each approach, and the issues left unaddressed. While this involves extensive discussion of the literature, the book is not intended to be the definitive literature survey of the area. My goal is the more modest (and more achievable) one of providing a general perspective on the development and evolution of market microstructure theory.

In pursuing this goal, I have chosen to focus on the topics that I find most interesting in the field. This has the somewhat unfortunate consequence that some work (particularly my own) is emphasized, while other work is perhaps not given the attention it deserves. My focus only on theoretical work also means that some of the most provocative work in market microstructure is not included simply because it is empirical in nature. I freely acknowledge these difficulties, and hope that the sheer dimension of the field provides at least some justification for these shortcomings.

Finally, I would like to acknowledge the assistance of a number of people who generously provided me with their insights and comments on these chapters. I am particularly grateful to Peter Carr, Michael Fishman, Doug Foster, Ananth Madhavan, Craig MacKinley, Duane Seppi, Matt Spiegel, and S. Viswanathan for all their help. I would also like to thank Joe Paperman for his assistance and his careful reading of the manuscript. Part of this manuscript was completed while I was at the University of Cambridge, and I acknowledge the support of Churchill College and the Department of Applied Economics. Above all, I owe a particular debt of gratitude to David Easley. His help with virtually every step of this project is thankfully acknowledged.

M.O'H.

1

Markets and Market Making

Market microstructure is the study of the process and outcomes of exchanging assets under explicit trading rules. While much of economics abstracts from the mechanics of trading, the microstructure literature analyzes how specific trading mechanisms affect the price formation process. These mechanisms may involve a specific intermediary such as a stock specialist or an order clerk (a saitori), employ a centralized location such as an exchange or a futures pit, or be simply an electronic bulletin board in which buyers and sellers indicate an interest in trading. Whatever the specific mechanism, however, prices emerge and buyers and sellers trade.

Interest in the role of trading mechanisms has undoubtedly been spurred by the fragility of markets revealed by the market crash in 1987. And the proliferation of new markets and exchanges occurring now with remarkable speed further contributes to the appeal of the microstructure area. But underlying the study of market microstructure is a more basic curiosity: the desire to know how prices are formed in the economy. This subject, long relegated to the "black box" of economics, is fundamental to understanding how economies work to allocate goods and services.

Market microstructure research exploits the structure provided by specific trading mechanisms to model how price-setting rules evolve in markets. This provides the ability to characterize not only how different trading protocols affect price formation, but also why prices exhibit particular time-series properties. As microstructure research is set in the markets for financial assets, this enhances our ability to understand both the returns to financial assets and the process by which markets become efficient.

In the abstract, market microstructure research is valuable for illuminating the behavior of prices and markets. This has immediate application in the regulation of markets, and in the design and formulation of new trading mechanisms. An even greater payoff, however, may come from the insights

1

market microstructure theories yield for empirical research. The increased availability of detailed, and in some cases real-time, data on prices, orders, and other market information allows for empirical investigations at a level of detail never before possible. But our knowledge of economic behavior over fine time intervals is not extensive, and there is need to formulate exactly what behavior is consistent with the actions of optimizing economic agents.

This book provides such a formulation by investigating the current state of theoretical work in market microstructure. The goal of this book is not to provide an encyclopedic reference of every issue addressed in market microstructure, but rather to analyze the general paradigms used to explain market behavior. With the extensive literature emerging in this area, as well as the burgeoning use of tools and techniques from information economics, market microstructure theory may appear an amorphous collection of models, with little in common but subject matter. Underlying much of this research, however, is a shared focus on the information implicit in market data, and on the learning process that translates this information into prices. It is my hope in this book to provide a unified framework for understanding these connections, and a consequent appreciation for the insights available from existing theoretical research.

One interesting aspect of market microstructure theory is its evolution. While the early work investigated issues relating to the stochastic nature of supply and demand, later work focuses more on the information-aggregation properties of prices and markets. These two approaches have not yet been wholly merged, meaning that many interesting and important dimensions of microstructure problems have not been addressed. These general paradigms have been applied to a wide range of issues, however, and it is useful to understand what these analyses have shown.

Perhaps more important are the many questions yet to be investigated in microstructure. The evolution of financial markets has raised innumerable policy issues relating to market structure and stability. And despite extensive modeling, theoretical analyses have not as yet provided definitive results on the empirical properties and behavior that security prices should possess. Such issues will undoubtedly be the focus of research agendas over the next decade. Before these issues can be understood, the more fundamental issue of how markets work must be addressed. It is to this task that we now turn.

In the remainder of this chapter, I consider the very basic question of how prices are set in markets. I illustrate the difficulties with the traditional view of price formation and, in particular, its failure to include any role for explicit trading mechanisms. I then provide a brief discussion of the types of markets used to trade financial assets. This serves as an introduction to our analysis in subsequent chapters of the various theoretical approaches used to explain the evolution of prices in markets.

1.1 PRICES AND MARKETS

What determines a price? In the standard economics paradigm, it is the intersection of supply and demand curves for a particular good. And certainly, in equilibrium, this must be the case. But how, exactly, is this equilibrium actually attained? What is it in the economy that coordinates the desires of demanders and suppliers so that a price emerges and trade occurs? Perhaps surprisingly, economics provides few answers to this question, and therein lies the beginnings of market microstructure research.

For economists, there were two traditional approaches to the mechanics of price formation. The first was to argue for its irrelevance. Since much of economics involves the analysis of equilibrium, what mattered for many questions were the properties of equilibrium prices. These properties could be determined by simply solving for a market-clearing price; how exactly this market clearing was achieved was not of interest. Such an agnostic approach to price setting can be found, for example, in the rational expectations literature.[1] There, the questions of interest involve how traders use information in prices to determine their equilibrium demands. Behavior out of equilibrium is not considered, in part because it is difficult to reconcile ever observing such behavior, let alone characterizing what its properties might be.

Two assets of this approach are its simplicity and its generality. Implicit in this approach, however, is the assumption that the trading mechanism plays no role in affecting the resulting equilibrium; that, whatever the trading mechanism employed, the same equilibrium would arise. This assumption is particularly troubling for markets in which traders have differential information. As Radner [1979] notes: "A thorough analysis of this [equilibrium] situation probably requires a more detailed specification of the trading mechanism than is usual in general equilibrium analysis. Nevertheless, it is tempting to try to obtain results that are as independent as possible of the specifics of the trading mechanism, by using some suitable concept of equilibrium." Subsequent researchers (see Blume, Bray, and Easley [1982] for discussion) would question whether this was, in fact,

---

1. A similar view can be found in the work of Hicks [1939], for example, who argued that there were actually two types of equilibrium: a temporary one in which at a given date supply equaled demand, and equilibrium over time, in which stationarity of supply and demand would result in prices realized being the same as those expected to prevail. This latter equilibrium was deemed of more importance, but in neither framework was the issue how such market clearing obtains given consideration. For more discussion, see Radner [1982].

achievable, but this abstraction from the trading mechanism dictated an indifference to the underlying mechanisms that generate equilibrium prices.[2]

An alternative approach to the mechanics of price setting is the fiction of a Walrasian auctioneer. As generations of economists learned, the price formation process could be captured by the general representation of a Walrasian auctioneer, who aggregates traders' demands and supplies to find a market-clearing price. The actual mechanism by which this occurs begins with each trader submitting his demand, or even his demand schedule, to the auctioneer. The auctioneer announces a potential trading price, and traders then determine their optimal demands at that price. No actual trading occurs until each trader has a chance to revise his order. A new potential price is suggested, traders again revise any orders, and the process continues until there is no further revision. Equilibrium prevails where each trader submits his optimal order at the equilibrium price, and at that price the quantity supplied equals the quantity demanded.

This representation views market prices as arising from a tattonement, or a series of preliminary auctions. There is no trading allowed outside of equilibrium and incentive issues are not considered, and so there is no difficulty of traders wishing to recontract once the "true" price is known. Because the price is adjusted until there is no excess demand, the Walrasian auctioneer does not take any trading position, but serves only to redirect quantities from sellers to buyers. Moreover, this auction activity is costless, so there are no frictions in the exchange process. The equilibrium price thus emerges as the natural outcome of an unseen trading game in which buyers and sellers costlessly exchange assets.

The Walrasian auctioneer provides a simple and elegant way to envision the price-setting process. But does it, in fact, capture the actual process by which prices are formed? Is it the case that prices evolve as naturally as is posited here, or are there other factors influencing price behavior? The answers to these questions are not immediate. As we shall discuss in the next section, in the case of financial assets, there are markets that bear at least an approximate resemblance to the Walrasian framework. But there are many other markets that differ dramatically, with specific market participants playing roles far removed from the passive one of the auctioneer. Perhaps more important is the issue of trader behavior. If trading involves more than simply matching supplies and demands in

---

2. In particular, researchers would investigate whether there is any trading mechanism that could implement a rational expectations equilibrium. The negative results found in this research suggest that the "temptation" noted by Radner may not have been a wise choice. This issue is discussed further in Section 4.3.

equilibrium, then the trading mechanism may have an importance of its own.

Such concerns were raised by a number of economists, for example, Working [1953] and Houthakker [1957]. The most direct analysis of trading, however, was that of Demsetz [1968], who examined the determination of prices in securities markets. Although Demsetz's focus was on the nature of transaction costs, his analysis of how the time dimension of supply and demand affected market prices set the stage for the formal study of market microstructure.

Demsetz began with the simple observation that trade may involve some cost. This cost could be explicit, arising, for example, from charges levied by a particular market, or it could be implicit, reflecting costs connected with the immediate execution of trading. These implicit costs, referred to as the price of immediacy, arose because, unlike in the Walrasian auction, trading had a time dimension. In particular, while over time the number of sellers might equal the number of buyers, at any particular point in time such an outcome was not guaranteed. If the number of traders wishing to sell immediately did not equal the number who wished to buy immediately, the imbalance of trade would make it impossible to find a market-clearing price at a given time *t*.

Demsetz argued that this lack of equilibrium could be overcome by paying a price for immediacy. Specifically, he argued that at any point in time there are two sources of supply and demand in the market. On the demand side, there is one demand arising from traders who want to buy immediately, and another coming from traders who want to buy but do not feel the need to do so at this particular time. The supply side of the market is defined analogously. If there is an imbalance of traders wanting to buy now, then either some buyers have to wait for sellers to arrive, or they can offer a higher price to induce those waiting sellers to transact now. Similarly, if there is an imbalance of sellers wanting to trade now, a lower price must be bid to induce more demanders to trade now. This results in two prices, not one, characterizing the equilibrium.

This idea that the price could contain a cost of immediacy captured an aspect of the price process not envisioned in the Walrasian framework. Now there were actually two supply curves and two demand curves, reflecting the two time frames of the trading process. While a trader willing to wait might trade at the single price envisioned in the Walrasian framework, trades occurring immediately would not share this outcome. This meant that even the notion of an equilibrium price was problematic. The price depended on whether one wanted to buy or to sell, and not simply on the willingness to trade.

Of perhaps equal importance was the implication that the specific structure of the market could affect the trading price. Since the size of the price concession needed to trade immediately, i.e., the spread, depended on the numbers of traders, factors such as volume could affect the cost of immediacy and thus the market price. These structure issues were addressed by Demsetz, who empirically investigated the relation of the size of the spread and the volume of trade on the NYSE. His work suggested that the behavior of markets, much like the behavior of firms, could only be understood by examining their structure and organization.

If the actual mechanism used to set prices is not merely a channel to an inevitable outcome, but rather is an input into the equilibrium price itself, then how such mechanisms work cannot be ignored. The Demsetz model analyzes the behavior of one simple trading mechanism, but its analysis is clearly limited. Actual mechanisms are far more complicated than that in this one-period model. Indeed, the list of features not included in the Demsetz analysis is seemingly endless. Equally important, however, are the interactions between the market mechanism and trader behavior. If the trading mechanism matters in setting prices, then so too will it matter in affecting traders' order decisions. Consequently, the exogeneity of the order process to the price-setting mechanism is unlikely to hold. The question of how prices are set thus takes on a complexity far removed from the simplicity of the Walrasian auctioneer.

In the remainder of this book, we examine how trading mechanisms affect the formation of prices. While all theoretical work involves some degree of abstraction from detail, microstructure research remains partially grounded by the features of actual market design. Consequently, at least a broad understanding of security market design is a prerequisite for the study of market microstructure. In the next section, we consider some general features of exchange markets and the alternative ways that price-setting rules are structured in actual markets. Our discussion will, by necessity, be incomplete; there are myriad ways markets are currently structured, and new market-clearing mechanisms are arising with surprising frequency. But many markets share common features, and it is these commonalties that we explore in subsequent chapters.

1.2 THE NATURE OF MARKETS

The process of exchange occurs in many ways. Buyers and sellers can contact each other directly. Traders can gather at a central setting or communicate through a computer screen. A single intermediary can arrange every trade, or there can be numerous individuals who meet to set prices. Whatever the setting, however, there are rules either explicit or implicit that govern the trading mechanism, and it is these rules that result in the formation and evolution of market prices.

As we discussed earlier, one simple set of rules could involve a sequential auction like that implicitly used by the Walrasian auctioneer. And, indeed, such a market approximates the London gold fixing.[3] There, every morning at approximately 10:30 representatives from each of the five London Bullion houses meet in the offices of N. M. Rothschild to determine the spot market price for gold. The fixing begins by the chairman of the session suggesting an opening price.[4] The representatives then indicate whether their firm is a net buyer or a net seller at that price. The chairman announces a new price, and net buying and selling is again determined. This process continues until a price is established at which net buying and selling are equal, and each representative has indicated his approval by lowering a small British flag on his desk. That price is the morning London gold fix. A similar process is repeated in the afternoon to establish the afternoon gold fixing.

This market captures the spirit of the Walrasian auction in that the market-clearing price is determined through a sequential process and no trades occur out of equilibrium. Unlike the Walrasian process, however, the actual quantity of gold trading at the equilibrium price is unknown. Because dealers only communicate their net positions, the total amount traded can be virtually any amount.[5] Consequently, while the gold fixing provides a price, it lacks at least one of the attributes (physical trading) that one might expect to find in a market. Nonetheless, by iterating from net supplies and demands to prices, the participants at the gold fixing establish a spot price for gold.

While this process determines a market price, it does so at some cost. The actual process takes place in one locale, there are a limited number of buyers and sellers actually determining the price, and it is time consuming. Only two prices are produced per day, so that intraday prices may be stale due to changes in events. Compared with a market such as foreign exchange (FX), where price quotes from a dozen or more dealers are outstanding at all times, the gold market appears archaic and inefficient. But the gold fixing and the FX market both produce market-clearing prices, and despite their differences they, like all trading mechanisms, share common features.

---

3. This description of the London gold market is drawn from O'Callaghan [1993].

4. The price is established for the sale of at least 2,000 ounces of gold in London deliverable in bars of 400 ounces.

5. O'Callaghan notes that while exact trading volume is not available, most of the London market's 100 to 200 tons of daily volume is believed to trade at the London fix. There are, however, many other larger markets in which gold trades, the most notable being Zurich, New York, and Hong Kong.

Any trading mechanism can be viewed as a type of trading game in which players meet (perhaps not physically) at some venue and act according to some rules. The players may involve a wide range of market participants, although not all types of players are found in every mechanism. First, of course, are customers who submit orders to buy or sell. These orders may be contingent on various outcomes, or they may be direct orders to transact immediately. The exact nature of these orders may depend upon the rules of the game. Second, there are brokers who transmit orders for customers. Brokers do not trade for their own account, but act merely as conduits for customer orders. These customers may be retail traders, or they may be other market participants such as dealers who simply wish to disguise their trading intentions. Third, there are dealers who do trade for their own account. In some markets, dealers also facilitate customer orders and so are often known as broker/dealers. Fourth, there are specialists, or market makers. The market maker quotes prices to buy or sell the asset. Since the market maker generally takes a position in the security (if only for a short time while waiting for an offsetting order to arrive), the market maker also has a dealer function. The extent, however, to which the market maker acts as a dealer can vary dramatically between markets.

These four categories include the main market participants, but they are by no means exhaustive. There are intermediaries such as block traders, who combine the brokerage and dealer functions with a broader search role. There are scalpers in futures markets who approximate the dealer role but hold no long-run market positions. The saitori, or order clerk, in Tokyo clears the market, but does so by matching orders rather than actively trading on his own account. The banks operating in the foreign markets may act as dealers for their customers, but as customers in the interdealer market. But while different markets have different specific players, their underlying functions can generally be described by the four groupings given above.

Where trading occurs is the second dimension of our trading mechanism. Traditionally, the most common setting is the exchange, which is simply a central location for trading. Orders are sent to the exchange, and all trade execution occurs there. Exchanges are used to trade equities in New York, Madrid, and Tokyo, futures in Chicago and Osaka, and options in San Francisco and Frankfurt. Such a central physical location, however, is clearly not necessary for trading to occur. Bonds trade primarily by computer screen and telephone, as does foreign exchange. Computerized trading networks such as Instinet and POSIT trade equities for institutional traders in the US, while Globex is struggling to establish computerized trading for futures. Indeed, the newly established Arizona Stock Exchange is nothing more than a computer network (which originally was not even based in Arizona!).

The proliferation of trading venues means that virtually any place can be a trading mechanism. What determines the operation of the market is thus not its location, but rather the rules by which trades occur. These rules, the third dimension of our trading game, dictate what can be traded, who can trade, when and how orders can be submitted, who may see or handle the orders, how orders are processed, and how prices are set. The rules may apply to every order submitted (such as the NYSE rule that all trades must execute on the floor of the exchange), or there may be differential rules governing various aspects of trading (such as the practice in London of clearing small volume stocks differently from large volume stocks). In any case, however, the rules determine how the mechanism works, and thus how the outcome of the trading game is decided.

Because each mechanism has its own distinctive set of rules, it is neither easy nor useful to describe how each trading mechanism works. But it is possible to discuss the operation of a specific mechanism, and detail, at least in principle, how mechanisms of that type actually work. The research in market microstructure has often focused on the behavior of the New York Stock Exchange, and so this seems a natural candidate to consider.

The NYSE currently trades equities for approximately 2,089 listed firms, with daily trading volume in 1992 averaging just over 202 million shares.[6] Equity trading is centered on the stock specialist, who is assigned particular stocks in which to make a market. While each listed security has a single specialist, the approximately 400 specialists may be assigned multiple stocks. Current exchange protocols assign stocks to specialists based on specialist performance and on the expected trading volume of the specific security. Lindsay and Schaede [1990] report that specialists handled an average of 3.7 stocks.

All trading on the exchange must go through the specialist, although the specialist may not be a participant in every trade. Estimates of the specialist's participation as either a buyer or seller in 1992 averaged around 19.4 percent of trades, with the specialist's role generally greater for less frequently traded stocks. In addition to all market orders (orders for immediate execution), the specialist also receives all public limit orders (orders that are contingent on price, time, etc.), and these orders are kept in the specialist's book. On the NYSE, the book is not common knowledge,

---

6. The data used throughout this discussion is drawn from the *New York Stock Exchange Fact Book* [1992]. It should also be noted that the New York Stock Exchange also trades a small number of bonds and, through the New York Futures Exchange, a range of futures contracts. Our discussion here considers only the equity trading mechanism.

although it is often available to traders to view at the discretion of the specialist.

Trading occurs from 9:30 a.m. to 4:00 p.m. (Eastern Standard Time) Mondays to Fridays, with the exception of designated holidays. Trading on the NYSE actually involves two different trading mechanisms, with a call auction used to open trading and a continuous auction used throughout the trading day.[7] In a call auction, orders accumulate and the specialist sets a single market-clearing price at which all executed orders transact. In a continuous auction, the specialist quotes bid and ask prices (i.e., the price at which he or she will buy the stock and the price at which he or she will sell), and trades occur individually.

The opening call is an important feature of the NYSE mechanism. Prior to the call auction, market-on-open orders and limit orders accumulate. The Opening Automated Report Service (OARS) receives all market orders up to 30,099 shares and matches the buy and sell orders. The specialist then knows the market order imbalance as well as the limit orders at every price, and he or she endeavors to set a single market-clearing price. At this price, the specialist may take a position for her own account, or she may rely entirely on the existing limit orders to offset any market order imbalance. One goal of the specialist is price continuity; large jumps from the previous day's closing price are to be avoided if at all possible.

On occasion, the imbalance in orders at the open may make it impossible to open the market without a large price movement. In this case, the specialist may delay the open and attempt to induce more liquidity by announcing a provisional opening price. In general, the specialist is not permitted to solicit orders but must instead use prices to influence order arrivals. Once a price is determined, the stock is opened with an initial trade of all relevant orders at the opening price.

Following the open, trading reverts to a continuous-auction mechanism. The specialist quotes bid and ask prices to buy and sell the stock up to some particular trade size, known as the depth. The specialist may not preempt a standing limit order, and so the actual quote may include orders on the book rather than the specialist's actual trading price.[8] There is some debate regarding the degree to which the specialist actually changes his quotes to

---

7. For infrequently traded stocks, the call auction might not be employed.

8. Limit orders are submitted contingent on a specific price. For a limit sell order, this price is above the current ask, and conversely it is below the current bid for a limit buy. Since there may be multiple orders submitted at a price, there must be rules for assigning priority of execution. On the NYSE, priority is assigned by price, quantity, and time. There are also other types of contingent orders in the market, and they, too, have priority over the market maker in execution. These issues are considered in more detail in Chapters 6 and 7.

reveal the "hidden" limit orders (see McInish and Wood [1991]), but in principle, at least, the quote should reflect the current trading prices.

Orders arrive at the specialist's post directly via floor traders and electronically via the Designated Order Turnaround System (part of the SuperDot system). Market orders of up to 2,099 shares and limit orders up to 99,999 shares may be sent by NYSE members to the specialist. Program trades are also submitted via the SuperDot system, and these orders currently account for approximately 11.5 percent of all orders. Orders also arrive via the Intermarket Trading System (ITS), which links nine US markets (the NYSE, the American Stock Exchange, Boston, Midwest, Cincinnati, Pacific, Philadelphia, the Chicago Board Options Exchange, and the NASD).

The specialist must clear any submitted orders at his outstanding quotes, but is free to change his quotes or depths at any time. A goal of the trading mechanism is price stability and continuity, and so the specialist is expected to move prices in minimal increments. The specific rules for price continuity are complex and vary depending upon the underlying stock's price and trading volume. For 1992, 96.4 percent of all transactions occurred with a price change of 1/8 or less. The specialist is also expected to stabilize the market, meaning that he should not contribute to market movements. This would preclude, for example, the specialist selling into a falling market.

Following the market crash of 1987, the NYSE instituted limit moves for prices, more commonly known as "circuit breakers." These rules are designed to restrict the behavior of the trading mechanism in periods of great market movement. When the Dow Jones Industrial Average declines 250 points from the previous day's close, all trading in stocks is halted for one hour. When the decline totals 400 points, all trading is halted for two hours. These procedures have never actually been used. Of more importance has been Rule 80A, which restricts index arbitrage (or program trading). When the Dow Jones Industrial Average declines 50 points from the previous close, index arbitrage-related sell orders can only be executed on a plus (or zero) tick, meaning that orders that would depress the market price further are not allowed; buy orders can only be executed on a minus (or zero) tick. For individual stocks, firm-specific events may also create difficulty in finding a fair market price, and a trading halt in that stock may be imposed. Trading is generally resumed once new information about the firm has been publicly released.

The rules of the NYSE define one mechanism for the trading of financial assets. It is, however, only one of many mechanisms used for trading securities, and, indeed, for trading equities. In Tokyo, for example, there are no specialists; instead, intermediaries known as saitori, or order clerks, handle the price-setting process.[9] These clerks match submitted orders and report the resulting transaction to the Exchange, but take no position themselves. Hence, unlike the specialist, who will trade to smooth out order imbalances, the saitori establishes a price only from the orders of other market participants. When, as may be the case, large imbalances arise, the saitori lowers or raises the prices until either new orders enter the market or the price movement reaches the market's preestablished limit.

As with the NYSE mechanism, the rules of the Tokyo Stock Exchange provide a mechanism for determining the trading price of an asset. So, too, do the rules of the London Stock Exchange, the Paris Bourse, and the Bolsa in Mexico City. Yet, while it is straightforward to write down the rules governing a trading mechanism, it is less apparent how it determines the equilibrium behavior of prices. The difficulty is that markets are influenced by myriad factors such as risk aversion, private information, and wealth constraints, all of which affect the buying and selling behavior of traders and market makers. As we will investigate in the remainder of this book, this devolves an importance to the structure of trading and of markets, and to the process by which prices are formed.

In the next chapter, we begin our study by examining the initial models in market microstructure. These models view the trading process as a matching problem in which the market maker must use prices to balance supply and demand across time. In this approach, a key factor is the market maker's inventory position. An alternative approach, which we investigate in later chapters, views the trading process as a game involving traders with asymmetric information regarding the asset's true value. Central to this approach is the learning problem confronting market participants. These inventory-based and information-based paradigms provide the general theoretical frameworks used in market microstructure theory, and it is to their derivation and application that we now turn.

---

9 This description of the Tokyo Stock Exchange is drawn from Lindsay and Schaede [1990], who provide an interesting description of the operations and differences of the Tokyo and New York markets.

2

Inventory Models

In traditional research on securities markets, securities prices were typically viewed as macroeconomic phenomena. This focus changed with the work of Demsetz, whose depiction of the nature of bid and ask prices focused attention on the underlying microfoundations of security markets. Viewing the behavior of securities prices from this microeconomic perspective provided a means of characterizing security price behavior as arising from optimizing behavior by economic agents. This, in turn, had two important benefits. First, since prices are typically set by a specific person or mechanism, the study of price formation becomes the study of the behavior of this individual or institution. The standard approximation of Walrasian equilibrium and its attendant lack of an explanation of how equilibrium prices actually arise can be discarded. Second, this microfocus permitted market behavior to be viewed as the aggregation of individual trader behavior, with the consequent ability to predict how prices would change given changes in those underlying decision problems.

In this chapter, we examine the initial theoretical analyses of the security market microstructure. Beginning with an important paper by Garman [1976], researchers focused on understanding how market prices arise given the nature of the order flow and the market-clearing protocol. In analyzing this problem, there are three distinct research paradigms that emerged in the literature. The first, beginning with Garman, focuses on the nature of order flow in determining security trading prices. The second approach, typified by the work of Stoll and Ho and Stoll, investigates explicitly the dealer's optimization problem. The third area, including work by Cohen, Maier, Schwartz, and Whitcomb, analyzes the effects of multiple providers of liquidity. Central to each of these approaches are the uncertainties in the order flow, which can result in inventory problems for the specialist or dealers and execution problems for the trader.

13

In this chapter, we discuss these general approaches and examine how the market maker deals with price and inventory uncertainty. Our focus is on ascertaining how market prices are set by specific price-setting agents in various market settings, and how these prices change as we introduce different types of uncertainty. As will be apparent, the market spread and the evolution of market prices can be explained in a variety of ways, with the result that a number of interesting properties can be predicted by these inventory-based approaches.

What may also be apparent, however, is that some of these approaches ultimately proved unproductive; they have been supplanted by other approaches and paradigms (which are investigated in later chapters of this book). Such is the nature of research, and understanding why this occurs and what contributes to a model's viability and longevity enhances our ability to build better and more useful models of microstructure phenomena. We begin by considering how a risk neutral market maker deals with the complex uncertainty introduced by stochastic supply and demand.

2.1 ORDER ARRIVAL AND MARKET MAKING

The equilibrium price is the price at which quantity demanded equals quantity supplied. Predicting that this price will prevail in the market has proven to be a useful first approximation to market outcomes. But a closer examination of trading in securities markets raises questions as to how to apply this paradigm as well as to its value in predicting the fine behavior of securities prices. For example, if buyers and sellers arrive at different points in time, to what time period do the supply and demand schedules refer? Similarly, if orders to buy or sell are not always balanced in the selected time period, how does the price change to reflect the order flow? Further, can a market-clearing mechanism survive in the long run given that short-run imbalances can arise between supply and demand?

These issues were the focus of research by Garman [1976]. Garman argued that an exchange market could be characterized by a flow of orders to buy and sell. These orders would arise as the solution to individual traders' underlying optimization problems, but the explicit characterization of such problems was not necessarily important. What mattered was that orders would be submitted to the market and imbalances between supply and demand could temporally arise. This imbalance gave an importance to the "temporal microstructure," or how the exchange between buyer and seller actually occurred at any point in time. Garman's focus on these intertemporal issues thus inaugurated the explicit study of market microstructure.

Treating supply and demand as stochastic processes allowed the exchange process to be viewed from a different perspective. While previous researchers (such as Demsetz) had noted the importance of trade imbalances, the focus on the trading desires of individual traders limited their ability to characterize how the market, as an entity, worked to resolve this clearing problem. Viewing the order flow in isolation made the exchange process appear more similar to stochastic matching problems found in inventory applications and in insurance markets. This perspective also provided a way to analyze the interaction between the specific market clearing mechanism (or price setter) and the behavior of the order flow. In particular, if the stochastic processes governing orders (i.e., the order arrival rates) were affected by the price prevailing in the market, then the optimal pricing mechanism must incorporate this relation. Moreover, since order imbalances were certain to occur, how the exchange mechanism operated would affect the provision of intertemporal liquidity. Such liquidity considerations are the focus of much subsequent work, and they are treated in more detail later in this chapter and in Chapter 8.

To examine these exchange issues, Garman considered two market-clearing frameworks, a dealer structure and a double auction mechanism. The double auction approach was a natural construct given the extensive research in auction theory, but its abstraction from explicit market characteristics was a drawback for studying specific market settings.[1] The dealer approach would prove more characteristic of the mechanism found in organized securities markets, and so we will concern ourselves with this specification.

In Garman's model, there is a single, monopolistic market maker who sets prices, receives all orders, and clears trades. The dealer's objective is to maximize expected profit per unit of time, subject to the avoidance of bankruptcy or failure. Failure arises in this model whenever the dealer runs out of either inventory or cash. The market maker's only decision is to set an ask price, p_a, at which he will fill orders wishing to buy the stock, and a bid price, p_b, at which he will fill orders wishing to sell the stock.[2] Orders are assumed to be for one unit of the stock. The dealer has an infinite horizon, but only selects bid and ask prices once, at the beginning of time.

---

1. The double auction approach views the market as a purely matching process. Other researchers also investigated such matching behavior, most notably Mendelson [1982].

2. This notation differs from that in Garman's paper: he denotes his ask price as p_b and his bid price as p_s. While certainly a reasonable way to define prices, this is confusing given the convention followed by subsequent researchers of denoting bids and asks differently. For clarity, I adopt the more standard approach.

The uncertainty in the model arises from the arrival of the buy and sell orders. These orders are represented as independent stochastic processes, where the arrivals of buy and sell orders are assumed to be Poisson distributed, with stationary arrival rate functions $\lambda_a(p)$ and $\lambda_b(p)$. Buy (or sell) orders follow a Poisson process if the waiting time between arrivals of buy (sell) orders is exponentially distributed. More formally, letting t be the time of the last buy order, the probability of a buy order arriving in the interval $[t, t + \Delta t]$ is approximately $\lambda_a \Delta t$ for small Δt. Representing orders as Poisson processes allows Garman to capture the randomness of the order arrival over time in a tractable manner.

With buy and sell orders following independent stochastic processes, the flow of buys and sells to the dealer will not be synchronous. It is this potential imbalance that is the crux of the dealer's problem. Since the order arrival processes are stationary but not identical, balancing his level of inventory and cash to avoid running out of either (and therefore failing) is not a trivial problem for the market maker. This is compounded by the assumption that the market maker is unable to change prices "midstream" to avoid imminent failure (an assumption both restrictive and unrealistic). In this model, therefore, the main problem for the dealer is simply "staying alive."

Garman's model involves several rather stylized assumptions. The market maker is not permitted to borrow either stock or money, dictating that his position at any point in time is completely determined by the order arrival rates. The level of demand associated with these order processes is also assumed exogenous to the market maker. Indeed, all market parameters except the order arrival rates are exogenous to the market marker.

These assumptions are not innocuous. While some restrictions can be justified as applying if not to all markets then to some, others, in particular the inability to borrow, are much less benign. The assumption of the exact structure of the order arrival processes is particularly restrictive. As Garman notes, Poisson order arrival rates essentially require that (1) there are a large number of agents in the market; (2) each agent acts independently in submitting her order; (3) no agent can generate an infinite number of orders in a finite period; and (4) no subset of agents can dominate order generation. This latter restriction would rule out, for example, any orders submitted by traders acting on private information, or any synchronized order strategies (such as portfolio insurance) that are followed by a subset of agents. What is required here is that the order flow be stochastic without being informative about future market or price movements. This is the general view taken in virtually all inventory-based microstructure models.

At time 0, the market maker is assumed to hold $I_c(0)$ units of cash and $I_s(0)$ units of stock. Let $I_c(t)$ and $I_s(t)$ be the units of cash and stock at time t.

Let $N_a(t)$ be the cumulative numbers of shares that have sold to traders up to time t (these are the executed buy orders), and let $N_b(t)$ be the cumulative number of shares that have been bought from traders as of time t (these are the executed sell orders). Then inventories are governed by

$$I_c(t) = I_c(0) + p_a N_a(t) - p_b N_b(t) \tag{2.1}$$

and

$$I_s(t) = I_s(0) + N_b(t) - N_a(t). \tag{2.2}$$

Characterizing the behavior of these inventory processes is not easy, as they each depend on the behavior of the underlying (separate) buy and sell order arrival processes. In general, we would like to know when these processes violate the bankruptcy bounds since this, in turn, would give us the expected time to failure. Similar problems involving the probability of "ruin" are the focus of extensive research in the insurance (and gambling) literatures. Unfortunately, calculating such a probability directly is intractable because of the multiple stochastic processes.

Garman argues, however, that we can approximate the market maker's position by analyzing how he changes his holdings of stock and cash over time. In particular, suppose we define the variable $Q_k(t)$ to be the probability that $I_c(t) = k$ and the variable $R_k(t)$ to be the corresponding probability that $I_s(t) = k$. Essentially, $Q_k(t)$ is just the probability that at time t the market maker has exactly k units of cash (or for $R_k(t)$, of stock). Now consider how this position could have arisen. In the case of stock, the market maker could have exactly k units at time t because:

1. the market maker held exactly $k - 1$ units of stock at time $t - \Delta t$ and in the next instant an order to sell one unit to him arrives; or
2. the market maker held exactly $k + 1$ units of stock at time $t - \Delta t$ and in the next instant an order to buy one unit from him arrives; or
3. the market maker is holding k units at time $t - \Delta t$ and in the next instant nothing happens.

It might also seem that the market maker could have exactly k units of stock at time t because at time $t - \Delta t$ he or she held some arbitrary position $k - z$ and over the next interval z units arrive (where z exceeds one, the minimum order arrival size). The assumption of a Poisson process, however, dictates that as Δt goes to 0, the probability of a jump greater than the smallest amount goes to zero even faster. It follows that the probability of being at exactly k units of stock or of cash at time t can then be decomposed into the three positions given above.

Suppose we now calculate the probability that the market maker has exactly k units of cash at time t. To determine this probability, Garman assumes that a unit of cash (say a dollar) arrives with rate $\lambda_a p_a$ and departs at rate $\lambda_b p_b$. Intuitively, this corresponds to a cash inflow resulting from the arrival of an order to buy stock from the dealer at price p_a, and conversely for the cash outflow. Using the three positions framework developed above, note that:

1. the probability the dealer had $k - 1$ units of cash and in the interval $t - \Delta t$ receives a cash inflow is $Q_{k-1}(t - \Delta t)[\lambda_a(p_a)p_a \, \Delta t][1 - \lambda_b(p_b)p_b \, \Delta t]$.

2. the probability the dealer had $k + 1$ units of cash and in the interval $t - \Delta t$ has a cash outflow is $Q_{k+1}(t - \Delta t)[\lambda_b(p_b)p_b \, \Delta t][1 - \lambda_a(p_a)p_a \, \Delta t]$.

3. the probability that the dealer is holding k units at of cash time $t - \Delta t$ and in the next instant nothing happens is $Q_k(t - \Delta t)[1 - \lambda_a(p_a)p_a \, \Delta t][1 - \lambda_b(p_b)p_b \Delta t]$.

The probability that the dealer has exactly k units of cash at time t is the sum of these probabilities, or

$$
\begin{aligned}
Q_k(t) = \; & Q_{k-1}(t - \Delta t)[\lambda_a(p_a)p_a \, \Delta t][1 - \lambda_b(p_b)p_b \, \Delta t] \\
& + Q_{k+1}(t - \Delta t)[\lambda_b(p_b)p_b \, \Delta t][1 - \lambda_a(p_a)p_a \, \Delta t] \quad (2.3) \\
& + Q_k(t - \Delta t)[1 - \lambda_a(p_a)p_a \, \Delta t][1 - \lambda_b(p_b)p_b \, \Delta t].
\end{aligned}
$$

To calculate the time derivative of the probability $Q_k(t)$, we take the limit as $\Delta t \to 0$ of $[Q_k(t) - Q_k(t - \Delta t)]/\Delta t$. This yields

$$
\begin{aligned}
\frac{\partial Q_k(t)}{\partial t} = \; & Q_{k-1}(t)[\lambda_a(p_a)p_a] + Q_{k+1}(t)[\lambda_b(p_b)p_b] \\
& - Q_k(t)[\lambda_a(p_a)p_a + \lambda_b(p_b)p_b].
\end{aligned} \quad (2.4)
$$

This differential equation (2.4) gives the dynamics of the market maker's cash position. As the orders arrive throughout the day, this cash position changes, and it is this dynamic movement that is important for the dealer. Since he cannot augment his cash (or, for that matter, his stock) except through trading, the question of interest is whether the market maker can avoid running his cash position to zero, and thus failing. Using equation (2.4), we can now address this issue.

2.1.1 The Gambler's Ruin Problem

Before proceeding to the solution for the market maker's failure probabilities, it is useful to consider how such problems are solved in general. In a typical gambler's ruin problem, the gambler is assumed to start with some initial wealth and wagers until either he reaches a certain threshold level or loses all his money. The failure probability is then calculated as a function of the odds of winning, the odds of losing, the threshold level, and the initial wealth. The market maker context considered here differs slightly, because there is no positive stopping point or threshold level; the market maker's maximum gain can be unbounded, and she stops only when she loses her cash (or stock). In this unbounded case, provided the odds of winning exceed the odds of losing, the ultimate failure probability can typically be expressed as

$$\left(\frac{\text{odds of losing} \; \times \; \text{amount of loss}}{\text{odds of winning} \; \times \; \text{amount of gain}} \right)^{\text{initial wealth position}} \tag{2.5}$$

If, on the other hand, the odds of losing exceed the odds of winning, then it is easy to show that this probability is one. In either case, the gambler faces a positive probability of ruin. But to the extent the gambler's initial stake is high or the odds of losing are small relative to the odds of winning, the gambler can expect to last longer.

To show why this is true, consider the following simple gamble involving units of stock. Suppose that a dealer "gains" a unit of stock (i.e., someone sells to the dealer) with probability p and loses a unit of stock (someone buys from him) with probability q, where $p > q$. If the dealer initially starts with S_0 units of stock, what is the probability that he runs out of stock (fails) at time t? Denote the probability of failing at time t given that the dealer currently has S units as $\Pr\{F|S\}$. Then, in the next transaction, there is a q chance that someone will take one unit away, leaving him with $S - 1$ units, while there is a p chance he will get a unit of stock, leaving him with $S + 1$ units. This implies that

$$\Pr\{F|S\} = q \Pr\{F|S - 1\} + p \Pr\{F|S + 1\}. \tag{2.6}$$

The solution to this difference equation yields the general expected failure probability

$$\Pr\{F|S_0\} = \left(\frac{q}{p} \right)^{S_0}, \tag{2.7}$$

which has the same general form as equation (2.5). Notice also that the difference equation in (2.6) is essentially the same as that derived in equation (2.4).

2.1.2 The Market Maker's Ruin Problem

In the continuous time context considered here, Garman shows that solving equation (2.4) for the approximate failure probability from running out of cash yields

$$\lim_{t \to \infty} Q_0(t) \approx \left(\frac{\lambda_b(p_b) \, p_b}{\lambda_a(p_a) \, p_a} \right)^{I_c(0)/\bar{p}} \quad \text{if } \lambda_a(p_a) \, p_a > \lambda_b(p_b) \, p_b,$$

$$= 1 \qquad\qquad \text{otherwise.} \tag{2.8}$$

where $\bar{p}$ is defined to be the average price (calculated as the mean of the bid and ask prices). The corresponding stock failure probability is given by

$$\lim_{t \to \infty} R_0(t) \approx \left(\frac{\lambda_a(p_a)}{\lambda_b(p_b)} \right)^{I_s(0)} \quad \text{if } \lambda_a(p_a) < \lambda_b(p_b),$$

$$= 1 \qquad\qquad \text{otherwise.} \tag{2.9}$$

Since $\lambda_a(p_a)$ is simply the probability of stock going out, $\lambda_b(p_b)$ is the probability of stock in, and $I_s(0)$ is our initial stock holdings, equation (2.9) is essentially the same failure probability as we derived for our example in equation (2.7). The cash failure probability is not as straightforward, however, as the bid and ask prices affect cash unequally. While equation (2.8) is essentially cash out over cash in, the initial cash level in the exponent must be normalized to account for the size of the "gamble" (i.e., the amount of the inflow or outflow). To solve the difference equation, Garman approximates the cash flow effect by scaling by some $\bar{p}$, where $\bar{p}$ is a price between the bid and the ask.[3]

---

3. Note that this transformation is not exact because there is a units problem in converting cash flow. In this approximation, $\bar{p}$ essentially scales the average cash flow effect. To see how this matters, return to our simplified example but let qp_b be cash out, and πp_a be cash in. Then, for equation (2.8) to be correct, there must be a $\bar{p}$ that solves the difference equation

$$\left(\frac{qp_b}{\pi p_a} \right)^{w/p} = q \left(\frac{qp_b}{\pi p_a} \right)^{(w - p_b)/p} + \pi \left(\frac{qp_b}{\pi p_a} \right)^{(w + p_a)/p}$$

While such a $\bar{p}$ may exist, the resulting solution only approximates the market maker's failure probability.

In this framework, as in more standard ruin problems, the dealer's failure probabilities are always positive. Consequently, no matter what price the dealer sets, there is no way to guarantee that he or she will not fail. Of perhaps more interest is that under certain conditions the dealer fails with probability one. Equations (2.8) and (2.9) imply that to avoid certain failure the market maker must set p_a and p_b so that they simultaneously satisfy

$$p_a \lambda_a (p_a) > p_b \lambda_b (p_b) \tag{2.10}$$

and

$$\lambda_b (p_b) > \lambda_a (p_a), \tag{2.11}$$

provided this is possible.

These conditions dictate that a single market maker set a lower price when he buys stock and a higher price when he sells. This results in a spread developing, and it implies the spread is an inherent property of this exchange market structure. This spread protects the market maker from certain failure, but it is not a panacea: he or she still faces a positive probability of failure.

What determines the size and placement of this spread is not immediately obvious. Since both the market maker's inventory and cash positions will have positive drift, characterizing price behavior or the market maker's inventory position is complex. To investigate the problem further requires limiting the scope of the uncertainty. Garman first simplifies the problem by assuming that the dealer pursues a zero-drift inventory policy. Given this assumption, the dealer's pricing strategy has some interesting properties. First, by assumption, the dealer sets prices to equate the order arrival rates. There are multiple pricing strategies that satisfy this condition, however; so where the dealer sets his prices depends on factors other than inventory. Given the dealer's objective, the exact prices he sets are those which maximize the dealer's expected profit.

These market-clearing prices are depicted in Figure 2.1. An important property of these prices is that the dealer does not set a single market-clearing price p^* but rather sets different buying and selling prices p_a and p_b, respectively. This allows the dealer to extract larger rents while still maintaining the zero-drift inventory requirement. As is typically optimal for a monopolist, this pricing strategy results in volume at the optimal prices being less than would occur with competitive prices.

This pricing strategy is reminiscent of that suggested by Demsetz. Where the analyses differ is that the Demsetz model did not incorporate the intertemporal nature of the dealer's problem; nor, for that matter, did it include a dealer. To address the dealer's intertemporal inventory problem, Garman considers a second simplification in which the profit maximization assumption is relaxed. Here, the dealer is assumed to set a single market-clearing price, p^*. With the dealer's pricing strategy specified, the effect of inventory on the dealer can be isolated.

From our earlier discussion of failure probabilities, it should not be surprising that pursuing this simple pricing strategy results in the dealer failing with certainty. One way to characterize the underlying difficulty is that the market maker fails if he or she runs out of inventory or runs out of cash. Since inventories follow a random walk, sooner or later a sequence of trades will force either his stock position or his cash position to their boundary. When this happens, the process meets an "absorbing barrier" and failure occurs.

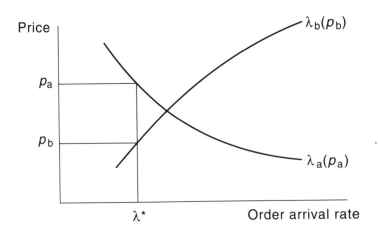

The λ functions depict the order arrival rates corresponding to orders to sell to the market maker (λ_b) and orders to buy from the market maker (λ_a). The market maker buys stocks at p_b and sells stock at p_a.

Figure 2.1   The Market Maker's Optimal Prices

Garman's characterization of the market-making process is thus simplistic but provocative. While the behavior of prices and inventories in this model is too mechanistic to be realistic, the demonstration of the dual complexity the dealer faces and its implications for market viability is insightful. This model provided an impetus for future research by demonstrating how, even with the simplest supply and demand specification, the actual price-setting problem faced by the dealer was quite complex. Equally important, the model demonstrated a frailty to the "exchange" process not suggested by previous work. One paradoxical aspect of this analysis is the role of inventory. As Garman's analysis demonstrates, inventory determines the dealer's viability. Yet in Garman's model, inventory per se plays *no* role in the dealers' decision problem since by assumption the dealer is allowed to set prices only at the beginning of trading. This restriction severely limits the applicability of this model to actual market settings in which prices continually evolve, and so the model's influence lies largely in its initial contribution.

A more realistic approach to the underlying problem is to consider how the dealer's prices change as his inventory position varies over time. This is the approach taken by Amihud and Mendelson [1980], who reformulate Garman's analysis to explicitly incorporate inventory into the dealer's pricing problem. Using essentially the same framework as Garman, Amihud and Mendelson show that the dealer's position can be viewed as a semi-Markov process in which the inventory is the state variable. The dealer's decision variables, again his bid and ask prices, depend on the level of the state variable and thus change over time depending on the level of the dealer's inventory position.

An important assumption in this analysis is that the inventory is bounded above and below by some exogenous parameters. This removes the possibility that the dealer can "run out" of inventory and so removes the failure considerations fundamental to Garman's analysis. Since the dealer need not worry about bankruptcy, his pricing policies are considerably simplified. This allows Amihud and Mendelson to characterize in more detail the link between the dealer's inventory and his prices.

Rather than focus on the specifics of their model (which retains much of the structure of Garman's model), it is perhaps more useful to consider the model's conclusions and then return to the issue of the underlying approach. The model yields three main results. First, the optimal bid and ask prices are monotone decreasing functions of the dealer's inventory position. As the dealer's inventory increases, he lowers both bid and ask prices, and conversely he raises both prices as inventory falls. Such a linkage between prices and inventory had been suggested by several authors (see, for example, Smidt [1971]) but had not been rigorously shown before. A second implication of the model is that the dealer has a preferred inventory position. As the dealer finds his inventory departing from his preferred position, he moves his prices to bring his position back. Subsequent research on dealer behavior (for example, Madhavan and Smidt [1993] and Hasbrouck and Sofianos [1993]) would examine this preferred position in more detail. Third, as was also the case in Garman, the optimal bid and ask prices exhibit a positive spread.

These latter two results raise interesting questions about the behavior of security prices and, by extension, about the appropriateness of the model. Whereas in Garman the spread arose partially because of the need to reduce failure probabilities, the spread here reflects the dealer's efforts to maximize profit. Since the dealer is assumed to be risk neutral and a monopolist, the spread reflects the dealer's "market power." In this model, however, if the dealer faces competition, then the spread falls to zero.[4] Consequently, the spread plays no role in the viability of the market but acts essentially as a transaction cost.

Similarly, the dealer's preferred inventory position arises because of the nature of the order arrival processes. The underlying asset value is irrelevant. What determines the optimal inventory position is the "variability" of the order arrival stochastic process, as inventory plays simply a buffer role. Hence, regardless of what is expected to happen to the value of the stock, the dealer holds the same preferred position. This may be an accurate depiction of the dealer's problem, but it seems likely that the preferred inventory position depends on factors other than the order arrival rates. The framework developed here, however, is not amenable to investigating such factors.

This suggests that additional insight into the price-setting problem requires greater emphasis on the nature of the dealer's decision problem, and this dictates departing from the simple stochastic process approach of Garman and Amihud-Mendelson. This statistical approach, however, did provide a new perspective on the difficult intermediation task required to clear markets, and in particular it focused attention on the dynamic behavior of markets. This dynamic focus would be an important direction for subsequent microstructure research, although the interesting failure difficulties posed by Garman would generally be ignored. In the next section, we consider the dealer-based approach for modeling price-setting behavior.

---

4. Interestingly, this same conclusion will arise in a much later model of liquidity, by Grossman and Miller [1988]. In both models, competition removes any role for the spread and hence suggests that the existence of a spread is due solely to fixed transactions costs or to market power.

2.2 THE DEALER'S PROBLEM

Analyzing the dealer's decision problem requires specifying the dealer's objectives and constraints in more detail. Of paramount importance is the need to delineate the risks the dealer faces and how these risks affect his decision making. From this perspective, the dealer's price-setting problem takes on the more natural characterization of choosing the optimal pricing strategy to maximize utility, with security prices arising as the outcome of the dealer's optimizing behavior.

One way to characterize this approach is to recognize that the dealer must be rewarded for providing specialist's services, in the same way that any intermediary must be compensated. By focusing on the supply of intermediary services, the dealer's decision problem reduces to determining the appropriate compensation to offset the costs the dealer faces in providing such services. This is the notion of the dealer as a supplier of immediacy. A formal analysis of this dimension of the dealer's problem was first undertaken by Stoll [1978].

Stoll's analysis departs from the order-based analyses discussed in the previous section by focusing on the portfolio risk the dealer function entails. For Stoll, the market maker is simply a market participant, or trader, who is willing to alter his own portfolio away from desired holdings to accommodate the trading desires of other traders. As a market participant himself, the dealer is assumed to be risk averse and therefore must be compensated for bearing this risk. This compensation arises from the bid and ask prices, and so the market spread reflects the "costs" the dealer faces in bearing this risk. This role of the dealer contrasts with that presented in the Garman and Amihud-Mendelson models, where the dealer is assumed to be a risk neutral monopolist whose prices reflect largely his market power.

Stoll focuses on determining the costs the dealer faces in providing dealer services, or, as Demsetz defined it, "immediacy." These costs arise from three sources. First, there are holding costs imposed by the suboptimal portfolio position the dealer must hold. These costs reflect the exposure risk of the dealer, which, since the dealer is assumed risk averse, now affects his decision making. Second, there may be order-processing costs that reflect the nature of the trading mechanism, such as exchange fees, transfer taxes, etc. Third, a cost may arise from trading with individuals who know more about the stock than the dealer. This latter asymmetric information cost will be the focus of much subsequent research (and indeed, the remainder of this book) but is addressed in a limited manner in this research.

Stoll considers a two-date model in which the dealer maximizes the expected utility of terminal wealth, where this wealth is a function of the dealer's initial wealth and his subsequent market-making positions. The dealer's decision problem is to set prices for one transaction in which he will buy or sell the asset at time 1, with liquidation of the asset occurring at time 2. The dealer finances his inventory by borrowing at the risk-free rate, R_f, and conversely can lend excess funds at R_f. As the time period considered is short and his borrowing ability is unlimited, the market maker's risk of bankruptcy is zero. An important assumption in the model is that the dealer has some exogenous (and unchanging) beliefs about the "true" price of the asset and about its "true" rate of return. This true price is invariant in the model.

The dealer is assumed willing to transact if his position in utility terms after the trade is at least as good as it would be if he did not trade. Let the dealer's initial wealth, W_0, be composed of the value of his initial position in the optimal efficient portfolio, the true value Q_p of his position in his trading account, and any remaining funds. Since the dealer knows the "true" value of the stock, let Q_i denote the true value of a transaction in stock i, where the true value is the true price times the number of shares, a positive (negative) number indicating a buy (sell). Following a trade, the dealer's terminal wealth is then given by

$$\widetilde{W} = W_0(1 + \tilde{R}^*) + (1 + \tilde{R}_i)Q_i - (1 + R_f)(Q_i - C_i), \qquad (2.12)$$

where $\tilde{R}^*$ is the rate of return on his initial portfolio, and $\tilde{R}_i$ is the rate of return on stock i. The last term in (2.12) includes the cost of carrying the inventory (or the return on the proceeds in the case of a sale), where C_i is defined to be the present dollar cost to the dealer of trading the amount Q_i. So, for example, if the dealer buys shares with a value Q_i, he need only borrow Q_i - C_i to finance the purchase. These costs, which are specified in more detail shortly, can be positive or negative depending on whether the trade in stock i raises or lowers the dealer's inventory holding costs, and they essentially capture the dealer's exposure cost of holding a nonoptimal portfolio.

The dealer is assumed to be willing to undertake any transaction that leaves his expected utility unchanged. That is, he requires

$$E\left[U\left(W_0\left(1 + \tilde{R}^*\right)\right)\right] = E\left[U\left(\widetilde{W}\right)\right]. \qquad (2.13)$$

Expanding both sides of (2.13) in a Taylor series expansion, dropping terms of order higher than two, setting $R_f = 0$, and simplifying the resulting expression yields

$$\frac{C_i}{Q_i} = c_i = \frac{z}{W_o}\sigma_{ip}Q_p + \frac{1}{2}\frac{z}{W_0}\sigma_i^2 \, Q_i, \tag{2.14}$$

where z is the dealer's coefficient of relative risk aversion, Q_p is the "true" dollar value of stocks held in the dealer's trading account (his total inventory), σ_{ip} is the correlation between the rate of return on stock i and the rate of return on the optimal efficient portfolio, and σ_i^2 is the variance of stock i's return. Equation (2.14) for $C_i(Q_i) = C_i/Q_i$ determines the percentage dollar cost that is necessary for the dealer to be willing to take that position Q stock i.

This cost function indicates that the dealer's cost of providing immediacy depends on several factors. First, the dealer's wealth and risk preferences enter directly, with greater initial wealth reducing his costs and greater risk aversion increasing them. Second, the level of the dealer's inventory position matters, with a larger position implying a greater cost for taking on more inventory. Similarly, the transaction size affects the total size of the costs; the larger the trade, the more it moves the dealer from his previous position. Of course, if the trade moves the dealer back toward his desired holdings, then this can reduce the costs of the trade. Finally, the characteristics of the stock as captured by its variance and correlation with other securities also affect the cost. Each of these factors affects the costs to the dealer of accepting a suboptimal portfolio position.

The dealer is compensated for bearing these costs through his trading prices. If the market is competitive, then his bid and ask prices must just compensate him for the costs of accepting the trade, and hence the bid and ask prices can be solved for as a function of the trading cost.[5] Expressing these costs in percentage terms relative to the true price P_i^*, the optimal bid price, P_b, for a transaction with true value Q_i^b is then

$$(P_i^* - P_b)/P_i^* = c_i(Q_i^b), \tag{2.15}$$

where Q_i^b represents the "true value" of a sale to the dealer. A similar expression can be used to derive the optimal ask price, P_a, with the resultant spread given by

$$(P_a - P_b)/P_i^* = c_i(Q_i^b) - c_i(Q_i^a) = [z/W_0]\sigma_i^2 \, | \, Q \, | \tag{2.16}$$

for $| \, Q_i^a \, | = | \, Q_i^b \, | = | Q |$.

---

5. One difficulty with such a competitive pricing assumption is that it implicitly requires dealers to be identical in every dimension, including their inventory holdings. This is unlikely to be accurate, but abstracting from this complication does indicate a lower bound on prices in this model.

There are several interesting features of these prices to consider. The linearity of percentage costs in trade size means that the spread increases linearly with trade size. And, as the spread equation does not include inventory as an argument, this spread does not change in response to the dealer's trades. Where the dealer's inventory matters is in affecting the placement of the bid and ask prices. A large (positive) inventory causes the dealer to face a higher cost for absorbing more inventory, and this increased cost lowers both bid and ask prices by the same amount. A negative inventory moves prices in the opposite direction. This prediction, that inventory would affect the placement of the spread but not its size, is an important and potentially testable hypothesis.[6]

While this analysis characterizes the effects of the dealer's portfolio exposure on trading prices, there can be other costs affecting prices as well. Stoll extends the analysis to incorporate order-processing costs, which are assumed to be a fixed fee per transaction. Such a fee structure results in a decreasing cost function with respect to order size. With portfolio costs increasing in trade size while processing costs decrease in trade size, the total dealer cost function becomes U-shaped. This has the intriguing implication that there is an optimal cost minimizing scale, or preferred trade size, for the dealer.[7]

This model thus provides a cogent analysis of the dealer's pricing behavior. In this model, inventory matters largely because of the dealer's inability to hedge his inventory exposure. This "risk aversion"-based spread contrasts with the "market power" role of the spread developed by Amihud and Mendelson or the "defense against bankruptcy" role described by Garman. The simplicity of the Stoll model, however, raises concerns about its generality. For example, if the dealer were risk neutral or able to diversify, then the cost of the providing dealer services would fall precipitously and, indeed, could fall to zero (or to the level of any order-processing costs). This implies a natural tendency for dealers to diversify their risk by incorporation or other means, a trend not observed on organized exchanges such as the NYSE.[8] This also suggests that differences

---

6. This implication is empirically examined by Hasbrouck [1988] and others.

7. Stoll also considers the effect of a simple adverse selection cost, which he assumes is independent of the scale of the transaction. This simply adds a fixed cost to the dealer's cost and hence widens his spread equally for every transaction. Subsequent researchers would expand this notion of the costs of informed trading significantly. In particular, Easley and O'Hara [1987a] would suggest that this adverse selection component would be increasing in trade size.

8. A related issue concerns the effect of competition on the dealer's spread. This issue is addressed in Ho and Stoll [1983].

in spreads between markets would be primarily due to risk-bearing abilities. While certainly possible, it is not clear that this provides the entire explanation. Furthermore, it is not obvious how this theory would explain phenomena such as differences in spreads during the trading day in the same stock.

A more fundamental difficulty is that the model minimizes the intertemporal dimension of the dealer's problem by assuming that the stock is liquidated at time 2. In this sense, it is a one trade-one period model because the dealer faces no uncertainty over how long he must hold any inventory position. If the order flow is random, however, this length of exposure may be an important dimension of the problem. Moreover, the assumed exogeneity of variables such as the stock's true price and the portfolio's return further restricts the risk that the dealer faces, because his ultimate return is not a random variable. The generality of the results is thus not apparent.

These concerns suggest that the intertemporal dimension so fundamental to Garman and Amihud and Mendelson must also be explicitly considered in formulating the dealer's decision problem. In the next section we consider the development of this approach by examining the models of Ho and Stoll [1981] and O'Hara and Oldfield [1986].

2.3 THE INTERTEMPORAL ROLE OF INVENTORY

The Ho and Stoll [1981] model extends the intuition of the Stoll [1978] analysis to a multiperiod framework in which both order flow and portfolio returns are stochastic. As in Garman [1976], buy and sell orders are represented by stochastic processes, whose order arrival rates depend on the dealer's pricing strategy. In this model, however, a monopolistic dealer is assumed to maximize the expected utility of terminal wealth, and consequently the dealer's attitude toward risk will affect the solution. This is a significant difference from the risk neutral intertemporal models of Garman [1976] and Amihud and Mendelson [1980].

The model employs a finite horizon (T period) dynamic programming approach to characterize the dealer's optimal pricing policy.[9] The dealer's optimal pricing strategy is actually a function that specifies bid and ask prices, p_b and p_a, given the level of those variables which affect the dealer's future utility. In this model, these state variables are the dealer's cash,

---

9. Readers unfamiliar with continuous-time dynamic programming may find it useful to read Chapters 4 and 5 in Merton [1990]. Those unfamiliar with discrete-time dynamic programming (which is employed later in this chapter) should see Hinderer [1970].

inventory, and base wealth positions. Since this is a finite horizon model, the time period itself also affects the dealer's choice.

As in Stoll [1978], the model assumes that the true value of the stock is fixed at some value p, and so the dealer's prices can be written as $p_a = p + a$ and $p_b = p - b$. It will often be more convenient to denote the dealer's choice variables by a and b rather than by the specific prices. In this model, transactions are assumed to evolve as a stationary continuous-time jump process, which, as in Garman, is assumed to be a Poisson process. The arrival rate of buy orders, λ_a, and that of sell orders, λ_b, will depend on the dealer's ask and bid prices, respectively.[10] Since orders are stochastic, however, the dealer's price influences the probability of the next trade being either a buy or a sell, but does not guarantee that such a transaction will occur. Consequently, the dealer faces uncertainty over the order flow and thus over the time he will have to carry any inventory position.

The dealer is also assumed to face uncertainty over the future value of his existing portfolio, X, implying that his future wealth is random. The return on the portfolio is assumed to follow a nonstandard Wiener process, so that the dealer earns some random return over time.[11] In the absence of any transactions, the portfolio growth, dX, is given by

$$dX = r_x X \, dt + X \, dZ_x, \tag{2.17}$$

where r_X is the mean return per unit time, and Z_X is a Wiener process with mean zero and instantaneous variance rate σ_X^2.

The dealer's portfolio consists of cash, stock, and any base wealth. The dealer's cash level changes as he buys and sells securities, with any balance in the account earning the risk-free rate r. The value of the cash account, F, is thus given by

$$dF = rF \, dt - (p - b) \, dq_b + (p + a) \, dq_a, \tag{2.18}$$

where q_b and q_a are dealer buys and sales of securities, respectively. Similarly, the value of the dealer's stock or inventory position, I, is assumed to follow

$$dI = r_I I \, dt + p \, dq_b - p \, dq_a + I \, dZ_I. \tag{2.19}$$

---

10. A Poisson process in which the intensity λ is stochastic is called doubly stochastic or a Cox process.

11. It is nonstandard in that the variance is not equal to one and there is a drift.

This specification includes several interesting features. First, inventory is always valued at the known intrinsic value of the stock, *p*, and not at the prices at which it actually trades. Hence, bid and ask prices play no role in the valuation of the inventory. Second, the value of the inventory does change due to both changes in its size (reflected in the q_b and q_a transaction terms) and changes in its value resulting from the diffusion term $I\, dZ_I$ and the drift term $r_I\, I\, dt$.

These latter fluctuations in the value of the stock pose a difficult technical problem, given that the price of the stock (and hence of the inventory) is assumed to remain constant at price *p*. This somewhat awkward construction dictates that any inventory return must take the form of a continuous stock, i.e., in-kind, dividend rather than the more standard cash dividend. While Ho and Stoll argue that this essentially captures the return uncertainty of the stock, this also removes any interaction between the dealer's pricing decision and the inventory value. We return to this issue later in the chapter.

Finally, the dealer's portfolio also includes base wealth, *Y*, whose change in value is described by

$$dY = r_Y Y\, dt + Y\, dZ_Y. \tag{2.20}$$

When the dealer begins trading, he is assumed to have no initial cash or inventory and hence holds only the initial portfolio. This construction is consistent with the interpretation of the dealer as a trader willing to provide dealer services in return for sufficient compensation. To avoid the failure complications noted by Garman, Ho and Stoll assume the dealer cannot go bankrupt over the *T*-period time horizon considered.

The dealer's pricing problem, therefore, is to choose bid and ask prices to maximize the expected utility of terminal wealth, where wealth is

$$W_T = F_T + I_T + Y_T. \tag{2.21}$$

The maximized value of this problem is given by the value function $J(\bullet)$ (the function that solves the Bellman equation) such that

$$J(t, F, I, Y) = \max_{a,b}[E[U(W_T)] \mid t, F, I, Y], \tag{2.22}$$

where *U* is the utility function, *a* and *b* are the ask and bid adjustments, and *t, F, I,* and *Y* are the state variables time, cash, inventory , and base wealth, respectively. The value function gives the level of utility given that the dealer's decisions are made optimally. Since there is no intermediate consumption before time T, the recursion relation implied by the principle of optimality is

$$dJ(t, F, I, Y) = 0 \quad \text{and} \quad J(t, F, I, Y) = U(W_t). \tag{2.23}$$

To find a solution to the dealer's problem, we need to find the ask and bid adjustments that solve (2.23) for each state.

The solution to this continuous time problem requires applying stochastic calculus, a technique painfully familiar to students of option pricing. While the complete derivation is beyond our purpose here, it is perhaps useful to demonstrate the basic solution technique. This involves an application of Ito's Lemma. Suppose we consider a smooth function

$$Y = f(x, t), \tag{2.24}$$

where t is time and x is some well-defined Ito process

$$dx = \mu \, dt + \sigma \, dz. \tag{2.25}$$

If we now wish to maximize Y by choosing x, we need to take the derivative of Y, and this is given by Ito's Lemma.[12] In particular, it will be the case that

$$
\begin{aligned}
dY &= \frac{\partial f}{\partial t} \, dt + \frac{\partial f}{\partial x} \, dx + \frac{1}{2} \frac{\partial^2 f}{\partial x^2} (dx)^2 \\
&= \frac{\partial f}{\partial t} \, dt + \frac{\partial f}{\partial x} [\mu \, dt + \sigma \, dz] + \frac{1}{2} \frac{\partial^2 f}{\partial x^2} \sigma^2 \, dt.
\end{aligned} \tag{2.26}
$$

Collecting the dt terms and rewriting yields

$$dY = \left[\frac{\partial f}{\partial t} + \frac{\partial f}{\partial x}\mu + \frac{1}{2} \frac{\partial^2 f}{\partial x^2}\sigma^2 \right] dt + \frac{\partial f}{\partial x}\sigma \, dz. \tag{2.27}$$

This is Ito's Lemma. It gives the formula for calculating the derivative of a function that depends on time and a stochastic process.[13]

----

12. To apply Ito's Lemma, f should be twice continuously differentiable in X and once continuously differentiable in t. Generalizations of Ito's Lemma relax these sufficient conditions.

13. For more discussion, see Merton [1990], Chapter 3, particularly 78-80.

In Ho and Stoll's model, the dealer's problem in equation (2.23) involves maximizing the value of the $J(\bullet)$ function, which depends on time and the three state variables cash, stock, and base wealth. Writing out the partial differential equation implied by (2.23) and applying Ito's Lemma yields

$$\frac{dJ}{dt} = J_t + LJ + \max_{a,b}\{\lambda_a[J(t, F + pQ + aQ, I - pQ, Y) - J(t, F, I, Y)]\}$$
$$+ \lambda_b[J(t, F - pQ + bQ, I + pQ, Y) - J(t, F, I, Y)] = 0, \qquad (2.28)$$

where J_t is the time derivative and L is the operator defined as

$$LJ = J_F rF + J_I r_I I + J_Y r_Y Y + \frac{1}{2}J_{YY}\sigma_Y^2 Y^2$$
$$+ \frac{1}{2}J_{II}\sigma_I^2 I^2 + J_{IY}\sigma_{IY}IY. \qquad (2.29)$$

Equations (2.28) and (2.29) can perhaps be better understood by comparing these equations with the simple example in equation (2.27). The first term in (2.28) is the time derivative corresponding to the $\partial f / \partial t$ term in the example. The first three terms of LJ are the mean terms of the state variables F, I, and Y. The next two terms in LJ contain the variance terms of the I (inventory) and Y (wealth) state variables (the third state variable, cash, earns the constant r and hence has no variance). The final term of LJ is the covariance term. The example in (2.27) also contains a dZ term, but the dZ term does not appear in (2.29). The reason is that in the problem considered here, the dealer is maximizing expected utility, and so the expectation of the dZ term is zero at the optimum.

The final term in equation (2.28) (i.e., the max term) gives the effect on the dealer's utility of transactions taking place at the bid and ask prices. It is here that the dealer's pricing decisions directly affect his utility. The first part (the λ_a term), for example, is the effect of a dealer sale, and hence it is the incremental utility effect of cash in and inventory out. The second part is the corresponding effect for a dealer buy.

While equations (2.28) and (2.29) determine the solution, finding the actual solution requires solving explicitly for the $J(\bullet)$ function. This is not straightforward, and Ho and Stoll do not solve the general problem. Instead, they introduce some transformations and simplifications into the problem in order to solve it. First, they consider the problem only at the endpoint, or when the time remaining, defined as τ, is equal to zero. Second, since it would be useful if the cash and inventory effects on utility could be handled explicitly, Ho and Stoll take a first-order approximation of the Taylor's series expansion of the max term in (2.22) such that

$$J(t, F + Q + aQ, I - Q, Y) = J(t, F + Q, I - Q, Y)$$
$$+ J_F(t, F + Q, I - Q, Y) aQ, \tag{2.30}$$

and similarly for the bid term.[14] Also, Ho and Stoll now assume symmetric linear demand and supply to the dealer, so that $\lambda_a = \lambda(a) = \alpha - \beta a$, and $\lambda_b = \lambda(b) = \alpha + \beta b$. Finally, they define the sell operator, S, by

$$SJ = S[J(t, F, I, Y)] = J(t, F + Q, I - Q, Y) \tag{2.31}$$

and the buy operator, B, by

$$BJ = B[J(t, F, I, Y)] = J(t, F - Q, I + Q, Y). \tag{2.32}$$

These functions give the effect of transactions on the dealer's utility excluding the bid and ask increments. The buy and sell operators are intended to capture the incremental effects on the dealer's utility of changing his holdings by Q units. So utility will decrease if the transaction takes the dealer farther from his desired portfolio, and it will increase if the transaction takes him closer to the desired position.

With these simplifications and substitutions (and suppressing the time arguments), the dealer's problem can be restated as

$$J_T = LJ + \max_{a,b} \{\lambda(a)aQSJ_F - \lambda(a)[J(\bullet) - SJ]$$
$$+ \lambda(b)bQBJ_F - \lambda(b)[J(\bullet) - BJ]\}. \tag{2.33}$$

The first-order conditions to this problem can be solved for the dealer's optimal prices, which in the case of the bid is simply

$$b^* = \frac{\alpha}{2\beta} + \frac{J(\bullet) - BJ(\bullet)}{2BQJ_F}, \tag{2.34}$$

where α and β are parameters of the linear supply and demand functions.

While equation (2.34) gives the dealer's bid optimal price, it depends explicitly on the $J(\bullet)$ function, which has not yet been determined. To characterize the dealer's pricing strategy, the optimal prices must be substituted back into equation (2.33) and the problem solved explicitly for the optimal $J(\bullet)$ function. Unfortunately, as is often the case in such

---

14. Note that the error of this approximation is on the order of a^2.

dynamic programs, there is no known closed-form solution to this problem. It is possible, however, to approximate the solution through a Taylor series expansion with some additional assumptions on the model's parameters. The most important of these is that Ho and Stoll now assume the dealer has a quadratic utility function. Rather than concentrate on the mechanics of the approximation, it is perhaps more useful now to analyze the resulting optimal policy.

Ho and Stoll demonstrate three important properties of the dealer's optimal pricing behavior. First, the spread depends on the time horizon of the dealer. As the dealer nears the end of trading, the risks in acting as a dealer decrease since there is less time in which the dealer must bear any inventory or portfolio risk. For the limiting case where the time remaining is essentially zero, the dealer sets the risk neutral, monopolistic spread. This spread simply depends on the slopes (or elasticities) of the supply and demand curves, with greater elasticity reducing the dealer's spread. As the time horizon lengthens, the spread increases to compensate the risk averse dealer for bearing inventory and portfolio risks.[15] This demonstration that the spread can be decomposed into a risk neutral spread plus an adjustment for uncertainty is an important feature of the analysis.

This risk adjustment depends on the dealer's coefficient of relative risk aversion, the size of the transaction, and the risk of the stock as measured by its instantaneous variance. These factors are the same as those determined by Stoll in his one-period model. One interesting finding in this model is that transactions uncertainty per se does not affect the spread. Although such uncertainty enters indirectly through the time horizon effects noted above, one might have expected a direct risk adjustment based on the variability of the order arrival processes. Ho and Stoll argue that this does not occur because transactions variability has no direct effect on the dealer but rather works indirectly through its effect on his overall portfolio position. Such a direct effect would arise, for example, if the dealer faced a fixed operating cost, so that having fewer transactions would pose cash flow problems for the dealer. As there is no such assumed cost, transaction uncertainty does not enter the spread.

The third property of this optimal pricing policy is that the spread is independent of the inventory level. This property, which was also a feature

---

15. This increase in the spread as the time horizon lengthens is somewhat paradoxical as the market maker has more opportunities with a longer horizon to alter his position. But since the market maker can liquidate his portfolio at a certain price at the end of the horizon, a short time period reduces the interim period in which the dealer is subject to risk, while giving the dealer the same end-of-period certainty. In the absence of a certain liquidation value, it is not obvious that this result would remain.

of Stoll's one-period model, means that the spread is not affected by the dealer's inventory position or even his expected change in inventory (since transaction uncertainty also does not matter). Although individual prices depend on inventory, the dealer affects the order arrival processes by moving the placement of the spread relative to the true price rather than increasing or decreasing the spread itself. Thus, if the true price is 50, the dealer may set first-period prices of 48 and 52. If the next order is at the bid, then the dealer increases his inventory, and he shifts both prices down, say to 47 and 51. How much the dealer shifts the prices is a function of his relative risk aversion, the riskiness of the stock, and his wealth.

These results are derived in a complex framework capable of including both multiperiod issues and dealer risk aversion. There are, however, a number of underlying restrictions in the model that are important to consider. Because the model employs a finite horizon, there is an explicit assumption that the inventory is liquidated at some known point in the future, in this case at time T. This ending certainty reduces the underlying risk of the inventory and introduces the time element into the dealer's spread equation. One implication of this behavior, however, is that the dealer's prices will exhibit deterministic patterns. For example, if the dealer's horizon were one trading day, spreads would be largest in the morning and would narrow steadily throughout the day. Indeed, traders would always be worse off dealing with a specialist who had a long time horizon as opposed to a market maker with a shorter horizon. Such dependence on the dealer's horizon seems unlikely to be a realistic feature of actual markets.

A second important assumption of the model is that there is a fixed "true" price for the stock. This assumption is fundamental to the analysis. If the underlying stock value could vary across time, then it would be formidable even to approximate the model's solution. Assuming a fixed intrinsic value of the stock, however, seems realistic only if the time horizon is fairly short. Ho and Stoll argue that the stochastic return on the inventory position allows for future differences in the stock value to affect the market maker, but as discussed earlier, it is not clear that this captures completely the interaction effects of security value uncertainty. Since the focus of the model is on the intertemporal behavior of security prices, it seems more realistic that this underlying value could itself be a random variable. If the price is variable, then it is unclear whether the authors' pricing results will all still hold. In particular, the movement of a fixed spread around the true price may no longer be optimal if the price itself is moving.

The model also assumes a specific underlying stochastic process for the order flow. Why orders would necessarily exhibit that specific process is not clear, but as an approximation to the order flow such a specification need not be unrealistic. It is the case, however, that the assumptions needed to justify the Poisson distribution effectively preclude the possibility that some traders know more about the future movement of prices (i.e., are informed traders) than do other traders. For the inventory focus in this paper, this is not important. But for subsequent work, the absence or presence of informed traders is a crucial element in affecting order flow behavior, and hence the applicability of this approach to that setting is not clear.

It should be noted that this order flow assumption implicitly restricts the analysis to consider only market orders. Market orders are orders to buy and sell for immediate execution, as opposed to limit orders, which are orders to buy or sell at some prespecified price. As the limit price is "better" than the current price, such orders are generally held in the specialist's book until the price moves to the designated level. Since limit orders are price-contingent, however, their representation by a simple stochastic process is problematic. Moreover, the collection of unexecuted orders in the specialist's book may provide valuable order flow information to the market maker.

These concerns are addressed in research by O'Hara and Oldfield [1986]. They consider the dynamic pricing policy of a risk averse market maker who receives both limit and market orders, and who faces order flow and inventory value uncertainty. Their analysis involves a discrete-time multi-period framework and hence differs from the continuous-time multiperiod models of Amihud-Mendelson and Ho-Stoll.[16] O'Hara and Oldfield model the trading day as containing n trading intervals, and they assume the dealer maximizes his utility over an infinite number of trading days. This essentially views the dealer's dynamic program as an infinite series of n finite period intervals. The dealer's payoff (in utility terms) occurs everyday, and not only at the terminal date as was the case in the models considered thus far in this chapter. Because the dealer operates with an infinite horizon, there is also no presumed date at which the dealer's inventory is liquidated, and the analysis does not assume a fixed value for the stock. Consequently, the "price" or value of the stock may vary, dictating that the value of the dealer's inventory is also not fixed.

Because of the model's discrete-time focus, the dealer's trading behavior differs from that discussed in previous models. The dealer's order flow is composed of both known limit orders and unknown market orders. The dealer is assumed to set bid and ask prices at the beginning of every period,

---

16. Discrete-time models of dealer behavior are also developed by Zabel [1981] and Bradfield [1979].

and in each period some quantity of market orders arrive. The dealer then clears all such orders as well as any qualifying limit orders at his posted prices, and he sets prices for the next trading interval. The last trading interval in the day is followed by an overnight market in which trades settle and the dealer can borrow or lend stock. Trading then begins anew the next trading day.

This framework allows incorporation of several "realistic" features of actual security markets. For example, traders can "hit the quote" by submitting market orders to trade at the specialist's current quote. The incorporation of an overnight market also allows trade settlement to be modeled independently of order processing. And the ability to include limit orders provides a dimension not yet incorporated in inventory models.

One drawback with this approach, however, is that the trading process is modeled as a series of call markets, and hence it only approximates the continuous trading process found on most organized exchanges.[17] As with all approximations, this can be made arbitrarily close by shortening the time period included in each of the n trading periods. A second limitation is that the limit orders are implicitly assumed to last one period, with new limit orders arriving for the book before each trading interval. This restriction reflects the difficulty of characterizing the piecewise optimization problem resulting from executed orders leaving the book. A similar assumption can be found in virtually every model incorporating limit orders, and we discuss such models in more detail in Chapter 7.

The dealer's problem is to set bid and ask prices, b_t and a_t, to solve

$$\max \ E\left[\sum_{j=0}^{\infty} \phi^j U\left(\sum_{t=1}^{n} \tilde{\pi}_{jt}\right)\right], \qquad (2.35)$$

where ϕ is a discount rate, j is the index for trading days, U is a strictly concave utility function, t is the index of trading periods in each day, and $\tilde{\pi}_{jt}$ is the trading profit in period t of day j (this trading profit will be defined in more detail shortly). Note that while the dealer is assumed to maximize expected utility, his portfolio outside of his trading account is not considered. Hence, this model does not include the portfolio considerations so fundamental to the Ho and Stoll analysis. The approach developed here

---

17. The timing of the model is also different in that the market maker sets prices before he sees his total order flow. As will become apparent, however, the market maker does know the structure of supply and demand because he uses the information in the book. This timing convention is also used by subsequent researchers to address information issues; see Admati and Pfleiderer [1989] and Easley and O'Hara [1992b].

instead views the dealer as an individual who specifically acts as a specialist, rather than as a trader who is willing to accommodate orders.

The market maker's order flow in any period is potentially composed of limit orders to buy or sell and market orders to buy or sell. The limit orders are assumed to be linear functions of the price, and they are represented by cumulative order functions defined as integrals of the incremental orders. The limit orders to buy from the dealer in period t, denoted A^L, are given by

$$A_t^L = \alpha^L - a_t\gamma^L = \int_{a_t}^{\bar{a}} q_a(a_t)\, da_t, \tag{2.36}$$

and the limit orders to sell to the dealer, B^L, are defined by

$$B_t^L = \beta^L + b_t\phi^L = \int_{\underline{b}}^{b_t} q_b(b_t)\, db_t. \tag{2.37}$$

In these equations, the L superscripted variables refer to the limit order book, α, γ, β, and φ are parameters of the limit order flow, the q functions are the incremental orders at each price, and the limits of integration $\bar{a}$ and $\underline{b}$ are the highest ask and lowest bid price, respectively, at which traders will submit orders. Intuitively, these functions can be understood as adding up the outstanding limit orders to buy at or below an ask price a, or to sell at or above a bid price b. The market maker is assumed to clear all qualified limit orders at the current quote, dictating that some orders actually transact at better prices than they were placed. This contrasts with their treatment in actual markets, where limit orders typically trade only at their specified prices. The issue of order form and price behavior is considered in more detail in Chapter 6.

A period's market order flow is composed of both price-dependent and liquidity-based orders. The market maker uses the information from his limit orders to form his expectation about the market order flow. Thus, the market order flow is represented as functions

$$\tilde{A}_t^m = \alpha^m - a_t\gamma^m + \tilde{\omega}_t, \tag{2.38}$$

$$\tilde{B}_t^m = \beta^m + b_t\phi^m + \tilde{\varepsilon}_t, \tag{2.39}$$

where the $\tilde{\omega}_t$ and $\tilde{\varepsilon}_t$ terms are random variables incorporating both deviations from the market maker's expected price-dependent orders and any liquidity-based orders. The total order flow in any period is just the sum of these limit and market orders.

Because the dealer must clear all relevant orders at his stated prices, it is likely that he will acquire either a positive or negative inventory position in the stock. In this model, all transactions settle at the end of the day. Gains and losses accumulate during the day, but neither shares nor cash change hands until close. At that time, the dealer delivers all securities sold and takes cash, and he accepts all securities bought and pays cash. If the dealer is short inventory, he can borrow in the overnight market; if he is long inventory, he can lend. This overnight market is a repurchase market that establishes a price $\tilde{p}$ and an interest rate r for transactions, which are reversed the next day. If the dealer is short, he pays $r\tilde{p}I_n$, and conversely he receives this amount if he is long.

This daily settlement means that inventory affects both the current cash flow and the dealer's future operations. Inventory thus represents the state variable of the system. The market maker's dynamic program for any trading day can then be expressed by

$$\max \ E\left[U\sum_{t=1}^{n} \tilde{\pi}_t + V\left(\tilde{I}_n\right)\right],\tag{2.40}$$

where V is the dealer's derived value function. This value function incorporates the effect of current actions on future expected utility given that future actions are chosen optimally. Since the value function depends on the dealer's inventory position, it follows that the dealer's expectation of this future value of the inventory affects his optimal strategy.

The dealer's optimal pricing policy can be found by working backward. The dealer's last decision is a trading day is to set a_n and b_n to maximize

$$E\left\{ \begin{array}{l} U\left(\displaystyle\sum_{t=1}^{n-1} \tilde{\pi}_t + a_n\left(\alpha - a_n\gamma + \tilde{\omega}_n\right) - b_n\left(\beta + b_n\phi + \tilde{\varepsilon}_n\right)\right. \\[2mm] + \ r\tilde{p}\left(I_{n-1} + \beta + b_n\phi + \tilde{\varepsilon}_n - \alpha + a_n\gamma - \tilde{\omega}_n\right) \\[2mm] + \ V\left(\tilde{I}_{n-1} + \beta + b_n\phi + \tilde{\varepsilon}_n - \alpha + a_n\gamma - \tilde{\omega}_n\right) \end{array} \right\},\tag{2.41}$$

subject to

$$\alpha^{L} - a_n\gamma^{L} \geq 0,\tag{2.42}$$

$$\beta^{L} + b_n\phi^{L} \geq 0.\tag{2.43}$$

Note that the dealer's profit in period n, π_n, is captured by

$$a_n\left(\alpha - a_n\gamma + \tilde{\omega}_n\right) - b_n\left(\beta + b_n\phi + \tilde{\varepsilon}_n\right) +$$
$$\tilde{r}p\left(I_{n-1} + \beta + b_n\phi + \tilde{\varepsilon}_n - \alpha + a_n\gamma - \tilde{\omega}_n\right), \tag{2.44}$$

where the first two terms are the direct cash flow effects, and the last term gives the cash flow cost of financing or lending the resulting inventory. The problem is a constrained maximization because the limit orders must be positive.

The first-order conditions can be solved for the optimal bid and ask prices for period n. Assuming interior solutions, these are given by

$$a_n = \frac{\alpha}{2\gamma} + \frac{E\left(U'\tilde{\omega}_n\right)}{E\left(U'\right)2\gamma} + \frac{rE\left(U'\tilde{p}\right)}{2E\left(U'\right)} + \frac{E\left(V'\right)}{2E\left(U'\right)}, \tag{2.45}$$

$$b_n = -\frac{\beta}{2\phi} - \frac{E\left(U'\tilde{\varepsilon}_n\right)}{E\left(U'\right)2\phi} + \frac{rE\left(U'\tilde{p}\right)}{2E\left(U'\right)} + \frac{E\left(V'\right)}{2E\left(U'\right)}. \tag{2.46}$$

These expressions are not explicit solutions for a_n and b_n, because they contain U' and V', both of which depend on a_n and b_n. The expressions do provide some interesting insights into the determinants of the bid and ask prices. The first terms in each expression derive from the known limit orders and expected market orders. As might be expected, these terms reflect the slope of the order flow, and a monopolistic dealer sets prices based on these demand and supply elasticities. The remaining terms reflect risk adjustments due to the randomness confronting the dealer. The second term, for example, incorporates the effect of the market order flow. Market orders affect the dealer directly by determining the scale of trading. For a risk averse dealer, however, the variability of the market order flow is also important. This is captured by the covariance between U' and ω and ε, and all else being equal, this variability effect shifts prices downward.

The effects of inventory are impounded in the third and fourth terms. Inventory affects the dealer directly through cash flow, and indirectly through the value of the position he takes into the future. Both effects can be seen in the price equations, as the third term captures the overnight effects of borrowing or lending at rp, while the fourth term impounds the value of carrying his inventory position into the future. An interesting feature of these inventory adjustments is that they affect the bid and ask prices equally. Hence, as we have seen in previous analyses, increases or decreases in inventory tend to shift prices in the same direction.

These trading prices can be solved for the spread, given by

$$a_n - b_n = \frac{\alpha\phi + \beta\gamma}{2\phi\gamma} + \frac{\phi E(\tilde{\omega}_n) + \gamma E(\tilde{\varepsilon}_n)}{2\phi\gamma}$$
$$+ \frac{\phi \, \mathrm{cov}(U', \tilde{\omega}_n) + \gamma \, \mathrm{cov}(U', \tilde{\varepsilon}_n)}{2\phi\gamma E(U')}. \tag{2.47}$$

The structure of this spread is similar to that of Ho and Stoll in that it can be viewed as a risk neutral spread plus adjustments for risk. The first two terms reflect the market maker's expected order flow, while the last term incorporates the effects of market order uncertainty. If the market maker is risk neutral, this last term is zero. For a risk averse market maker, this term can be either positive or negative depending on the relative magnitudes of the covariances. This has the intriguing implication that a risk averse dealer can set a smaller spread than a risk neutral specialist.

Significantly, the spread equation has no explicit inventory terms, nor does any value function term appear. At first glance, this might appear to reinforce the finding of Ho and Stoll that the spread is independent of inventory. The spread does include a marginal utility U' term, however, and this implicitly contains the inventory variables. To delineate exactly how inventory affects utility, we need to impose more structure on the dealer's preferences. One commonly used approach for doing so is to assume that the dealer's preferences exhibit constant absolute risk aversion. Such preferences can be represented by a negative exponential utility function.

In this problem, a difficulty in interpretation immediately arises, because while the utility function may be negative exponential, it is not immediately obvious that the value function will be as well. Hakansson [1970] has shown that, under some fairly general conditions, exponential preferences lead to an indirect utility function that is exponential in wealth. Consequently, O'Hara and Oldfield assume that the dealer's problem can be represented by

$$\max \, E\left[-\exp\left(-c\sum_{t=1}^{n} \tilde{\pi}_t\right) - \exp\left(-d\tilde{p}\,\tilde{I}_n\right)\right], \tag{2.48}$$

where the parameters c and d are the market maker's coefficients of absolute risk aversion associated with trading profits and overnight inventory, respectively. Since the value of taking inventory into the next trading day depends on both its size and market value, some price must be attached to the overnight inventory position. For simplicity, it is assumed that the market maker values his overnight inventory at the random repurchase market price. Since this price is not known to the dealer until after the close of trade, it is a random variable at the time the dealer is making his buying and selling decisions.

If trading profits and inventory value are jointly normally distributed, the dealer's expected utility is linear in means and variances. Consequently, the explicit effect of inventory on dealer marginal utility can be calculated as a function of these two moments. These inventory effects are quite complex, as inventory imposes two types of risk on the dealer. First, the variability in market orders means that the dealer is never entirely sure what the size of his inventory position will be. This quantity exposure means that the dealer can finish the trading day with a large negative or positive inventory position. Second, the price of the stock is also a random variable, dictating that the value of the inventory position is also unknown. These two effects on the dealer can be isolated by solving separately for the optimal spread.

First, suppose that there were no market order variability, so that the market maker faced only price variability. Then solving the dealer's problem reveals that the optimal spread is simply the risk neutral spread derived earlier, but the individual bid and ask prices do *not* equal their corresponding risk neutral values. Hence, the market maker incorporates uncertainty about future inventory value by moving the bid and ask prices symmetrically. With his supply and demand fixed, the dealer can control his inventory position, and so he incorporates variation in the stock's price by moving the placement of his trading prices.

Alternatively, suppose that the market maker faced market order variability but not price variability. This would occur if the inventory could be valued at a constant *p,* corresponding to the framework analyzed by Ho and Stoll. There are two interesting results that emerge in this case. First, the spread now contains a risk adjustment term that can be either positive or negative. Second, the level of inventory does not affect the spread. This suggests that faced with either order uncertainty or price uncertainty alone, the market maker moves his prices symmetrically, and his spread remains invariant with respect to his inventory.

In general, however, the market maker faces simultaneous order and price uncertainty, and his pricing policy changes to reflect this dual uncertainty. Of particular importance is that now solving the dealer's problem reveals that both the placement and the magnitude of the spread depend on his inventory position. The reason is that with multiple uncertainty the market maker cannot adequately control his risk by simply moving his trading prices. By allowing the size of the spread to change as well, the market maker gains more flexibility to offset what can be complex changes in both the size and value of his inventory. This result, that the spread is not independent of the market maker's inventory, suggests a complexity to the dealer's pricing problem not envisioned in previous work.

These results relate to the dealer's period n problem. Given these optimal prices, the dealer's $n - 1$ period problem can then be solved. While the solution is shown in the paper, the complexity of the problem defies easy characterization. Moreover, solving for earlier periods rapidly becomes intractable, illustrating the practical difficulties with applying a discrete-time multiperiod model to analyze the dealer's problem. Interestingly, this same difficulty arose in the continuous-time framework of Ho and Stoll [1981], and as noted earlier, their solution involved analyzing only the last time instant before the end of the horizon.

The dealer-based models considered in this section thus illustrate the complexities of the pricing problem faced by the dealer. In each model, inventory introduces risks for the dealer, and his pricing strategy reflects at least partially his efforts to minimize those risks. The spread plays a role related to the inventory, but the extent of this role differs in the various frameworks considered. What is true in every model, however, is that inventory imposes some cost on the dealer, and it is this cost that is reflected in market bid and ask prices.

One feature common to the models considered here is that the dealer acts as the sole provider of liquidity in the market.[18] In markets in which there is only a single specialist and all trades arise from market orders, such models may accurately describe market behavior. But many, indeed perhaps most, markets do not fit this simple description. Some markets have multiple market makers, allowing for alternatives to any particular dealer's prices. Even if there is only one specialist in a market, however, competition may arise through the guise of order form. In the next section we consider these issues by first analyzing how traders' order strategies affect price behavior. We then consider the interaction between inventory and prices in markets with competitive dealers.

2.4 PRICES AND INVENTORIES IN COMPETITIVE MARKETS

In the models considered thus far in this chapter, the main activity of the specialist is the provision of immediacy to traders. If there exist other traders who are willing to provide such immediacy, however, then a specific "specialist" need not be necessary in the market. For example, if

---

18. Recall, however, that Stoll [1978] used the notion of potential competition to find the market maker's prices. Thus, that model included the effects of potential competition on prices.

traders can submit limit orders, then any market orders requiring immediate execution can be crossed with such orders, leaving no role for the specialist. This suggests that the interaction of market and limit orders may provide sufficient liquidity to result in a viable security market in much the way suggested by Demsetz. Equally important, analyzing the properties of these two order types may indicate how liquidity arises in markets in ways other than directly from the market maker.

These issues are addressed in an interesting paper by Cohen, Maier, Schwartz, and Whitcomb (CMSW) [1981]. Their model examines the order strategies of traders who can choose between submitting a market order for immediate execution or a limit order that specifies a specific price for execution. In this model, there is no active specialist, and so market prices evolve as a result of orders crossing between traders.[19] What is an important feature of this market, however, is the existence of exogenous transaction costs. These transactions costs influence the order decisions of traders and hence determine the trading prices of the underlying asset.

The underlying investor problem is highly structured. The investor is assumed to maximize the expected utility of terminal wealth by allocating funds between a risky asset and a risk-free asset. There are assumed to be transactions costs that impede the trader's ability to continuously alter his portfolio. These costs dictate that the trader will make trading decisions only periodically, and in particular, he will trade only at a discrete set of decision points. These decision points are assumed exogenously given and are presumably identical for all traders. At each decision point, the trader may trade via a market order, he may submit a limit order, or he might not trade at all.

What the trader opts to do depends partially on the properties of the alternative order forms. CMSW assume that the market ask (or bid) price depends only on the last previous market ask and hence is a Markov process. With some additional assumptions, the market ask price generation process can be modeled as a Poisson process.[20] Now, let a trader consider submitting a limit order between the current market bid and ask. What is the probability that the limit order will in fact execute over the next trading

---

19. Such crossing networks are now a common feature in many markets. For example, both POSIT and Instinet function this way, while many European markets (such as the Helsinki Stock Market) also operate as crossing networks. Much current research is being directed to the behavior of such markets, but it is interesting to note that this issue was first addressed in the early microstructure literature.

20. Again, this assumption of a Poisson process makes sense here because orders cannot be information related. If there could be such orders, then the robustness of this approach is not clear.

period? If it is one, then it will clearly be optimal for the trader to submit a limit order and hence reduce the price at which he trades.

The authors show that such is not the case; no matter how close the trader places his limit order to the current market price, the probability of the limit executing is always less than one. Since a market order always executes, this implies that there is a jump in the probability as the price approaches the ask. This jump, however, is crucially dependent on the existence of transaction costs. CMSW show that without such costs, the underlying price process becomes a Wiener process and the "jump" property disappears. One way to view this result is simply that the existence of trading costs limits trading activity and hence discretizes the price process. The greater the trading intensity, however, the less this happens and the more the process becomes like a Wiener process. This has the important implication that in inactive (or thin) markets the probability jump is larger, dictating that the probability of a limit order executing is also correspondingly lower.

Given these properties of the price process, the optimal order strategy for an investor can be determined. To address this issue, CMSW assume that all orders are for the same quantity and that any limit orders last only one trading period and are then canceled if not executed. This latter assumption is a serious simplification; most limit orders are active for much longer periods, and the cost of submitting an order is an important factor in the model. Incorporating such intertemporal properties, however, would preclude finding a closed-form solution for the model. Allowing one-period limit orders does allow the trader's decision between trading for certain or pursuing a contingent order strategy to be investigated, and hence it captures the execution uncertainty implicit in the limit order.

CMSW assume a particular cost structure such that the trader pays a cost for submitting a limit order and an additional cost if the order executes. Alternatively, if the trader submits a market order then he faces a single transaction cost (as well as the implicit bid-ask spread). Perhaps not surprisingly, the trader's optimal order strategy is shown to depend on factors such as transaction costs, the parameters of his utility function, and the existing market spread. What matters for this analysis is that under some parameterizations the trader will submit a limit order. Consequently, the interaction between these orders and market prices is nontrivial, and indeed it influences what will be the actual market spread.

In this model, the limit orders held in book determine the market "spread" because the spread is essentially the "hole in the book." If the spread is wide, then a trader has much to gain from submitting a limit order; if it executes, the trader will have transacted at a much better price. This will induce traders to shift from using market orders to using limit orders, and this will tend to decrease the spread. As the spread narrows, however, the probability jump property discussed earlier means that at some point the trader will prefer to take the certain execution with a market order to the uncertain execution of a limit order. The resulting influx of market orders will cross with existing limit orders from the book, which in turn widens the spread.

There are two important properties of this process to note. First, the "gravitational pull" of the market orders dictates that a nonzero spread is an equilibrium property of the market. This spread exists because it is not optimal (given the underlying transaction costs) to continuously trade, and hence the certain execution of the market order induces some traders to enter market orders rather than limit orders. This occurs in a neighborhood of the market prices, and hence the spread does not collapse to zero.

Second, the size of the spread depends on the movement of traders between limits and markets, and this in turn partially depends on the execution probability of the limit order. In the absence of transaction costs, all orders would be limits because the continuity of the price process would guarantee execution, but with transaction costs this probability falls with trading intensity. In thin markets, limit execution is low, and hence even with a large spread traders may prefer to enter market orders rather than limit orders. This trading strategy dictates that larger spreads will be an equilibrium property of thinner markets.

This analysis suggests a number of interesting insights into the behavior of market prices and spreads. In this model, spreads arise as a natural consequence of transaction costs. If there were no such costs, there would be no bid-ask spread. What limits the size of the spread are the gains available to providing immediacy. As the spread widens, more traders find it optimal to enter limit orders and thereby increase the liquidity available to the market. As spreads narrow, the gains to such trading decrease, and traders switch to demanding liquidity via market orders. This suggests that the behavior of traders provides a natural bound on the size of the market bid-ask spread.

In this model, unlike in the other models considered in this chapter, inventory does not play an explicit role. This reflects the highly stylized structure of the model, as well as the model's focus on competitive traders essentially endeavoring to minimize transaction costs in meeting their own trading needs. If traders were willing to act as dealers, however, then the inventory position of each dealer might be expected to affect at least his willingness to buy or sell the asset. This issue is investigated by Ho and Stoll [1983], who examine price setting in a model with competitive dealers.

The Ho and Stoll [1983] model does not include limit orders per se, but instead allows market makers the ability to trade either directly with the public or between themselves in an interdealer market. While this might appear to be very different from the issues we have been considering in this section, the fundamentals of these processes are the same. The interdealer market allows the dealer to lock in a certain price by trading with another dealer, while trading in the public market provides the dealer with better prices (his bid or ask) but uncertain execution. This trade-off dictates that the dealer's price may reflect more than the simple order-balancing issues analyzed previously. And the existence of competitive dealers means that the dealer does not have an exclusive franchise on clearing the order flow; so inventory positions can expose the dealer to substantial risk.

Introducing competing dealers into the models analyzed thus far is not a trivial exercise. Since traders will presumably transact with the dealer with the best price, each dealer's pricing problem should in principle depend on the actions of every other dealer. This dictates solving for the dealer's optimal strategy given his expectations over the actions of the other dealers. Over multiple periods with uncertain order flows, this would constitute an extremely complicated decision problem. Moreover, if dealers differ in their risk preferences, expectations of the stock's future value, or knowledge of the order flow, then a dealer's price-setting problem could be so complex as to be intractable.

Ho and Stoll do not analyze this general problem. Instead, they consider a simpler model in which two competing market makers, each trading two stocks denoted N and M, choose bid and ask prices to maximize their expected utility of wealth. This model shares features with both the Stoll [1978] and Ho and Stoll [1981] models, in that the dealer cares about his overall portfolio and not simply his trading activity. For each stock, each dealer chooses a buying fee, b_i, $i = N, M$, and a selling fee, a_i, $i = N, M$. These buying and selling fees are selected so that the dealer's utility from trading at those prices is no lower than if he did not trade at all. It is also implicitly assumed that there is perfect information regarding each dealer's inventory and wealth positions. While Ho and Stoll set up the general multiperiod model, they explicitly solve a simpler one-period model in which the intertemporal dimensions of the dealer's inventory are not included. The strategic element one might expect to find in such a problem is also not a feature of this model.

These assumptions result in each dealer's pricing functions having a very simple form. Assuming transactions in stocks M and N are independent, then a dealer with inventories of M dollar value in stock M and N dollar value in stock N has a reservation buying fee for stock M of

$$b_M = \frac{1}{2}\sigma_M^2 R\,(Q + 2I_M) \qquad (2.49)$$

and a selling fee for stock M of

$$a_M = \frac{1}{2}\sigma_M^2 R\,(Q - 2I_M), \qquad (2.50)$$

where Q is a fixed transaction value (rather than a size), and R is the discounted coefficient of dealer absolute risk aversion. In these equations, $I_M = M + (\sigma_{NM}/\sigma_M^2)N$ is the overall value of the dealer's inventory position, which depends on the return variance of stock M (σ_M^2) and the covariance of return between stocks M and N. Given these buying and selling fees, the dealer's spread for stock M is simply $s = \sigma_M^2 RQ$. Thus, the value of the dealer's inventory affects the placement of the spread, but not its size. This also implies that the dealer's spread is independent of the number of stocks he trades, and so the diversification of the dealer's trading activities does not affect the spread. Notice that these pricing and spread functions do not include expectations of the other dealer's actions, or even the size of the other dealer's inventories. In a more complete model or even in this model with a two-period horizon, such interactions would arise.[21]

Where the market spread lies does depend on the spreads quoted by each of the dealers. Ho and Stoll argue that the market buying and selling fees will reflect the second best prices rather than each dealer's reservation prices. In particular, suppose that one dealer's reservation price to sell is 50, while the other dealer's reservation price is 51. The first dealer can clearly outbid the second for order flow, but could do so at any price up to 51. Thus, the first dealer will quote 51 (or an epsilon below), and the market spread will reflect the second best price.[22] This means that the spread need also not reflect its reservation price level. Ho and Stoll argue that with two dealers the spread can exceed $\sigma_M^2 RQ$, with three dealers it will equal $\sigma_M^2 RQ$, and with more than three it can be below that level.

---

21. Subsequent research (for example, Pagano [1989a]; Biais [1993]) addresses these effects in more detail. We consider this issue further in Chapters 8 and 9.

22. This second best pricing is characteristic of a Dutch auction, and this is essentially what Ho and Stoll argue occurs in the competitive market. Biais [1993] provides an interesting analysis along similar lines by looking at how fragmenting orders between exchanges affects prices in fragmented and centralized markets. He shows that prices in the two settings correspond to those arising in English and Dutch auction, and that in general the type of mechanism does not affect prices. He argues that this irrelevance result is reminiscent of Vickrey's finding of the irrelevance of auction mechanisms.

An interesting feature of this model is that interdealer trading is permitted. Such trading is extensive in markets for foreign exchange (see Lyons [1993]) and is also important in many other markets. If interdealer trading is permitted, then a dealer can lay off an unwanted position by trading at another dealer's quote. In this model, if there are only two dealers, then such trading does not arise, because each dealer essentially acts as a monopolist on his side of the market. The dealer in a better position to buy thus quotes the highest price he can, which results in his price being essentially the same as that of the other dealer. Since selling at this price cannot improve the utility position of the first trader, no interdealer trade occurs, and each dealer instead waits to cross his position against a market order. The market spread is then essentially the monopoly spread, with its width determined by the inventory positions of the dealer on each side of the market.

If there are more than two dealers, however, then bids and asks need not be at the "worst" prices, and a smaller spread arises. Ho and Stoll argue that this spread will not go to zero because of the interdealer trades. In particular, since a sale to a dealer raises that dealer's inventory position, this should also lower his bid price and thereby widen the spread. As the market spread narrows, therefore, a gravitational pull of orders from other dealers will arise. This causes the best bids and asks to worsen, resulting in a widening (and nonzero) spread. This gravitational pull is similar to that in Cohen, Maier, Schwartz, and Whitcomb, and it suggests that the spread reflects factors relating to the supply of liquidity.

One caveat that should be stressed, however, is that Ho and Stoll do not actually show that such an equilibrium occurs. In a one-period model, such dynamic effects are not really possible. Perhaps more important, to find such an equilibrium really requires a formal game-theoretic structure, and that is not a feature of this analysis. Subsequent microstructure research would employ such a game-theoretic approach, and we analyze several such models in the next three chapters. That inventory would affect the placement of the spread differentially among dealers, however, is an interesting and important insight of this paper.

In the next chapter, we consider an alternative theory of market prices and spreads in which explicit inventory costs play no role at all. Before proceeding to that, however, it may be useful to summarize some remaining issues and concerns in the inventory literature.

2.5 INVENTORY MODELS AND MARKET MAKER BEHAVIOR

The models examined in this chapter present a varied view of the behavior of market prices and spreads. In each of the approaches we have discussed, a spread arises between the market maker's buying and selling prices. The explanations for this phenomenon differ widely, however, ranging from "market failure" and "market power" explanations of the spread to more transaction cost-related "dealer risk aversion" and "gravitational pull" theories. These divergences reflect the many dimensions of the price-setting problem, and they suggest that, at least to some degree, all these factors may be present in market spreads.

Despite the apparent differences in the various approaches, there is an underlying similarity to the inventory-based approach to market making. In an inventory model, the specialist faces a complex balancing problem in that he must moderate random deviations in inflows and outflows. These deviations are by assumption unrelated to the future value of the stock, but in the short run they determine the behavior of the market. For the long run, however, assuming the dealer can adjust his position and prices, these stochastic inflows and outflows are irrelevant. Consequently, the dealer's effect on prices is also always temporary, with prices ultimately reverting to "true" levels that prevail when order flows are balanced.

For empirical researchers, this behavior dictates a need to focus only on the short run in characterizing market behavior. Joel Hasbrouck (see, for example, [1988, 1991a, 1991b]) has used this property to separate price movements into short-run inventory-related effects and longer-run effects related to other factors such as information. There remain, however, several puzzling issues in characterizing exactly how the dealer formulates his strategy for dealing with his inventory, and hence there are still a number of unresolved issues in understanding even the short-run behavior of market prices.

One of the most important of these unresolved issues concerns the dealer's preferred inventory position. As Amihud and Mendelson demonstrated, it may be that the dealer simply operates so as to keep his inventory position at some specific level. If this is the case, then inventory will be mean-reverting, and the dealer's inventory control measures will induce serial dependence in the security price process. What this desired level is, however, is not obvious, nor is it clear what, if anything, would change the level. Moreover, if the dealer could speculate on the stock (even assuming the absence of private information in the market), it seems likely that this preferred level need not be stationary even over longer time periods.

One reason this matters is that the recent availability of databases containing dealer inventory positions suggests at least the possibility of testing for the effect of dealer inventory positions on bid and ask prices. To formulate any test, however, requires specifying how the dealer's optimal strategy translates into his prices, and as we have seen, the complexity of such problems defies easy (or in some cases, any) characterization. Moreover, the results we do have often rely on specific restrictions (such as Poisson) on the order arrival process, and hence their generality is not apparent. Research articles by Madhavan and Smidt [1991, 1993] and Hasbrouck and Sofianos [1993] provide interesting empirical evidence to bear on this issue. These authors find evidence of preferred inventory positions, but also that the dealer is willing to depart from these preferred positions over long (i.e., several weeks) cycles. Such behavior is not yet predicted by extant inventory models.

One simple prediction of the inventory models is that since a dealer will prefer to sell if he is long inventory and buy if he is short, there should be mean reversion in security prices due to inventory effects. These predictions have been the focus of extensive research by Madhavan and Smidt [1991], Manaster and Mann [1992], Lyons [1993], Laux [1993], and many others. Interestingly, while Lyons finds evidence of inventory effects in foreign exchange markets, Madhavan and Smidt find little evidence of inventory effects in equity markets, and Manaster and Mann find similarly little evidence of inventory effects in futures markets.

These conflicting results may be due to differences in market structures and data sources, but they may also reflect the difficulty of specifying empirical tests given the simplicity of current inventory models. Further, if inventory can be correlated with factors related to future stock price movements (a property not allowed in the inventory models considered in this chapter), then testing for inventory effects can be extremely complex. We consider this issue more fully in later chapters, but it remains the case that many aspects of the market maker's behavior have not been fully resolved in the inventory literature.

3

Information-Based Models

The inventory approach discussed in the previous chapter provides a number of important insights into the behavior of market prices. One implication of these models, however, is that transaction costs (albeit augmented to include a wide variety of inventory costs) still determine the bid-ask spread. Beginning with an insightful paper by Bagehot [1971], a new theory emerged to explain market prices that did not rely on transaction costs, but rather posited an important role for information. These information-based models used insights from the theory of adverse selection to demonstrate how, even in competitive markets without explicit transaction costs, spreads would exist.

In the next three chapters, we analyze the major information-based models with a view to understanding how these models explain price behavior. One important aspect of the information-based models is that they allow for examination of market dynamics and hence provide insights into the adjustment process of prices. These adjustment issues will be examined in more detail in Chapter 6. Another aspect of information-based theories is that they allow for potential strategic behavior for informed and uninformed traders. These issues are considered in Chapters 4 and 5.

3.1 INFORMED TRADERS AND UNINFORMED TRADERS

The origin of the information models is usually credited to a simple paper by Bagehot [1971]. His starting point was noting that there is a distinction in the market between market gains and trading gains. The former concept is the familiar notion that when market prices go up in general, most investors gain; when they fall, most investors lose. Since over time prices tend to both rise and fall, one might expect that investors play a fair game and hence receive a neutral market rate of return. The latter concept of trading gains, however, suggests otherwise: information costs will make

53

this average investor actually lose money relative to the market return over time.

This information loss arises because of the presence in the market of traders who have superior information. In particular, the market maker, who is in the middle of all trades, knows that some traders may have better information than he does. These informed traders buy when they know the stock's current price is too low; they sell when they know it is too high. Moreover, these informed traders have the option not to trade, unlike the market maker, who must always quote prices to buy and sell. Consequently, the market maker knows that when he is trading with an informed trader, he always loses. To remain solvent, he must be able to offset these losses by making gains from uninformed traders. These gains arise from the bid-ask spread.

That the spread reflects a balancing of losses to the informed with gains from the uninformed represented a fundamental insight into the nature of market making. While, undoubtedly, inventory and transaction costs are important factors, the notion that information costs also affect prices provided a new and important direction for market structure research. Perhaps most significant, it provided a way to explain market bid-ask spread behavior without relying on exogenous technological specifications of transaction costs.

The first attempt to formalize this concept of information costs was by Copeland and Galai [1983]. Their analysis develops a one-period model of the market maker's pricing problem given that some fraction of traders have superior information. The Copeland and Galai paper includes two almost distinct approaches to viewing the bid-ask spread. The first approach assumes a risk neutral dealer who sets bid and ask prices to maximize expected profit. The second views the bid and ask prices as call and put options provided by the dealer to the traders. Although the second approach captures a potentially important characteristic of the dealer's position, it would not prove as tractable as explicitly solving the dealer's maximization problem.[1] Hence, we consider how the dealer's decision problem can be formulated in a world of asymmetric information.

Copeland and Galai consider a very simple model. There is a single risk neutral dealer, who trades with a population of traders. The stock price, denoted P, is drawn from some known density, $f(P)$, which is exogenous to the market. Some traders are assumed to know the actual value of the stock and hence are informed. Other traders know only the general price process

---

1. In particular, using the latter approach, Copeland and Galai demonstrate that the volatility of the underlying value is an important determinant of the spread. They also demonstrate that higher priced stocks have lower percentage spreads.

and not the actual value, and hence they are uninformed, or liquidity, traders. How information arises in this model and who gets to know it are left unspecified. Similarly, why liquidity traders trade is also left unspecified. This general approach of viewing liquidity traders' motivations as exogenous to the model is similar to the approach taken in the inventory models considered in the last chapter. As in those models, traders' utilities, risk preferences, etc., are all left unspecified. The recognition, however, that the informed traders have a clear and quantifiable reason for trading allowed this model to capture an aspect of order flow not considered in the inventory models.

As in the inventory models, traders are assumed to arrive at the market according to some exogenous probabilistic framework that is independent of the stock price process. Since some traders know more about *P*, this assumption now is not innocuous, as it might seem likely that informed trader behavior depends on what they know about the stock relative to what the market thinks. This aspect of the problem is not addressed in this simple one-period framework. Copeland and Galai do introduce the notion, however, that the dealer's order flow may include information-based trades. In particular, while individual traders are anonymous to the dealer, the market maker knows that any given trade comes from an informed trader with probability π_I and from an uninformed trader with probability $1 - \pi_I$. This probabilistic structure is an important contribution of the model.

Once a trader arrives at the market, Copeland and Galai assume that there is some probability an uninformed trader will buy (π_{BL}), some probability he will sell (π_{SL}), and some probability he will not trade at all (π_{NL}). The informed trader is assumed to make the trade (either buy or sell) that maximizes his profit. All trades are for the same fixed size. Traders are allowed to have price-elastic demand functions, and so the uninformed are not forced to trade.[2] This latter feature is important; it means that whether a trade actually occurs depends on the bid-ask spread, and so the price-setting problem for the market maker must take account of this elasticity.

In an instantaneous quote framework, the market maker sets his quotes, and trades occur with no intervening time passing. Given this structure, the market maker can calculate his expected gain or loss from trading with any trader over the next instant. If the trader is informed (which occurs with probability π_I), the market maker can expect to lose

$$\int_{P_A}^{\infty} (P - P_A) f(P) dP + \int_0^{P_B} (P_B - P) f(P) dP, \qquad (3.1)$$

2. Note that the uninformed do not consider any strategic issues in their decision to trade, such as whether it makes sense to trade if other traders in the market are informed. This issue is addressed by Milgrom and Stokey [1982].

where P_B and P_A are the dealer's bid and ask prices and P is the "true" stock price.

Conversely, if the trader is uninformed, then the market maker's expected gain is given by

$$\pi_{BL}(P_A - P) + \pi_{SL}(P - P_B) + \pi_{NL}(0). \qquad (3.2)$$

Implicit in the trading probabilities of both equations are the respective demand elasticities of the informed and uninformed traders. Since the dealer does not know the type of trader he is facing, he weights his expected gains and losses by the probability of informed and uninformed trading. Hence, $-\pi_I$ times (3.1) plus $(1 - \pi_I)$ times (3.2) gives the dealer's objective function. The optimal bid and ask prices then emerge as the solutions to the dealer's maximization problem, provided these prices are positive (otherwise, the market closes).

This model captures the information notion suggested by Bagehot in that it allows the explicit calculation of the market maker's expected gains and losses to traders to influence the size and placement of the spread. The model also makes clear that calculating these gains and losses requires knowing the trading probabilities of the informed and uninformed, the stochastic behavior of the stock, and the elasticities of traders' demands. Indeed, this focus on elasticities is reminiscent of the earlier Demsetz analysis. The decision problem described here is for a monopolistic dealer. The framework, however, can include competition by incorporating a zero-profit constraint into the dealer's problem.

The most important result that emerges from this model is that even with risk neutral, competitive dealers, a spread arises. The size of this spread differs with various market parameters, in particular the elasticities of traders' demand functions and the population parameters of the uninformed and informed traders. As long as there is a positive probability that some traders are informed, however, the spread is never zero. Consequently, a market spread will exist without either risk aversion, market power on the part of the market maker, or the inventory effects so extensively analyzed by previous researchers. The Copeland and Galai framework thus quantifies the intuitive concept introduced by Bagehot that information alone is sufficient to induce market spreads.

While the model provides an interesting characterization of the bid-ask spread, it does so in a static one-trade framework.[3] Because the dealer's

---

3. The authors also consider an interesting extension by casting the dealer's problem in an option pricing framework. Here, the dealer can be thought of as writing a call option at his bid price and writing a put option at his ask price. If both prices are the same, then an

decision problem in this framework is simply to balance gains and losses, his problem is isomorphic to the inventory control problems discussed earlier. This similarity disappears, however, once dynamic considerations are introduced. With asymmetric information, the nature of the order flow is not exogenous to the dealer's problem, and consequently *the trade itself conveys information.* Moreover, the continued trading of the informed provides at least the potential for other uninformed market participants to infer the underlying information. This concept of trades as "signals" of information is developed in papers by Glosten and Milgrom [1985] and Easley and O'Hara [1987a].

3.2 THE INFORMATION CONTENT OF TRADES

If some traders have superior information, then the market maker loses on average to those traders. In the one-trade world considered by Copeland and Galai, it is easy to quantify the size of this expected loss. If the new information, however, is not instantly revealed after the trade, the issue of losses to the informed is not so easily resolved. Instead, the size of the loss will depend not only on the current bid and ask price, but also on how quickly those prices reflect the new true value.

The effect of information on market prices, therefore, takes on added dimension as the possibility of multiple rounds of trade is considered. What makes this problem particularly interesting is that it cannot be viewed as a simple repeated version of the problem solved by Copeland and Galai. If it were, then the losses to the informed would simply be the cumulative total of the (constant) loss per trade times the number of trades. The reason for this is that the market maker has no reason to change bid and ask prices, because the parameters affecting his decision (the probability of trade by the informed, the stochastic process of the stock, and the elasticities of demand) remain unchanged. What is missing in this framework is the realization that the trades, in themselves, could reveal the underlying information and so affect the behavior of prices.

It is this insight that Glosten and Milgrom develop in their model of the market maker's pricing decision. They focus on the fact that in a

---

informed trader essentially exercises an in-the-money option. An uninformed trader, conversely, exercises an out-of-the-money option. Balancing these gains and losses requires the dealer to write options at different prices (a "reverse strangle"), and hence the spread can be solved for as optimal put and call prices. This approach certainly captures an important aspect of the dealer's problem. One difficulty in extending it further is that the option pricing framework requires exogeneity of the underlying order processes, and as will be apparent, it is this exogeneity that future researchers would relax to characterize the dynamics of the market making process.

competitive market, informed agents' trades will reflect their information, either selling if they know bad news or buying if they know good news. If someone wants to sell to the market maker, therefore, it could signal that the trader knows bad news. It could also mean, however, that the trader is uninformed and simply needs liquidity. Since the market maker cannot tell which is the case, he protects himself by adjusting his beliefs about the value of the stock, conditional on the type of trade that occurs. As the market maker receives trades, therefore, his expectation of the asset's value changes, and this, in turn, causes his prices to change. Glosten and Milgrom demonstrate that over time the preponderance of informed trades on one side of the market results in the market maker eventually learning the informed traders' information, and his prices converge to the expected value of the asset given this information.

This focus on the learning problem confronting the market maker was a new, and important, direction in microstructure research. In previous research, the exogeneity of order flow and asset value uncertainty dictated that the market maker's decision problem essentially concerned setting prices to balance risks over time. The resulting market prices reflected these exogenous parameters, as well as the market maker's preferences or market power. Now, however, the ability to learn from the market meant that the price path was not independent of private information on the asset's true value. This linkage of price setting to underlying asset values meant that the process by which information was impounded into prices could be addressed. This issue, long the focus of both the efficient markets and the rational expectations literatures, could now be addressed in the context of the actual mechanisms used to set prices in security markets.

The focus of market microstructure research thus moved to analyzing how the market maker learns from the order flow and how this, in turn, affects the movement of prices over time. While the specific market setting of this learning problem could differ, all asymmetric-information micro-structure models essentially solve a Bayesian learning model. Such models provide a cogent, and tractable, mechanism for solving dynamic learning problems. The Appendix to this chapter examines the mechanics of Bayesian learning models and demonstrates several fundamental properties of Bayesian dynamics. The reader unfamiliar with such models may find it useful to read the Appendix before continuing with the rest of this chapter.

3.3 THE GLOSTEN-MILGROM MODEL

The sequential trade framework used by Glosten and Milgrom begins with similar assumptions to that of Copeland and Galai. The market maker and all market participants are assumed to be risk neutral and act competitively.

The asset being traded has an eventual value given by the random variable V. Trades involve one unit of the asset, and all trades take place at either the market maker's bid or ask prices. There are no inherent transactions costs to trade (i.e., no commissions, taxes, etc.), nor are there any explicit costs to holding inventory or maintaining short positions.

Indeed, an important characteristic of both models is that inventory does not matter by construction; the assumptions of market maker risk neutrality, unlimited capital, no bankruptcy, and a short time horizon negate any meaningful inventory-carrying effects. This specification provides a convenient way to specify how information per se affects prices without the compounding distraction of inventory. But if, as seems likely, both information and inventory matter in actual markets, then this dichotomization is also a weakness; to incorporate both effects as well as the interaction between them requires a richer model than either that of Copeland and Galai or Glosten and Milgrom.

In the Glosten-Milgrom model, some traders have information about V, while others do not. The uninformed traders face an interesting problem because, if the informed are profiting on their information, it must be at the uninformeds' expense. An important paper by Milgrom and Stokey [1982] demonstrates that if the uninformed trade for speculative reasons, then it is always optimal for them to forgo trading rather than face a certain loss transacting with an informed trader. This "no trade equilibrium" result necessitates that the uninformed must trade for reasons other than speculation. A useful construct to achieve this is that of the liquidity trader who trades for reasons exogenous to the model.

In this model, trade takes place sequentially, with one trader allowed to transact at any point in time. How traders actually arrive at the market is an important issue. Informed traders profit from trading if prices are not at full-information levels, and so any informed trader will prefer to trade as much (and as often) as possible. Since such behavior would quickly indicate the information of the informed, the market maker would quickly (perhaps instantly) adjust prices to reflect this information. Such a revealing outcome is a problem in the rational expectations models, which are discussed in the Appendix to Chapter 4. One way to avoid this instantaneous revelation outcome is to assume that traders are chosen to trade probabilistically, and that once selected, a trader may trade at most one unit of the asset. If a trader desires to trade further, he must return to the pool of traders and wait to be selected again to trade.

This probabilistic selection process dictates that the population of traders the market maker actually faces is always the same as the population of potential traders. This distinction is important because it means that, despite the informed traders' informational advantage, the market maker can always calculate the probability that he is trading with an informed trader. Note that this does implicitly rule out some plausible trading scenarios. For example, if information is likely to become more dispersed over time, then the fraction of informed trades would also increase with time, giving the market maker yet another parameter to learn. This is not considered in the simple framework developed here, but the general sequential trade approach can be developed to include this and other trade specifications. We consider some of these trading frameworks later in this chapter and in Chapters 6-8.

The specialist in the Glosten-Milgrom model sets prices such that the expected profit on any trade is zero. The general rationale for this zero-profit condition is that competition combined with risk neutrality dictates that any rents earned on trades would be bid away by a competing specialist. Indeed, since dealers compete through supply-and-demand schedules, two competing agents are sufficient to create the competitive outcome (see Mas-Colell [1980]). In effect, each market maker selects an expected profit-maximizing supply-and-demand schedule (his strategy) given his competitors supply-and-demand schedules. Market makers thus play a game, in these strategies, against each other. Since each market maker starts with the same prior belief and trade information is common knowledge, every market maker can calculate every other market maker's optimal prices.[4] This results in all market makers quoting the same bid and ask prices.

An important implication of this competitive pricing is that prices are set equal to the specialists' conditional expectation of the asset's value given the type of trade that occurs. In equilibrium, bid and ask prices are "regret-free" in the sense that given the trade that actually occurs the market maker believes the price is fair. Hence the bid price is simply the market maker's expected value of the asset given that a trader wants to sell the asset to the market maker; the ask price is the expected value given that a trader wants to buy the asset from the market maker. Such "regret-free" prices retain the property typically found in rational expectations models of incorporating the information the trade itself reveals. Since the type of trade has signal value, following the trade the market maker revises his beliefs and sets new trading prices. These new prices reflect his beliefs given what he has learned from the trade outcomes.

---

4. Notice that this would not be true if inventory mattered (as would be the case with risk aversion or capital constraints) or if the order flow were not observable to all specialists. In this case, the market maker's prices might reflect idiosyncratic information known only to himself. With risk neutrality, such inventory-based pricing effects will not arise, but the order flow constraint could be violated if there were limit orders known to one specialist and not to all. Such market structure and order form issues are considered in more detail in Chapter 7.

Viewing bid and ask prices as conditional expectations allows the adjustment of prices over time to be seen as isomorphic to the change in the market maker's beliefs. Consequently, to understand the behavior of bid and ask prices, we need to analyze the market maker's learning problem. The Appendix to this chapter examines this learning problem in more detail, but it is useful here to illustrate the basic problem. While Glosten and Milgrom derive their results in a more general framework, their results are more easily illustrated by examining a simple version of their model.[5]

Suppose that informed agents know the true value of the stock will be either low or high, denoted $\underline{V}$ or $\bar{V}$. Let S_1 denote the event that a trader wants to sell the stock to the market maker and B_1 the event that someone wants to buy from the market maker. The market maker sets bid and ask prices such that

$$a_1 = E[V|\ B_1] = \underline{V}\ \Pr\{V = \underline{V}|B_1\} + \bar{V}\ \Pr\{V = \bar{V}|B_1\}. \tag{3.3}$$

$$b_1 = E[V|\ S_1] = \underline{V}\ \Pr\{V = \underline{V}|S_1\} + \bar{V}\ \Pr\{V = \bar{V}|S_1\}. \tag{3.4}$$

Hence, the ask price at time 1 is the conditional expectation of V given that a trader wishes to buy from the market maker, with the bid price defined similarly given that a trader wishes to sell.

To determine the bid price, for example, the market maker calculates $\Pr\{V = \underline{V}|S_1\}$ and the corresponding $\Pr\{V = \bar{V}|S_1\}$. The approach taken here is standard Bayesian learning, and so these probabilities are found by applying Bayes Rule. This first probability is given by

$$\Pr\{V = \underline{V}|S_1\} =$$
$$\frac{\Pr\{V = \underline{V}\}\ \Pr\{S_1|V = \underline{V}\}}{\Pr\{V = \underline{V}\}\Pr\{S_1|\ V = \underline{V}\} + \Pr\{V = \bar{V}\}\ \Pr\{S_1|V = \bar{V}\}}. \tag{3.5}$$

The corresponding probabilities $\Pr\{V = \underline{V}|B_1\}$, $\Pr\{V = \bar{V}|S_1\}$, and $\Pr\{V = \bar{V}|B_1\}$ can be calculated similarly. The initial bid and ask prices then follow from simple calculations.

One important characteristic of these prices is that they explicitly depend on the probability of a sale (and a buy). In previous theoretical models and in many empirical analyses, the assumption made (either implicitly or

---

5. The Glosten-Milgrom model makes extensive use of the law of iterated expectations to demonstrate when one information set results in a finer partition than another. This allows them to demonstrate how trader and market maker behavior evolves given their respective information sets. In that setting as in here, the basic approach is Bayesian learning.

explicitly) is that buys and sells are equally likely. As should be apparent, in this framework this cannot be true. If there is good news, there will be more buy orders; if there is bad news, there will be more sell orders. And it will not be the case that the market maker's prices will adjust to offset this imbalance. As long as prices are not at full-information equilibrium levels, the expected order flow will differ depending on the market maker's beliefs regarding the asset's true value.[6]

Calculating these probabilities of receiving a buy or a sale can be greatly simplified by constructing a simple tree diagram. In this tree, nature makes the first move and chooses whether the information will be good or bad. This is represented in Figure 3.1 as the first node on the tree. The second node corresponds to what fraction of traders learn the information, and as is apparent this is assumed to be symmetric with respect to good and bad information. The third node corresponds to the trading decision each trader will make if given the opportunity to trade. Here the difference between informed and uninformed enters directly, as informed traders will not buy if they know bad news (or sell if they know good news), while uninformed traders are assumed equally likely to buy or sell whatever the information.

In the tree diagram, the end of each branch gives the probability of being at that point of the tree, and hence it corresponds to the likelihood of observing a particular outcome. As our interest is in the probability of a particular trade occurring (a buy or a sale), this can be calculated by simply adding up the various ways a sell (buy) order can occur. For example, in the tree in Figure 3.1, the probability of observing a sale is $(1 - \mu)\gamma^S + (1 - \theta)\mu$, while that of observing a buy is $(1 - \mu)\gamma^B + \theta\mu$. In both expressions, the first terms are the probabilities the trade is from an uninformed trader, while the latter terms give the probabilities the trade is from an informed trader. As is apparent, more complex trading games can be represented by adding nodes to the tree corresponding to any additional decision points.[7]

Given the initial price quotes, some trade occurs at time 1. Suppose that this actual time 1 trade is a sale. The market maker must then use the information conveyed by the trade to construct his posterior probability that $V = \underline{V}$. This is just the value $\Pr\{V = \underline{V} \mid S_1\}$ calculated above. To set his

---

6. In the limit, however, when everyone is informed, buys and sells will be equally likely. Recall that in the Garman model the market maker ultimately failed because she either ran out of stock or money. In this setting such failure cannot occur because the market maker is assumed to have access to unlimited amounts of either commodity. If the order flow is informative, it will also be the case that the market maker may learn the true value rather quickly, suggesting that very large imbalances in stock or cash may not develop even over short periods.

7. For examples of more complex decision trees in microstructure applications, see Diamond and Verrecchia [1987] or Easley and O'Hara [1992a].

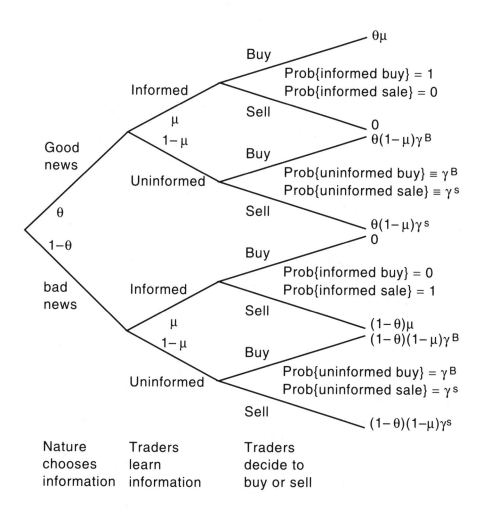

In the diagram θ is the probability the signal is good news, $1 - \theta$ the probability it is bad news; μ is the probability a trader is informed, $1 - \mu$ the probability he is uninformed; γ^B is the probability an uninformed trader buys and γ^s the probability he sells.

Figure 3.1   The Probability Structure of Trade

trading prices for time 2, the market maker updates his beliefs by using this posterior in place of his prior in the formulae above. A specific example of this is given in the Appendix.

The determination of beliefs and prices for subsequent periods proceeds in the same way. An important characteristic of this learning process is that revision of beliefs can be expressed as a simple updating of the market maker's prior belief by Bayes Theorem. The eventual convergence of beliefs and thus of prices to full-information levels follows from standard Bayesian learning results.

There are several important results that Glosten and Milgrom demonstrate in this framework. The first is that, as in Copeland and Galai, a spread arises that is independent of any exogenous transaction or inventory costs. There is, however, an important difference in interpretation between the two models. For Copeland and Galai, the spread merely balances expected gains and losses. The spread in the Glosten and Milgrom model arises because the fact that someone wishes to buy causes the market maker to revise his expectation of the asset's value upward and his quotes move accordingly; the willingness of someone to sell causes the opposite revision. The assumption of competitive behavior dictates that the specific prices set will balance the market maker's expected gains and losses in much the way it does in the Copeland and Galai framework, but here these prices are the *expected values* given publicly available information. Glosten and Milgrom characterize the specific factors influencing the spread, and in particular they demonstrate how it depends on the nature of the underlying information, the number of informed traders, and traders' elasticities.

A second important result of the model is that transaction prices form a Martingale. The stochastic process of prices follows a Martingale with respect to the market maker's information if $E[p_{t+1} \mid I_t] = p_t$, for I_t the market maker's information set at time t. Intuitively, this means that a market observer following prices cannot do better in predicting the future price than by simply using the current price. This property is important because it suggests a linkage between the price behavior in the model and the concept of market efficiency. As it is usually defined, prices are strong-form efficient if they reflect all private information, semi-strong-form efficient if they reflect all publicly available information, and weak-form efficient if they reflect the information in their own past values.[8] As the Appendix demonstrates, in Bayesian learning models it will be the case that prices ultimately converge to the true value, and hence they become strong-

---

8. These concepts of efficiency are suggested by Roberts [1967] and are formally tested by the research of Fama [1976], Leroy [1972], and others.

form efficient. Given that some traders have superior information, however, it is clear that prices along the way do not exhibit strong-form efficiency. The Martingale property dictates that prices will be semi-strong form efficient in that they reflect all the information available to the market maker.

An interesting point to consider, however, is that it is not entirely clear what market efficiency tells us in a dynamic setting. Depending upon the information the market maker sees, there can be very different price adjustment paths, with some price paths closer to the true value than others. Each path, however, has the property that prices are a Martingale, and so the notion of efficiency is somewhat limited. This issue was raised in a provocative article by Black [1989] and is considered in a microstructure setting by Easley and O'Hara [1992b].

An interesting implication of the Martingale property is that the first differences of the transaction price process will be serially uncorrelated. As Glosten and Milgrom discuss, this contrasts with the negative serial correlation that arises from transaction costs such as inventory carrying costs, or from risk aversion or market power by the market maker. Roll [1984] used this negative serial correlation property to estimate the effect of transaction costs on the bid-ask spread. With asymmetric information, however, future prices are *not* independent of the current transaction, and so Roll's technique is no longer applicable. Glosten and Milgrom derive an alternative estimator that incorporates the presence of asymmetric information. This divergence in serial correlation properties also provides a means to estimate empirically the impact of asymmetric information on security prices. Such empirical testing would be the focus of subsequent research by Hasbrouck [1988], Harris [1990], and Glosten and Harris [1988].

Another result that arises from the Glosten and Milgrom model is that under some conditions the adverse selection induced by asymmetric information can cause the market to collapse or shut down. The intuition for this result is similar to the classic reasoning of Akerloff [1970]. If there are too many informed traders, then the market maker may have to set the spread so large as to preclude any trading at all. Since information is reflected in prices through trades, however, this lack of trade results in a breakdown of the market system. One application of this is in considering whether there exist alternative market structures that avoid this unpleasant feature. A second application is in considering whether institutional features such as trading halts or circuit breakers are useful in dealing with information-based problems. These issues in market structure are addressed in Chapter 7, but it is important to note that their genesis is to be found in this early paper.

In both the Copeland-Galai and Glosten-Milgrom models, the central result can be stated as showing that asymmetric information induces a bid-ask spread. With this as a starting point, two obvious questions arise. First, how robust is this result to the trading environment? Is it the case that the presence of informed traders always induces a bid-ask spread? A second, and perhaps more intriguing, question is, can other market phenomena be explained by the presence of asymmetric information?

One area where both issues converged was in the role of trade size. In the models considered thus far, traders are assumed to buy or sell one unit of the asset. If traders could chose to transact different quantities, is it the case that spreads would still arise? Moreover, since empirical research (for example, Dann, Mayers, and Raab [1977], Holthausen *et al.* [1987, 1990]) has found interesting price patterns connected with large trade quantities (or block trades), could an information-based approach provide insight into this security price behavior? These questions are addressed in research by Easley and O'Hara [1987a].

3.4 TRADE QUANTITIES AND PRICE BEHAVIOR

The approach taken by Easley and O'Hara involves a sequential trade model similar in spirit to that of Glosten and Milgrom. Traders are assumed to trade an asset with competitive, risk neutral market makers. The market makers quote bid and ask prices and adjust quotes across time based on the trades that occur. Inventory effects do not matter, and trades take place sequentially according to a probabilistic structure.

The Easley-O'Hara model differs from previous asymmetric information models along two dimensions. First, traders are allowed to transact different trade sizes. This ability to transact orders for large or small quantities provides the potential to address the effects of trade size on security prices. The ability of traders to choose order sizes also introduces a simple strategic element into the trading game, and this, in turn, requires the development of a more sophisticated equilibrium concept. A second difference in the models lies in the nature of the information uncertainty. Unlike in previous analyses, the existence of new information is not assumed. Instead, in this game, nature essentially has two moves in deciding first whether there will be new information and then, if there is, what it will be. This dual uncertainty means that the market maker's learning problem involves determining both the existence and direction of new information.

In the Easley and O'Hara model, an information event is defined as the occurrence of a signal, s, about the value of the asset. The probability that a signal occurs is α, and if a signal occurs, it is assumed to do so before the trading day begins. The signal can take on two possible values, low and high. If a signal occurs, some fraction μ of the traders receive the signal. Of course, if no signal occurs, all traders will be uninformed. Since the market maker does not know if there is new information, he cannot know for certain when such an uninformed outcome occurs. Such information-event uncertainty seems a natural representation of how private information may exist in markets. In cases where information is known to exist but its particular level is not known to the public, it is common practice to halt trading in the stock until the information is revealed.

Trade occurs sequentially, with the individual trader chosen to trade based on the probabilities of trader types in the population. The model allows for different-sized orders, and so a trader whose turn it is to transact may either buy a small or a large quantity (denoted B_1 and B_2), sell a small or a large quantity (S_1 or S_2), or simply not trade. Because of the "no trade" equilibrium results of Milgrom and Stokey [1982], some informed traders will trade the large quantity only if uninformed traders want to trade the large quantity. If they did not, then a large trade could only be from an informed trader, and the market maker's "regret-free" prices for large trades would then be the full-information values (for good and bad news). After each transaction, the market maker sets new trading prices.

Informed traders are assumed to be risk neutral and trade to maximize their expected profits. Because there are multiple trade sizes, the behavior of the informed takes on a dimension not found in the previous papers. In particular, since the informed profit at the market makers' (or the uninformed traders') expense, the larger the trade size, the larger is their gain all other things remaining equal. Consequently, trade size induces an adverse selection problem, because at the same price the informed trader always prefers to trade larger quantities. Since uninformed traders do not share this size bias, a rational market maker will interpret large orders as a signal of information-based trading and adjust prices accordingly.

The idea that the informed could choose to transact in certain ways introduces a simple strategic element into the market making problem. Much subsequent research would involve analyzing more complex strategic decisions, but even in this simple structure the effect of allowing the informed to select among trade sizes means that the equilibrium need not be that of the Copeland-Galai or Glosten-Milgrom models. In particular, how the market maker sets prices now depends on where he believes the informed will be trading. But, of course, where the informed trade depends on the prices the market maker sets. This requires finding a fixed point at which, in addition to the competitive constraints noted earlier, the market maker's conjectures regarding the location of the informed are correct.

One aspect of the Easley-O'Hara model that should be stressed is that the informed are assumed to act competitively. This competitive behavior greatly simplifies the informeds' decision problems and facilitates the construction of a well-behaved equilibrium. In the absence of competitive behavior, with multiple informed traders the equilibrium can be intractable, if it exists at all. In the next two chapters we consider models in which informed traders act strategically, and these equilibrium issues are discussed in more detail.

Easley and O'Hara demonstrate that in this framework, two types of equilibria are possible. The informed traders could all choose to trade only the large quantity and hence be "separated" from the small uninformed traders. Alternatively, informed traders could choose to submit both large and small orders and thus be "pooled" with the uninformed traders. Of course, even in the separating equilibrium some uninformed traders must be active in the large trade market, suggesting that a "semiseparating" equilibrium is actually a better description of the separating outcome. Such pooling and separating equilibria are common constructs in many areas of economics and finance (such as in search models or in more general signaling analyses), but heretofore had not been applied to market microstructure issues.

Determining which outcome occurs is done by first solving the market maker's pricing problem assuming that the informed traders all trade large quantities. The market maker's decision problem is then solved again assuming instead that the informed are trading both quantities. The two outcomes then provide a means to determine when it is rational (i.e., optimal) for informed traders to choose one strategy over the other, thus dictating the conditions under which each outcome prevails. Solving each pricing problem involves the same general approach used in all Bayesian learning problems, with the specific trade probabilities adjusted to reflect the market maker's conjecture as to where the informed are trading.

If the informed are trading the large quantities, then the market maker's pricing policy in the separating equilibrium has the following properties. First, there is no spread for trades of the small quantity. Since informed traders do not trade small quantities, there is no reason for the market maker to protect himself from information-based trading by setting a spread. Second, prices for large trades do exhibit a spread. These prices are given by

$$b^* = V^* - \frac{\sigma_v^2}{\overline{V} - \underline{V}} \left[\frac{\alpha\mu}{X_S^2(1 - \alpha\mu) + \delta\alpha\mu} \right], \qquad (3.6)$$

$$a^* = V^* + \frac{\sigma_v^2}{\overline{V} - \underline{V}} \left[\frac{\alpha\mu}{X_B^2(1 - \alpha\mu) + \alpha\mu(1 - \delta)} \right], \qquad (3.7)$$

where V^* is the expected value of V with $V \varepsilon [\underline{V}, \bar{V}]$, X denotes the fraction of uninformed traders who trade the large quantity (subscripted to indicate buy or sale), δ is the probability that V is equal to $\underline{V}$, $\sigma^2 v$ is the variance of V, and $\alpha\mu$ represents the probability of informed trading (which depends on the probability of an information event and the fraction of traders who are informed if there is an event).

Given these trading prices, it follows that the informed choose to trade large sizes only if doing so results in larger profits than trading the small amount. Since there is no spread at the small quantity, the informed trader must be able to offset the better price by the ability to trade more shares, albeit at a worse price. If this does not occur, then the optimal strategy for the informed does not involve only trading the large quantity, and the separating equilibrium cannot prevail. For the prices in (3.6) and (3.7) to constitute an equilibrium, therefore, the following conditions must hold:

$$S^2/S^1 \geq 1 + \alpha\mu\delta/X_S^2(1 - \alpha\mu) , \tag{3.8}$$

$$B^2/B^1 \geq 1 + \alpha\mu(1 - \delta)/X_B^2(1 - \alpha\mu) , \tag{3.9}$$

where S^2 (B^2) denotes the larger sell (buy) size and S^1 (B^1) is the smaller sell (buy) size.

These conditions guarantee that the informed traders' profit is higher trading the larger quantity at the "worse" price than it is trading the smaller quantity at a better price. If the large quantity is large enough or there is little threat of information-based trading, then the market will be in a separating equilibrium. In both conditions, the left side gives the relative size of the large and small trades, and it reflects the simple fact that trading enough shares, even at poor prices, may still be preferred if the amount is large enough. In many active markets, huge blocks often transact, suggesting that in such markets a separating equilibrium might be expected to prevail. The right sides of (3.8) and (3.9) reflect the effects of informed trading on the price. If the market maker knows that most large trades are uninformed, then he can "break even" on these trades with only a small spread. In this case, the informed trader pays little penalty for trading the large amount and so profits more by trading large.

If these conditions do not hold, then the market cannot be in a separating equilibrium. It may, however, be in a pooling equilibrium. If the informed are assumed to pool with the uninformed, then the market maker's pricing strategy can again be determined. With the informed trading both large and small quantities, the market maker now sets a spread at both large and small trade sizes. The small trade spread is smaller than the large trade spread, however, resulting in a similar better price-bigger trade trade-off as occurs in the separating equilibrium. For this to be an equilibrium, it must again be the case that the informed make a larger profit by pooling than by separating. Solving for the conditions under which this is true results in conditions exactly the opposite of those in equations (3.8) and (3.9). This dictates that the market is always either in a separating or a pooling equilibrium, depending on the market parameters.

That spreads could vary across trade sizes, and indeed could even be zero in some cases, provides several important insights into the behavior of market prices. Indeed, one difficulty it reveals is that there is no one market price: *the price will depend on the size of the trade.* A second, and related, implication is that using market spreads as measures of market "goodness" can be very misleading. Since spread size will depend partly on the nature of the equilibrium, examining only the small-trade spread cannot provide a good indication of the extent of asymmetric information or of the costs of trading.

The model also provides an information-based explanation for the observed empirical regularity that large trades transact at worse prices. One traditional explanation for this phenomenon was that the large inventory exposure such trades imposed on the market maker required additional compensation, and this was accomplished by the trade clearing at a worse price. One difficulty with this story, however, is that the specialist rarely takes the other side of such trades, and indeed he or she may not participate in the trade at all. Instead, many large trades (known as blocks) bypass the specialist system completely and are handled via syndication. The mechanics of this alternative trading process are examined in Chapter 8. Since the information-based explanation given by the Easley and O'Hara is equally applicable whether the trade takes place at the risk neutral specialist's quote or clears in the "upstairs market," this model provides an explanation that is robust to trading venues.

One additional implication of the analysis is that the extent to which the market maker revises his beliefs, and hence his prices, following a trade also varies with trade size. As in the Glosten-Milgrom framework, the revision process in this model involves a Bayesian updating approach. Because of the dual uncertainty in the model over the existence and direction of new information, however, the revision process results in a different price process than that which arose in the Glosten-Milgrom framework. Easley and O'Hara demonstrate that this revision process can explain not only the immediate price drop associated with block trades, but also their puzzling subsequent price behavior as well.

In particular, suppose that the market is in a separating equilibrium and that the initial trade of the day is a large sale. In setting quotes for the next trading interval, the market maker again sets bid and ask prices equal to the (revised) conditional expectation of the asset given the type of trade. It is straightforward to see that the occurrence of two large sales leads the market maker to increase his belief that there is adverse information, and so he sets the next large sale price below the current large sale price.

Where he sets the small-trade price is more intriguing. In a separating equilibrium, the market maker knows that only uninformed traders trade small amounts. With no possibility of trading with an informed trader, therefore, there is no need for a spread, and the market maker sets the new small-trade bid and ask prices equal. But that the trader wants to trade a small quantity rather than a large amount may, in itself, provide information to the market maker regardless of whether the trade is a buy or a sell. If there is uncertainty over the existence of information, then even an uninformed trade can have information value, because it may signal that no new information exists. In particular, if there has been no information event, then the probability of a small trade rises because there are no informed traders in the market. A small trade following a block trade thus causes the market maker to revise downward his belief that there is new information, and this causes the price path to differ from what it is if there is no information-event uncertainty.

Figure 3.2 depicts these price path effects for the trade sequence small trade, block sale, small trade. Figure 3.2(a) gives the market maker's prices when new information is known to exist. As expected, the price for the block sale falls, and the price for the next small trade is set at the market maker's new expected value of the stock, which is, of course, the block price. In this path, the stock price is permanently lower following the block trade because the market maker believes it more likely that the new information is bad news. And, since small trades do not cause the market maker to revise his beliefs, the price stays at this level until a new block trade causes a revision in his beliefs.

Figure 3.2(b) gives the price path when there is uncertainty as to whether there is new information. Again, the block sale trades at a lower price, but now the price partially recovers if the next transaction is a small trade. This recovery reflects the market maker's revision of his beliefs regarding the existence of information, and whether the next trade is a small buy or a small sale, the price recovers. What is particularly intriguing about this effect is that such a recovery is consistent with the observed empirical behavior reported by numerous researchers (see, for example, Kraus and Stoll [1972], Dann, Mayers, and Raab [1977]).

This "existence" uncertainty introduces a new complexity into the analysis of asymmetric information. Now, the price effect of a trade depends not only on the trade and the current, but also on the sequence of past trades. In statistical parlance, this means that while prices are

Martingales, they are not Markov. A Markov process is one in which the future movement of the process does not depend on the history of the process, but only on its current state. Thus, the price process is Markov if $E(p_{t+1} \mid p_t) = E(p_{t+1} \mid p_t, p_{t-1}, \ldots, p_1)$. For empirical researchers, the result that prices are not Markov has the unpleasant implication that price observations cannot be viewed as independent of the prior sequence of prices. Because prices will move differently depending upon the sequence of trades preceding the current observation, this makes empirical investigations of specific economic events of interest extremely difficult. This issue of the role of price sequences is considered in more detail in Chapter 6. What this sequence result suggests for our focus here, however, is that the effects of information on security prices may be more complex than the simple "balancing" idea suggested by Bagehot.

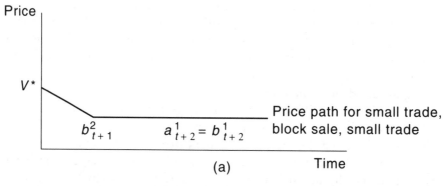

Figure 3.2a is the price path for a market in a separating equilibrium when there is no information-event uncertainty.

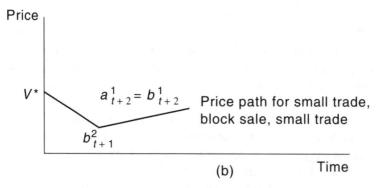

Figure 3.2b is the price path for a market in a separating equilibrium when there is information-event uncertainty.

Figure 3.2   The Time Path of Prices

3.5 SEQUENTIAL TRADE MODELS AND PRICE BEHAVIOR

The sequential trade models of Glosten and Milgrom and Easley and O'Hara provide a framework for addressing issues related to the adjustment of prices to information. The strength of these models is that they allow the learning problem of the market maker and the uninformed trader to be analyzed explicitly. This allows price behavior to be characterized on a trade-by-trade basis without ignoring the dynamic linkages between trades and information. Moreover, this approach allows the process of market maker quotes to be separated from the process of transaction prices, thereby allowing greater insight into the movement of beliefs across time. In concluding our discussion of these models, it is useful to consider the strengths and limitations of these models in more detail.

Perhaps the greatest advantage of these models is their ability to characterize the bid-ask spread. By demonstrating how market parameters such as the size of the market or the ratio of large to small trades affect quotes and spreads, these models explicitly detail how asymmetric information affects market behavior. And this, in turn, should provide at least some guidance to empirical researchers examining security market behavior.[9] These models also demonstrate that there may be an important distinction between quotes and prices. This issue, which will be addressed in more detail in Chapter 6, takes on particular importance for empirical researchers employing transaction data. Since trades across securities do not take place synchronously, the existence of a continuous quote process provides a mechanism to deal with this problem.

Another important aspect of the sequential trade approach is that it is possible to demonstrate that prices do indeed converge to full-information values. In the absence of this, concepts such as market efficiency would be problematic. This actual convergence, however, takes place only in the limit. Hence, one limitation of these two models is that they provide little insight into how long this adjustment process takes. Although more general results provided in the Appendix give more structure to this convergence issue, it remains the case that "how long" it takes is not easily determined. One reason this is important is that knowing how quickly information is assimilated into security prices might yield new insights into the nature of market efficiency. A more applied benefit is that it might suggest how institutional market design features contribute to or impede this attainment of efficiency. Subsequent research, discussed in Chapter 7, addresses some

---

9. This approach also distinguishes an important role for trades. This has been investigated in the work of Hasbrouck [1988, 1991a, 1991b].

of these issues, but it remains the case that the actual adjustment paths remain difficult to characterize precisely.

A third aspect of these models that deserves consideration is the actual mechanics of the sequential trading process. In both the Easley-O'Hara and Glosten-Milgrom models, traders essentially form a queue and trading takes place sequentially. How traders arrive at the queue is problematic. One simple scenario is that a trader is selected from a pool of traders according to the population probabilities. Hence, if there are x percent informed traders in the trader population, then there is an x percent chance that an informed trader will be transacting. That trader is allowed to transact once and then must rejoin the end of the queue if he wishes to trade further.

There are two obvious difficulties with this approach. Presumably, any informed trader would prefer to continue to trade until the price has adjusted. If this were the case, however, then once a single informed trader began to transact, the uninterrupted sequence of trades all on one side of the market would quickly convey to the market maker the underlying information, and prices would adjust almost immediately. Moreover, if the fiction of a queue is abandoned, an informed trader acting competitively would simply submit so many orders that again prices would adjust so quickly that returns to informed traders would be minuscule. The solution to this problem is to assume that, however trades occur, the intensity of the informed trades is such that x percent of trades arise from informed traders. This allows prices to reflect the uncertainty of underlying information, but avoids specifying (and thus understanding) the actual mechanism by which traders transact.

A related problem is that informed and uninformed traders are both assumed willing to continue to transact. For an informed trader, such repeat trading is certainly optimal, but it is less believable that a randomly selected uninformed trader's behavior remains the same after trading as it was before. But if the uninformed trader "drops out" of the market, the probabilistic framework used in these models is not correct. One way to characterize this difference is that informed traders should be sampled with replacement while uninformed traders should be sampled without replacement. The sequential trade models, however, assume that the percentage of trades that are information-based is constant, which can only be true if the number of uninformed traders is constant. While likely to be approximately true in some markets, it is not clear that this holds in general.

A final issue relates to the ability to incorporate strategic behavior in these models. In these models, traders and market makers are assumed to behave competitively. For uninformed traders, the lack of any coherent trading motivation is clearly an area of major weakness in the model. In the case of informed traders, the competitive assumption rules out broad categories of behavior that could be rational under a wide range of conditions. For example, if only one or even a few traders know the new information, a strategy of trading to disguise the true information might lead to higher trading profits.

In the sequential trade models, this issue is difficult to address for two reasons. First, since traders never know for certain that their turn to trade will arrive, delaying or disguising trades is only optimal if the information is extremely long-lived. A more serious problem is that it is not generally possible to compute the return to information in these models. Because the adjustment path depends on the specific trade sequence and prices are known to converge only in the limit, the trading gains to the informed depend on the specific outcomes of numerous random variables. Indeed, it is not even generally possible to determine how many times the informed will transact, let alone how much they make on each trade.

This inability to compute the exact return to information means that the sequential approach is not useful for some problems. In the next chapter, we consider another class of models designed to address these issues. In these models, the trading environment departs from the sequential trade-by-trade approach and considers a batch framework. In batch models, the payoff to strategic behavior can be calculated since trades clear at a single price. This structure, however, necessarily means that the information contained in single trades or in the bid-ask spread is removed. We return to these issues in later chapters.

Appendix:
Bayesian Learning Models

In microstructure models with asymmetric information, the key to understanding the dynamics of price adjustment is Bayesian learning. The market maker (and potentially other uninformed agents) knows that the order flow is correlated with the value of the asset but does not know what this "true" value is. What he or she must do is use the indirect evidence from the order flow to infer what this underlying value must be. This order flow may be a single trade (as in the sequential trade models) or it may be the outcome of a call market in which orders are batched together and only the net demand is observable (as in a Kyle model). In either case, the learning problem is solved via an application of Bayes Rule.

The mechanics of this learning problem are straightforward. Each trader has a prior belief about the value of the asset. One can think of this prior belief as being the probability that the value of the asset, denoted by the random variable V, has a realized value x. The trader then observes some data (say a trade) and based on this data will calculate the conditional probability that the event $(V = x)$ has occurred given the data he has seen. This conditional probability is his *posterior* probability of the event, and hence it incorporates the new information he has learned from observing the trade. The posterior then becomes his new prior, he observes more data, and the updating process continues.

There are three important aspects of this learning process that this appendix will address. First, the updating process is done according to Bayes Rule, and we will review how this actually transpires. Second, because the movement of beliefs (and prices) over time is determined by Bayes Rule, it is important to understand what we know about the dynamics of this updating process and, in particular, its convergence properties. This will allow us to determine what aspects of price behavior follow simply from the nature of Bayesian learning, and which reflect other factors such as dealer-specific preferences or market structure constraints. Third, because many problems involve random variables with continuous distributions, it is useful to understand how Bayes Rule applies in those settings. To conclude the appendix, we will examine the more general learning problem, with a particular emphasis on Bayesian learning with normally distributed random variables.

3.A.1   BAYES RULE

To determine the probability of an event occurring given the data we observe, we need two pieces of information. First, we need to know the likelihood of seeing the data, given that the event has occurred (i.e., Pr{data|event}). And we need to know the likelihood of seeing the data, given that the event did not occur (i.e., Pr{data|not event}). Using these, we can calculate the marginal likelihood function of the data having occurred:

$$Pr\{data\} =$$
$$Pr\{data|event\} \; Pr\{event\} + Pr\{data|not \; event\} \; Pr\{not \; event\}. \tag{3.10}$$

We know that the probability of both seeing the data and the event having occurred has the symmetric property that

$$Pr\{data, event\} =$$
$$Pr\{event|data\}Pr\{data\} = Pr\{data|event\}Pr\{event\}. \tag{3.11}$$

This means

$$Pr\{event|data\} = \frac{Pr\{data|event\}Pr\{event\}}{Pr\{data\}.} \tag{3.12}$$

But Pr{data} is simply given by (3.10), and so

$$Pr\{event|data\} =$$
$$\frac{Pr\{data|event\}Pr\{event\}}{Pr\{data|event\}Pr\{event\} + Pr\{data|not \; event\} \; Pr\{not \; event\}} \tag{3.13}$$

This is Bayes Rule. It gives the updating formula to use to form the posterior probability that an event has occurred given the observation of some data. Another way to state this is

$$\text{Posterior belief} = Pr\Big\{event|data\Big\} = \frac{\text{Prior belief} \times Pr\Big\{data|event\Big\}}{\text{Marginal likelihood of the data}}, \tag{3.14}$$

where the marginal likelihood of the data is simply the denominator in equation (3.13).

An Example

Suppose that the market maker believes that an asset's value is either high or low (for simplicity, let this be 0 or 1) and that his prior probability that the value equals 0 is δ. Now either a buy or a sale occurs. What do we need to know to set our posterior, $\Pr\{V = O|Q_1\}$, when we observe a trade of Q_1?

First, suppose that the trade at time 1 is a sale (i.e., $Q_1 = S$). Then, Bayes Rule dictates that

$$\Pr\{V = 0|S\} = \frac{\Pr\{V = 0\} \Pr\{S| V = 0\}}{\Pr\{V = 0\} \Pr\{S|V = 0\} + \Pr\{V = 1\} \Pr\{S| V = 1\}} \tag{3.15}$$

To solve this explicitly, we need to specify some parameter values. Suppose that initially $\Pr\{V = 0\} = 1/2$ and $\Pr\{V = 1\} = 1/2$, so that $\delta = 1/2$. Since we learn from the order flow, the trading propensities of informed and uninformed traders are also important. For simplicity, suppose that half of the traders are informed and half are uninformed. Further, assume that any uninformed trader is equally likely to buy or sell.

Given these probabilities, we can calculate $\Pr\{S|V = 0\}$. First, note that if $V = 0$, then the informed all know bad news and, hence, will sell with probability one. The probability that an uninformed trader sells is 1/2. So, since informed and uninformed are equally likely to trade, the probability of seeing a sale if $V = 0$ is

$$\Pr\{\text{in. trader}\} \Pr\{\text{in. trader sells}\} + \Pr\{\text{un. trader}\} \Pr\{\text{un. trader sells}\}$$
$$= (1/2)(1) + (1/2)(1/2) = 1/2 + 1/4 = 3/4$$
$$= \Pr\{S| V = 0\}. \tag{3.16}$$

In similar fashion, we can calculate $\Pr\{S|V = 1\}$. Now the informed know good news and so sell with probability 0, while the uninformed continue to sell with probability 1/2. Hence, the probability of seeing a sale if the true value is 1 is

$$\Pr\{\text{in. trader}\} \Pr\{\text{in. trader sells}\} + \Pr\{\text{un. trader}\} \Pr\{\text{un. trader sells}\}$$
$$= (1/2)(0) + (1/2)(1/2) = 1/4$$
$$= \Pr\{S| V = 1\}. \tag{3.17}$$

We now have sufficient information to solve our updating equation (3.15). Substituting for the probabilities yields

$$\Pr\{V = 0|S\} = \frac{(1/2)(3/4)}{(1/2)(3/4) + (1/2)(1/4)}$$
$$= \frac{3/8}{4/8} = \frac{3}{4} \quad \rightarrow \quad \text{Posterior.} \tag{3.18}$$

This is the posterior belief on $V = 0$ given that a sale occurs. A similar updating process gives us the posterior if the first trade is a buy. In this case, Bayes Rule dictates

$$\Pr\{V = 0|B\} =$$
$$\frac{\Pr\{V = 0\}\Pr\{B|V = 0\}}{\Pr\{V = 0\}\Pr\{B|V = 0\} + \Pr\{V = 1\}\Pr\{B|V = 1\}}. \tag{3.19}$$

Solving for the probability of observing a buy proceeds as before. If $V = 0$, then the probability that the

$$\left.\begin{array}{l} \text{Uniformed buy} = 1/2 \\ \text{Informed buy} = 0 \end{array}\right\} \Pr\{B \mid V = 0\} = 1/4. \tag{3.20}$$

If $V = 1$, then the probability that the

$$\left.\begin{array}{l} \text{Uniformed buy} = 1/2 \\ \text{Informed buy} = 1 \end{array}\right\} \Pr\{B \mid V = 1\} = 3/4. \tag{3.21}$$

Substituting into equation (3.19) gives

$$\Pr\{V = 0|B\} = \frac{(1/2)(1/4)}{(1/8) + (1/2)(3/4)} = \frac{1}{4}. \tag{3.22}$$

Given these conditional expectations, where does the market maker set his prices? We know that if the market maker sees a buy, he believes the probability that the asset value is 0 is now 1/4, while if he sees a sale he believes this probability is 3/4. Thus, setting prices equal to conditional expected values yields

$$E\left[V|B\right] = (1)(3/4) + (0)(1/4) = 3/4, \tag{3.23}$$

$$E\left[V|S\right] = (1)(1/4) + (0)(3/4) = 1/4, \tag{3.24}$$

These are the market makers ask and bid prices, respectively. They are "regret-free" prices in the sense that if a buy does occur, then its trading price (the ask) is at the market maker's expected value given the trade, and similarly for a sale at the bid.

Now, suppose there actually is a buy. We know this trade takes place at $E[V \mid B]$. Where does the market maker set the next price? Again, starting from his new prior (which is now 3/4) the market maker calculates the conditional expected values:

$$\Pr\{V = 0|B, B\} =$$
$$\frac{\Pr\{V = 0 \mid B\}\Pr\{B|V = 0\}}{\Pr\{V = 0|B\}\Pr\{B|V = 0\} + \Pr\{V = 1|B\}\ \Pr\{B|V = 1\}} \tag{3.25}$$
$$= \frac{(1/4)(1/4)}{(1/4)(1/4) + (3/4)(3/4)} = \frac{1/16}{10/16} = 1/10,$$

$$\Pr\{V = 0|B, S\} =$$
$$\frac{\Pr\{V = 0 \mid B\}\Pr\{S|V = 0\}}{\Pr\{V = 0|B\}\Pr\{S|V = 0\} + \Pr\{V = 1|B\}\ \Pr\{S|V = 1\}} \tag{3.26}$$
$$= \frac{(1/4)(3/4)}{(1/4)(3/4) + (3/4)(1/4)} = \frac{3/16}{6/16} = 1/2,$$

Notice that if the latter event occurs (the buy is followed by a sale), this moves the new posterior back to its original value (the beginning prior). It is also useful to note that these posteriors can be calculated directly from the prior, without going through the intermediate step of updating after the first observation. That is, for example,

$$\Pr\{V = 0|B, B\} =$$
$$\frac{\Pr\{V = 0\}(\Pr\{B|V = 0\})^2}{\Pr\{V = 0\}(\Pr\{B|V = 0\})^2 + \Pr\{V = 1\}\ (\Pr\{B|V = 1\})^2}. \tag{3.27}$$
$$= \frac{(1/2)(1/4)^2}{(1/2)(1/4)^2 + (1/2)(3/4)^2} = 1/10$$

Given these posterior beliefs, what are the ask and bid prices?

$$E\left[V \mid B, B\right] = \Pr\{V = 0\}(0) + \Pr\{V = 1\}(1)$$
$$= (.1)(0) + (.9)(1) = .9, \tag{3.28}$$

$$E\left[V \mid B, S\right] = \Pr\left\{V = 0\right\}(0) + \Pr\left\{V = 1\right\}(1) = .5. \qquad (3.29)$$

The evolution of quotes for this trade history can thus be depicted as follows:

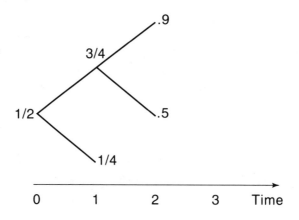

Figure 3.A.1 The Evolution of Quotes in the Market.

3.A.2 THE DYNAMICS OF BAYESIAN LEARNING

As updating occurs, it follows that beliefs (and thus prices) change over time. Since this price movement corresponds to the market maker's learning about the underlying information, several important questions arise. First, where are the prices going? Does the price process eventually go to a single point, or can prices continue to cycle? A second, and related, issue concerns the speed of price adjustment. If prices do converge to some value, how long does this take?

To address these issues, we must analyze how the updating process behaves over time. In particular, we will demonstrate two important properties of the dynamics of Bayesian learning:

1. the posteriors converge almost surely to the true value; and
2. the posteriors of a Bayesian observing an independent and identically distributed process over time converge exponentially.

This first property has the important implication that prices will eventually be at the full-information value, and so they will be strong-form efficient (for a discussion of efficiency definitions, see Section 3.3). From a finance perspective, this is clearly a desirable property, as it suggests that markets are efficiently impounding information into prices. The second property, suggests that, while this adjustment is not instantaneous, it is possible to quantify how long it will take. Consequently, it may be possible to analyze (and compare) the speed of price adjustment in alternative market settings. To demonstrate these properties, we need first to consider the Strong Law of Large Numbers.

The Strong Law of Large Numbers

Let X_t be an i.i.d. sample from some distribution with mean μ. Then

$$\lim_{T \to \infty} \frac{1}{T} \sum_{t=1}^{T} X_t = \mu \tag{3.30}$$

Intuitively, this says that if you take the average, as the sample gets large the average observation goes to the true mean. By almost surely (denoted a.s.) it is meant that

$$\Pr\left\{ \lim_{T \to \infty} \frac{1}{T} \sum_{t=1}^{T} X_t = \mu \right\} = 1 \tag{3.31}$$

or that, on a set of sample paths, with probability one the limit of the sample average is the true mean μ.

Now, let's return to our market maker problem. We want to look at what happens to prices as we look at a sequence of trades. To do so, we need to specify a few definitions.

Definition: Let $b = \#$ buys, $s = \#$ sales.

Because the trades are i.i.d., we need not worry about the sequence of trades and so can keep track of simply the aggregate numbers of buys and sales. These are sufficient statistics for the sample. Let us retain the structure introduced earlier of letting V take on values either high or low, but now let these values be denoted $\underline{V}$ and $\bar{V}$.

Definition: Let

$$q = \Pr\{B|\underline{V}\}, \ 1 - q = \Pr\{S|\underline{V}\},$$
$$p = \Pr\{B|\bar{V}\}, \ 1 - p = \Pr\{S|\bar{V}\},$$

where B denotes the event that a specific trade is a buy, and S that it is a sale.

Now, we can write the general updating formula as

$$\Pr\{\underline{V} \,|b, s\} = \frac{(\text{Prior}) \Pr\{\text{data}|V = \underline{V}\}}{\text{Marginal likelihood of the data}}$$

$$= \frac{\overbrace{\Pr(\underline{V})}^{\text{prior}} \overbrace{q^b(1-q)^s}^{\Pr\{\text{data}|V=\underline{V}\}}}{\underbrace{\Pr\{\underline{V}\} \, q^b(1-q)^s + \Pr\{\bar{V}\}p^b(1-p)^s}_{\text{Marginal likelihood for data}}}. \tag{3.32}$$

This formula gives us our posterior belief on the event $V = \underline{V}$ given the information we have learned from b buys and s sales. Notice that it has the same form as equation (3.27) but is now based on more than simply two trades. The formula for $\Pr\{\bar{V} \mid b, s\}$ is calculated similarly.

We now establish our first proposition that the posterior belief in equation (3.32) converges to the true value. Suppose that the event $V = \underline{V}$ has occurred. To prove our convergence result, we first look at the posterior odds (the ratio of the probability that $V = \bar{V}$ to the probability that $V = \underline{V}$):

$$\frac{\Pr\{\bar{V} \mid b, s\}}{\Pr\{\underline{V} \mid b, s\}} = \frac{\Pr_0\{\bar{V}\}p^b(1-p)^s}{\Pr_0\{\underline{V}\}q^b(1-q)^s}. \tag{3.33}$$

Second, take log of both sides:

$$\begin{aligned}
\log\left(\frac{\Pr\{\bar{V}|b, s\}}{\Pr\{\underline{V}|b, s\}}\right) &= \log\left(\frac{\Pr\{\bar{V}\}}{\Pr\{\underline{V}\}}\right) + \log p^b(1-p)^s \\
&\quad - \log q^b(1-q)^s \\
&= \log\left(\frac{\Pr\{\bar{V}\}}{\Pr\{\underline{V}\}}\right) \\
&\quad + b\log p + s \log(1 - p) - b \log q \\
&\quad - s \log(1 - q) .
\end{aligned} \tag{3.34}$$

The third step is to look at this average after many transactions. So divide both sides by the total trades $b + s$ and take the limit as $b + s$ goes to ∞:

$$\frac{1}{b+s} \log\left(\frac{\Pr\{\overline{V}|b,s\}}{\Pr\{\underline{V}|b,s\}}\right) = \underbrace{\frac{1}{b+s}}_{} \log\left(\frac{\Pr_0\{\overline{V}\}}{\Pr_0\{\underline{V}\}}\right) + \underbrace{\frac{b}{b+s}}_{} \left(\log\frac{p}{q}\right)$$

This goes to 0 as $b + s \to \infty$, and so the term $\to 0$.	If $V = \underline{V}$, then this goes to q by definition of q, a.s.

$$+ \underbrace{\frac{s}{b+s}}_{} \left(\log\frac{1-p}{1-q}\right). \tag{3.35}$$

This goes to $1 - q$, by definition (i.e., proportion of trades that are sales when $V = \underline{V}$ is $1 - q$, a.s.).

This implies that

$$\frac{1}{b+s} \log\left(\frac{\Pr\{\overline{V}|b,s\}}{\Pr\{\underline{V}|b,s\}}\right) \overset{a.s.}{\to} q \log\left(\frac{p}{q}\right) + (1-q) \log\left(\frac{1-p}{1-q}\right). \tag{3.36}$$

Now suppose the right hand side of equation (3.36) is negative. How can this happen? Only if $\log\left(\frac{\Pr\{V=\overline{V}\,|b,s\}}{\Pr\{V=\underline{V}\,|b,s\}}\right)$ is going to minus infinity. This will happen when $\left(\frac{\Pr\{V=\overline{V}\,|b,s\}}{\Pr\{V=\underline{V}\,|b,s\}}\right)$ goes to 0, or $\Pr\{V = \overline{V}|b,s\}$ goes to 0, which is what we wished to show. This suggests that to establish our result, we need only determine the sign of the right-hand side. As will be apparent, the right hand side of the equation is related to the standard statistical concept of entropy.

3.A.3   ENTROPY

Entropy is a measure of distance between probabilities. Entropy is defined as

$$I_q(p) \equiv q \log\left(\frac{q}{p}\right) + (1-q) \log\left(\frac{1-q}{1-p}\right) \tag{3.37}$$

There are three useful properties of entropy measures to note:

(1) $I_q(p) \geq 0 \quad \forall q, p,$ \hfill (3.38)

(2) $I_q(q) = 0$ \hfill (3.39)

(3) $I_q(p) \neq 0 \quad$ if $p \neq q$. \hfill (3.40)

The first property states that entropy is always positive, while the second states that its minimum is at zero. The third property dictates that the measure will not be zero unless $p = q$. To see the intuition for these claims, note that $I_q(p)$ is strictly convex in p and attains its minimum at $p = q$.

Let us now return to our market maker problem. What is the right-hand side of equation (3.36)? The negative of the entropy. So

$$\frac{1}{b+s} \log \left(\frac{\Pr\{V = \overline{V}|b, s\}}{\Pr\{V = \underline{V}|b, s\}} \right) \overset{\text{a.s.}}{\to} -I_q(p), \tag{3.41}$$

which is <0 if $q \neq p$. Note that if $q = p$, then trade data is not informative, and beliefs will remain at our original prior. If trades are informative, then beliefs do go to the true value, and this establishes our convergence result.

The second property we wish to establish is the speed of convergence. This, too, can be derived from our entropy measure. Since trades take place sequentially and there is one trade per period, letting t index time we can substitute t for $b + s$. Then equation (3.41) can be written

$$\frac{1}{t} \log \left(\frac{\Pr\{V = \overline{V} |b, s\}}{\Pr\{V = \underline{V} |b, s\}} \right) \to -I_q(p), \quad \text{a.s.} \tag{3.42}$$

So $\left(\frac{\Pr\{V=\overline{V} |b, s\}}{\Pr\{V=\underline{V} |b, s\}} \right)$ converges exponentially at rate $-I_q(p)$ to zero almost surely. This establishes our second result.

3.A.4 BAYESIAN UPDATING WITH CONTINUOUSLY DISTRIBUTED RANDOM VARIABLES

Our analysis thus far has demonstrated the updating method and convergence properties of Bayesian learning models in which the underlying random variables have discrete distributions. Many decision problems, however, involve continuously distributed random variables, and hence it is useful to consider how Bayesian updating occurs in those settings. To conclude this appendix, we review the general updating procedure and then derive the posterior distribution for the case of normally distributed random variables. Since many microstructure and rational expectations models involve such a normal structure, examining Bayesian learning in this context is particularly useful for understanding the evolution of prices and beliefs in those models.

To specify the learning problem, suppose we have a prior belief on a parameter μ, given by the density $g(\mu)$. We observe independently and identically distributed draws of a random variable x. Let the conditional density of x given μ be given by $f(x|\mu)$. To find the posterior distribution on μ given an observation x, recall that

$$\text{Posterior belief} = \frac{\text{Prior belief x Conditional probability of the data}}{\text{Marginal likelihood of the data}}$$

which for continuous distributions is

$$g(\mu|x) = \frac{g(\mu)f(x|\mu)}{\int f(x|\mu)g(\mu)\, d\mu}. \tag{3.43}$$

This is Bayes Rule for updating beliefs with continuously distributed random variables.

Example: Normally Distributed Random Variables

Suppose that the prior density $g(\mu)$ is $N(m, \sigma_\mu^2)$ and that $f(x\mid\mu)$ is $N(\mu, \sigma_x^2)$. Then

$$g(\mu) = \frac{1}{\sqrt{2\pi}\,\sigma_\mu} \exp\left[-\frac{1}{2\sigma_\mu^2}(\mu - m)^2 \right], \tag{3.44}$$

$$f(x|\mu) = \frac{1}{\sqrt{2\pi}\,\sigma_x} \exp\left[-\frac{1}{2\sigma_x^2}(x - \mu)^2 \right]. \tag{3.45}$$

Applying equation (3.43), the posterior density is given by

$$\left(\frac{\sigma_x^2 + \sigma_\mu^2}{2\pi\sigma_x^2\sigma_\mu^2} \right)^{1/2} \exp\left[-\left(\frac{\sigma_x^2 + \sigma_\mu^2}{2\sigma_x^2\sigma_\mu^2} \right) \left[\mu - \frac{\frac{m}{\sigma_\mu^2} + \frac{x}{\sigma_x^2}}{\frac{1}{\sigma_\mu^2} + \frac{1}{\sigma_x^2}} \right]^2 \right] \tag{3.46}$$

and so the posterior distribution is

$$N\left(\frac{\frac{m}{\sigma_\mu^2} + \frac{x}{\sigma_x^2}}{\frac{1}{\sigma_\mu^2} + \frac{1}{\sigma_x^2}}, \left(\frac{1}{\sigma_\mu^2} + \frac{1}{\sigma_x^2} \right)^{-1} \right). \tag{3.47}$$

There are several important properties to note about this example. First, the posterior is a normal. Hence if we begin with a normal prior and observe a normally distributed random variable, our posterior remains normal. This is a particularly useful property for tractability, and as we will see in the Appendix to Chapter 4, this feature is extensively exploited in rational expectations models.

Second, the mean of the posterior distribution reveals that the updating essentially involves weighting the prior and the signal by their respective precisions, where the precision is defined as the inverse of the variance. Hence, the posterior mean can be written as

$$\left[m\frac{1}{\sigma_\mu^2} + x\frac{1}{\sigma_x^2}\right] \bigg/ \left[\frac{1}{\sigma_\mu^2} + \frac{1}{\sigma_x^2}\right], \tag{3.48}$$

where the denominator is simply the sum of the precisions. Rather than calculate the integral in equation (3.43), therefore, a simpler method for finding the mean of the posterior belief is to multiply the prior and the signal outcome by their precisions and divide by the sum of the precisions.

Just as in the discrete case, the Bayesian's posterior beliefs converge to the truth when he sees repeated draws of x. After T independent draws $x_1, \ldots, x_T$ from $N(\mu, \sigma_x^2)$, the posterior is

$$N\left(\frac{\frac{m}{\sigma_\mu^2} + \frac{\Sigma_{t=1}^T x_t}{\sigma_x^2}}{\frac{1}{\sigma_\mu^2} + \frac{T}{\sigma_x^2}}, \ \left(\frac{1}{\sigma_\mu^2} + \frac{T}{\sigma_x^2}\right)^{-1}\right). \tag{3.49}$$

Using the Strong Law of Large Numbers, we again see that the mean of the posterior converges a.s. to μ and the variance of the posterior converges to zero.

4

Strategic Trader Models I: Informed Traders

The sequential trade models analyzed in the previous chapter characterize the behavior of security prices when all agents act competitively. The existence of private information, however, means that an informed trader may have an incentive to act strategically to maximize his profits. In this chapter, we consider the main models that analyze these information-based trading strategies. Because strategic models allow agents to time their trades or to choose their trade size, the equilibrium in these models can differ dramatically from that of the competitive outcome characterized in the sequential trade models.

One aspect of the strategic trader models that differs from the earlier microstructure models is their explicit link to the rational expectations literature. In rational expectations models (for example, see Grossman and Stiglitz [1980]), an important aspect of an agent's decision problem is the inference he makes from market statistics about others' information. In the market microstructure context analyzed here, it is the informed agent's conjecture about the market maker's pricing policy as well as the market maker's inference about the informed agent's information that plays a crucial role in determining the nature (and even the existence) of the equilibrium. For the reader unfamiliar with the rational expectations approach, the Appendix to this chapter provides a review of the basic framework and a discussion of its properties.

In the next two chapters we consider how this approach has been developed to address strategic issues in market microstructure. As a starting point, we consider the basic question of how a single informed trader can best exploit his informational advantage to maximize his profit. This strategic behavior was analyzed by Kyle [1985] in an important model of batch trading in securities markets. We then examine more complex strategic issues involving multiple informed traders and the nature of the trading mechanism. In the next chapter, we extend the analysis to incorporate strategic behavior by uninformed traders, and we analyze the effect of uninformed strategic behavior on security prices.

4.1 THE STRATEGIC BEHAVIOR OF AN INFORMED TRADER

In the models considered thus far, a trader who has superior information simply submits an order at each trading opportunity until prices eventually adjust to the new full-information value. If there are numerous traders acting in a competitive market, this strategy may accord well with actual market behavior. If there is one or even a few informed traders, however, this depiction is unlikely to be accurate. The problem is that a single informed trader possesses a valuable commodity, and as an "information monopolist" he should act to exploit that advantage. In particular, the trader will want to select his order size and trading intensity to explicitly take account of the effect that his trades will have on the movement of prices. This requires the informed trader to incorporate expectations of the market maker's pricing strategy, as well as any possible strategic actions by uninformed traders, into his optimal order strategy.

The first models to address theses strategic aspects of information in a market microstructure context were Kyle [1984, 1985]. Kyle's initial paper [1984] was directed at analyzing the behavior of informed speculators in a futures market and so includes multiple speculators and multiple market makers. Because of this slightly different focus, we consider this work more fully later in this chapter. Kyle's [1985] analysis involves a simpler framework in which a single risk neutral informed trader and a number of uninformed liquidity traders submit orders to a risk neutral market maker. The market maker aggregates the orders and clears all trades at a single price. Hence, unlike the sequential trade models, Kyle's batch-trading model does not allow for a bid-ask spread nor does it analyze the transaction price for individual trades. What his model does allow, however, is the explicit characterization of how an informed trader would choose to transact to maximize the value of private information. This, in turn, provides a way to characterize how information is incorporated into security prices across time given the strategic use of information by an informed trader.

In Kyle's model, a single risk neutral informed trader receives private information about the *ex post* liquidation value, v, of an asset. This liquidation value is assumed normally distributed with mean p_0 and variance Σ_0. Initially, Kyle considers a single trading period in which the informed trader submits his optimal order along with the orders submitted by uninformed traders. Kyle then temporally extends the model to consider sequential-auction and continuous-auction frameworks. As the intuition is the same, we focus on the simpler version of the model.

4.1.1 *The Single-Auction Setting*

In this batch-clearing model, the market maker does not see individual orders but rather sets a market-clearing price given the aggregate net order flow. As this order flow includes both informed and uninformed trades, it can provide a signal to the market maker of the underlying information in much the same way as it does in the sequential trade models. The actual learning process differs, however, in that it is the aggregate trade quantity that affects price behavior and not the size of any individual trade.

As was also true in the sequential trade models, there must be some uninformed traders who transact for nonspeculative reasons. If not, then the only equilibrium is a fully revealing one in which the price is set at the new, full-information, value. In the Kyle model, this requirement is met by assuming the existence of "noise" traders. Kyle assumes that these noise traders do not act strategically but rather submit a trade quantity that is a normally distributed random variable μ with mean 0 and variance σ_μ^2. This random variable is assumed independent of the distribution of the asset value v.

The informed trader knows the distribution of μ and hence can attempt to use the uninformed volume to hide his trades. An important aspect of the Kyle framework, however, is that the informed trader does not know the actual realization of the uninformeds' demands. Consequently, the informed trader cannot condition on the uninformed trade quantity when he submits his order.[1] This represents a significant departure from the typical approach taken in rational expectations models. As the Appendix demonstrates, in those models it is commonplace for an informed trader to condition on the equilibrium price in deciding on his optimal order. Since in actual markets this is not observed, Kyle's framework captures the uncertainty that more naturally surrounds security trading.

The trade protocol in this model involves a two-step process. In the first step, v (the asset's true value) and μ (the uninformed traders' order flow) are realized, and the informed trader chooses his trade quantity, x. In the

---

1. Rochet and Vila [1994] analyze a model related to that of Kyle in which the informed trader does know the uninformed demand before submitting this order. They view this model as essentially allowing the informed trader to submit a limit order. Their focus lies in determining the uniqueness of equilibrium, and they show that in their model the equilibrium is unique. See also the discussion in Section 4.3

second stage, the market maker observes the aggregate net order flow quantity $x + \mu$ and sets a single price p to clear the market. In equilibrium, the informed trader's profits are then simply given by $\pi = (v - p)x$.

The equilibrium in this model is more complex than in the sequential trading models because it involves analyzing the strategies of both the informed trader and the market maker. In equilibrium, the market maker is assumed to set prices so that, given the order flow $(x + \mu)$, prices are efficient. This means that the price is set equal to the conditional expected value of the asset given the aggregate order quantity. This condition is similar to that found in the sequential trade models, but here the market maker only observes and conditions on aggregate net trades. This changes the specific learning problem from that analyzed in the previous chapter, where each trade was observable. Because, however, the market maker sets a "regret-free" price and earns zero expected profit, the learning problem is solved using the same Bayesian framework, and the general results of Bayesian learning models apply.

Let the market maker's pricing strategy be represented by a function $p = P(x + \mu)$. Then the equilibrium price must satisfy

$$P(x + \mu) = E[v \mid x + \mu]. \qquad (4.1)$$

The informed trader's order strategy, $X(\bullet)$, depends on this pricing rule as well as on the parameters of the uninformed traders' order distribution. Although the informed trader does not know the actual uninformed trader order flow, he does know the parameters of its distribution and he has an expectation of how the market maker will set prices given any order flow realization. Given this pricing rule, the order strategy of the informed trader must satisfy

$$E\Big[\pi(X(\bullet), P) \mid \tilde{v} = v\Big] > E\Big[\pi(X'(\bullet), P) \mid \tilde{v} = v\Big], \quad \text{for each } v, \qquad (4.2)$$

or simply that the expected profit of the informed trader from following the strategy $X(\bullet)$ is greater than that from following any other order strategy $X'(\bullet)$.

This strategic behavior by the informed trader means that he explicitly takes into account the effect his trade will have on the equilibrium price set by the market maker. In this sense, the informed trader acts as an "information monopolist" by attempting to extract the most rent from his unique private information. If, instead, the informed trader acted competitively, then the absence of constraints on trade size combined with the trader's risk neutrality would result in prices in the batch market immediately adjusting to new, full-information values. With strategic behavior, however, this immediate adjustment need not occur, and the informed trader obtains a positive trading profit.

Kyle demonstrates that there is an equilibrium in this model in which the strategies of the informed trader and the market maker are given by

$$X(v) = \beta(v - p_0) \tag{4.3}$$

and

$$P(x + \mu) = p_0 + \lambda(x + \mu) \tag{4.4}$$

where

$$\beta = \left(\frac{\sigma_\mu^2}{\Sigma_0}\right)^{1/2} \text{ and } \lambda = 1/2 \left(\frac{\sigma_\mu^2}{\Sigma_0}\right)^{-1/2} \tag{4.5}$$

Before analyzing the derivation of this solution, it is useful to note two important properties of this equilibrium. First, the informed trader's optimal order quantity depends on the variance of the uninformed trader order flow. Since the informed trader does not know the actual uninformed order quantity, he uses the variance to "hide" his trade from the market maker. This, in turn, means that the informed trader's expected profit also depends on the uninformed order variance. As is apparent from the equations, the larger this uninformed variance, the better the informed trader is able to "hide" his trades and, hence, the larger his profit is.

That the optimal trading quantity also depends on the signal variance arises because of the strategic link between the order size and price adjustment. In particular, in this equilibrium the pricing rule is linear in the aggregate order quantity. Since this order flow is composed of both informed and uninformed trades, the λ variable reflects how much the market maker adjusts the price to reflect the information content of trades. Because the order flow variables x and μ are independent continuous random variables, this price adjustment is based on the convolution of their densities. Consequently, the adjustment of prices depends on the ratio of the amount of noise trading to the amount of private information the informed trader is expected to have. And since the informed trader conditions his trade on this pricing rule, his optimal trading strategy also depends on these variables.

A derivation of this equilibrium follows from a straightforward application of the laws of conditional distributions of normally distributed random variables. In particular, if $\vartheta = <\vartheta^{(1)}, \vartheta^{(2)}>$ is distributed $N(\mu, \Sigma)$, and Σ is nonsingular, then

$$E\left(\vartheta^{(1)} \mid \vartheta^{(2)}\right) = \mu^{(1)} + \Sigma_{12}\Sigma_{22}^{-1}\left(\vartheta^{(2)} - \mu^{(2)}\right). \qquad (4.6)$$

In the context considered here, this can be applied by defining

$$\vartheta \equiv \begin{pmatrix} \tilde{v} \\ \tilde{y} \end{pmatrix}, \quad \mu = \begin{pmatrix} E(v) \\ E(x + \mu) \end{pmatrix} = \begin{pmatrix} p_0 \\ \alpha + \beta p_0 \end{pmatrix}, \qquad (4.7)$$

where $\tilde{y}$ is the aggregate (net) order flow and

$$\Sigma = \begin{pmatrix} \Sigma_{11} & \Sigma_{12} \\ \Sigma_{21} & \Sigma_{22} \end{pmatrix} = \begin{pmatrix} \Sigma_0 & \beta\Sigma_0 \\ \beta\Sigma_0 & \sigma_\mu^2 + \beta^2\Sigma_0 \end{pmatrix} \qquad (4.8)$$

Then applying (4.6) dictates that

$$
\begin{aligned}
E(v \mid y) &= \mu^{(1)} + \Sigma_{12}\Sigma_{22}^{-1}\left(y - \mu^{(2)}\right) \\
&= p_0 + \frac{\beta\Sigma_0}{\sigma_\mu^2 + \beta^2\Sigma_0}(y - \alpha - \beta p_0) \qquad (4.9) \\
&= p_0 + \lambda y.
\end{aligned}
$$

The value of λ derived here is simply that of the equilibrium solution noted in equation (4.5) (after appropriate substitutions). The other equilibrium values can be determined similarly.

While this mechanistic approach to the model leads to the equilibrium solution, it does not lend much intuition into how the underlying decision problem results in the equilibrium outcome. This can, perhaps, be better understood by examining the learning problem the market maker faces in setting the market-clearing price given the order flow realization $x + \mu$. Just as in the sequential trade models, the market maker makes an inference about the underlying information from the trades he observes. While the trading mechanisms in the two approaches result in different trade information, the learning problem in both approaches involves an application of Bayes Rule. In particular, before trade begins, the market maker has a prior belief about the value of the asset, which is given by the normal distribution $N(p_0, \Sigma_0)$. The market maker will observe some net order flow $x + \mu$, which is composed of both uninformed and informed orders. The uninformed orders are normally distributed as $N(0, \sigma_\mu^2)$, but the informed orders depend on what the informed trader has seen.

Suppose that the market maker believes the informed trader will follow the linear order strategy, $x = \beta(v - p_0)$. The market maker does not observe x but rather sees $x + \mu$, which we shall call θ. Then $\theta = x + \mu = \beta(v - p_0) + \mu$. Rearranging terms yields

$$\theta/\beta + p_0 = v + \mu/\beta. \tag{4.10}$$

Let the left-hand side of the equation be denoted Z; so

$$Z \equiv \theta/\beta + p_0 = v + \mu/\beta. \tag{4.11}$$

Note that Z is distributed as $N(v, \sigma_\mu^2/\beta^2)$ and its distribution depends on v and known variables. (It shall be clear shortly why the market maker knows β.) Hence Z is a transformation of the observed order flow that has the same mean as the underlying asset.

Given Z, the market maker revises his beliefs about the asset's value v and sets the market-clearing price. This new price will be his posterior belief, and so the market maker updates his prior belief using Bayes Rule.[2] Thus the new posterior mean is

$$p_1 = \frac{p_0/\Sigma_0 + Z\left(\beta^2/\sigma_\mu^2\right)}{1/\Sigma_0 + \beta^2/\sigma_\mu^2} \tag{4.12}$$

and the variance is

$$\Sigma_1 = \left(1/\Sigma_0 + \beta^2/\sigma_\mu^2\right)^{-1}. \tag{4.13}$$

Rearranging terms and substituting for β in the price equation yields

$$p_1 = \frac{p_0\sigma_\mu^2 + \sigma_\mu^2 Z}{\sigma_\mu^2 + \sigma_\mu^2} = \frac{1}{2}(p_0 + Z)$$

$$= \frac{1}{2}(p_0 + \theta/\beta + p_0). \tag{4.14}$$

Recall that $\theta = x + \mu$; thus this can be written as

---

2. Recall from the Appendix to Chapter 3 that this is given by the prior mean times its precision plus the new observation Y times its precision, divided by the sum of the precisions.

$$p_1 = p_0 + \frac{x + \mu}{2\beta} = p_0 + \frac{1}{2}\left(\frac{\sigma_\mu^2}{\Sigma_0}\right)^{-1/2}(x + \mu)$$

$$= p_0 + \lambda(x + \mu), \quad \text{where } \lambda = \frac{1}{2}\left(\frac{\sigma_\mu^2}{\Sigma_0}\right)^{-1/2}.$$

$$(4.15)$$

Hence the market maker's price will, in fact, be linear in the order flow. This linearity is what allows the β variable to be known to the market maker. In particular, because the informed trader conjectures that prices will be linear in quantities, his objective function is quadratic in trade size. The optimal order strategy X that results from solving the maximization problem is then linear in the value of the asset, or $X(v) = a + \beta v$. The market maker can thus solve for what this value of β must be if he follows a linear pricing schedule.

What makes this equilibrium so easy to characterize is its linear structure. This linearity in order strategy is important because it means that the informed trader will not pursue a more complex mixed strategy or submit orders that are linked to the underlying signal value in a nonlinear manner. Consequently, given this strategic behavior by the informed trader, the market maker knows that the relationship between the aggregate order flow and the underlying signal value must also be linear. Since in equilibrium the market efficiency condition requires the market maker to set prices equal to the conditional expected value, this, in turn, means that market prices will also be linear in volume.

One way to interpret this pricing relation is that large volume results in a "worse" price, but not an increasingly worse price. Hence, a large volume outcome need not cause the market maker to instantly adjust the price to the full-information value as would occur if prices could be nonlinear in volume. Of course, an unfortunate implication of the linearity of prices and volume is that for a large enough negative trade imbalance the market maker would wish to set a negative price. This suggests that, as a description of actual price behavior, a linear pricing rule is, at best, an approximation.

A second feature of this linear price-volume relationship is that given the expected uninformed volume, the informed trader always chooses his order size so that his relative share is the same. Thus, if *ex ante*, the uninformed volume were to double, the informed trader would also double his order size.[3] This can be seen by noting that the informed trader's order strategy is

---

3. Note that the definition of uninformed volume in this market is somewhat confusing because the order flow is assumed to be a random variable with mean zero. The expected volume, however, will involve the absolute value of the orders and, and hence the volume

$$x = \left(\frac{\sigma_\mu^2}{\Sigma_0}\right)^{1/2} (v - p),$$ (4.16)

and his *ex ante* profit is given by

$$\pi = \frac{1}{2}\left(\Sigma_0 \sigma_\mu^2\right)^{1/2}.$$ (4.17)

Thus, doubling σ_μ simply doubles the order submitted by the informed trader, and this doubles the informed trader's expected profit.

With the uninformed and the informed both trading twice as much, an interesting question is, what happens to prices? Intriguingly, in this model, there is no *ex ante* change in the price. To see this, note that market maker's price can be written as

$$p = p_0 + \frac{1}{2\left(\frac{\sigma_\mu^2}{\Sigma_0}\right)^{1/2}} \left[\left(\frac{\sigma_\mu^2}{\Sigma_0}\right)^{1/2}(v - p_0) + \mu\right].$$ (4.18)

Because changes in σ_μ^2 affect both the optimal x and the optimal λ, these effects offset in the pricing equation. This implies that price behavior in markets is independent of factors such as market volume. As will be discussed later, this result is crucially dependent on the assumption of a fixed number (in this case, one) of informed traders.

Rational expectations requires that the pricing rule the informed trader conjectures is in fact the pricing rule the market maker uses. In the equilibrium noted above, this requirement is met in that the informed trader conjectures a linear pricing rule and the market maker in fact uses that linear pricing rule. But is this is the only equilibrium that can prevail? In particular, if the informed trader conjectured a different pricing rule, could that also result in an equilibrium?

In general, this question of uniqueness of equilibria is impossible to answer. In the Kyle framework, there are no other linear equilibria, but there could be nonlinear equilibria. In a nonlinear equilibrium, the market maker would not attach a linear relation between prices and volume (and by extension, to the underlying asset value), and so the informed trader's order strategy need not be linear or, indeed, even be a pure strategy. A more practical difficulty is that the linearity that provides much of the model's

---

will depend on the variance of the order flow. It is this uninformed order variance that is used throughout the model.

tractability would be lost, so that even characterizing these other equilibria would be formidable.

Since the objective of the Kyle model is to describe how an informed trader could trade on information, this potential for multiple equilibria does not raise a serious difficulty. In other applications of rational expectations models to microstructure issues, however, such problems are of more importance. In particular, ascribing policy implications is highly problematic if more than one equilibrium outcome is possible. A related difficulty is the reliance in this and in many other rational expectations-based models on the assumption of joint normality of random variables. While this assumption is needed for tractability, it directly affects predictions regarding factors such as the optimal trade size and the effects of volume. We return to these issues in more detail in later chapters.

In the single-auction framework described above, the informed trader's optimal order strategy results in the market maker's new beliefs reflecting some, but not all, of the informed trader's information. This information revelation, however, does not mean that the new market price p_1 is necessarily closer to the true value v. What price comes to be depends on the actual net order flow. An unexpectedly large uninformed buy imbalance could overwhelm the informed trader's sell order, causing the market maker to set a high price even though the full-information value is low. Where the information affects price behavior is through the variance. Recall that the variance of the posterior distribution is

$$\Sigma_1 = \left(\frac{1}{\Sigma_0} + \frac{\beta^2}{\sigma_\mu^2} \right)^{-1}. \tag{4.19}$$

Substituting for β and rearranging, this becomes

$$\Sigma_1 = \frac{\Sigma_0 \sigma_\mu^2}{\sigma_\mu^2 + \sigma_\mu^2} = \frac{1}{2}\Sigma_0 \tag{4.20}$$

Hence, regardless of the actual trade outcome, the new variance is exactly one-half of the prior variance. This is what is meant by Kyle's claim that the trader's optimal order strategy will result in half of his information being revealed by the market price. Note that this variance effect is deterministic, so that the market maker's new beliefs about v have half their previous dispersion, though their new realized mean need not be more accurate.[4]

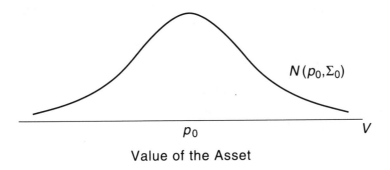

$$N(p_0, \Sigma_0)$$

p_0 V

Value of the Asset

The time 0 prior beliefs of the market maker are depicted above. This is also the expected posterior (before trade occurs). At time 1, the actual posterior depends on the trade outcome.

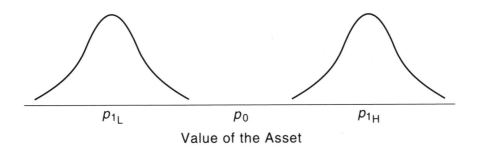

p_{1L} p_0 p_{1H}

Value of the Asset

Depending on the net order flow (depicted here as high or low) the market maker's beliefs shift to either p_{1L} or p_{1H}. The new variance is $\Sigma_1 = \Sigma_0/2$.

Figure 4.1. The Evolution of the Market Maker's Beliefs

---

4. This variance property is a direct result of the normality assumptions in the model. If the normality assumption were relaxed, then the variance would not have the deterministic pattern found in this paper. Foster and Viswanathan [1993] investigate such variance effects by enlarging the set of allowable distributions to include all elliptically contoured distributions (which includes the normal distribution as well as others). Their results provide intriguing evidence that the price behavior depicted in the Kyle model is greatly dependent on the assumption of normal distributions. Their work also suggests that price adjustment with nondeterministic variances may be a great deal more complex.

Figure 4.1 illustrates this variance effect by considering how the market maker's beliefs (and prices) change. At time 0, the market maker's beliefs are given by $N(p_0, \Sigma_0)$. Following the trade outcome, the market maker's beliefs change so that their new distribution is centered on p_1 and has exactly half the variance of the prior distribution: $N(p_1, \Sigma_0/2)$. Note that since prices in this model will be a Martingale, before the trade outcome at time 1, the expected posterior mean is p_0. On average, of course, the posterior mean is moving toward v. To see this, note that from (4.18) the expectation of p_1, conditional on v, is $E[p_1 \mid v] = (p_1 + v)/2$.

It is easy to see that the variance will converge to zero given enough rounds of trading. It will also be the case that the posterior mean will converge (almost surely) to the true value v. This follows because the sample mean of the aggregate order flow, Y_t, is given by

$$\frac{1}{T}\sum_{t=1}^{T} Y_t = v + \frac{1}{\beta}\frac{1}{T}\sum_{t=1}^{T}\mu_t. \tag{4.21}$$

By the Strong Law of Large Numbers,

$$\frac{1}{T}\sum_{t=1}^{T}\mu_t \to 0, \quad \text{almost surely,} \tag{4.22}$$

and so

$$\frac{1}{T}\sum_{t=1}^{T} Y_t \to 0, \quad \text{almost surely}, \tag{4.23}$$

Hence, given multiple rounds of trading, prices converge to their full-information value.

If there were multiple rounds of trading, however, it is not clear that the equilibrium analyzed thus far actually prevails. The difficulty is that in a one-shot trading model the informed trader need only consider the impact of his trades on that period's price, whereas with repeated trading opportunities the multiperiod impacts must also be considered. This creates a much more complicated decision problem, and consequently it necessitates a richer model. Incorporating multiple periods into the model can be done either as a sequence of auctions or as a continuous auction. We first consider the sequential auction framework in Kyle, and then we examine the continuous trading model developed by Back [1992].

4.1.2 The Multiple Trading Period Equilibrium

Kyle addresses this issue of multiple periods by looking at a sequential auction in which N rounds of trade occur in a trading day. This is a discrete time setting, but as the number of periods becomes large, it approximates a continuous auction. In a multiperiod setting, the informed trader faces the problem that his trading decisions in each period are linked because of their effect on the informativeness of prices. If the trader opts to trade large amounts in early periods, then this is penalized in later periods by "worse" prices. The trader's optimal order strategy, therefore, must take account of future as well as current trading opportunities and profits. Since these opportunities depend, in part, on the behavior of the uninformed, their behavior must be specified in more detail.

Kyle assumes that as the number of periods becomes large, the uninformed trades $\tilde{u}(t)$ follow a Brownian motion, so that $\Delta\tilde{u}_n$ is normally distributed with mean zero and variance $\sigma_\mu^2\Delta t_n$. One implication of this assumption is that the uninformed quantity traded at one auction is independent of the uninformed quantity traded at the other auctions. Since this will not be true of the quantity traded by the informed trader, it is this linkage of information and quantity that will ultimately cause prices to reflect all underlying information.

The informed trader's profit in this setting now depends on his trading behavior and the prices over the N sequential auctions. The informed trader's profits for auctions $n, \ldots, N$ is given by

$$\tilde{\pi}_n = \sum_{k=n}^{N}(\tilde{v} - \tilde{p}_k)\Delta\tilde{x}_k. \tag{4.24}$$

The equilibrium solution to this recursive model involves the same general linear form as in the single-auction model. In this equilibrium, prices are linearly related to the order flow and the informed order strategy is linearly related to the true asset value. As trades occur, the market maker updates his beliefs using Bayes Rule and sets the market-clearing price equal to the mean of his posterior belief. The market maker's and the informed traders' strategies are then given by

$$\Delta X_n(\tilde{v}) = \beta_n(\tilde{v} - p_{n-1})\Delta t_n \tag{4.25}$$

and

$$p_n = \lambda_n(\Delta x_n + \Delta\mu_n), \tag{4.26}$$

and the informed trader's expected profit is

$$E\{\pi_n \mid p_1, \ldots, p_{n-1}, v\} = \alpha_{n-1}(v - p_{n-1})^2 + \delta_{n-1}. \qquad (4.27)$$

The constants in equations (4.24)-(4.27) are now the unique solutions to the difference equation system

$$\lambda_n = \frac{\beta_n \Sigma_n}{\sigma_\mu^2}, \qquad (4.28)$$

$$\beta_n \Delta t_n = \frac{1 - 2\alpha_n \lambda_n}{2\lambda_n(1 - \alpha_n \lambda_n)}, \qquad (4.29)$$

$$\alpha_{n-1} = \frac{1}{4\lambda_n(1 - \alpha_n \lambda_n)}, \qquad (4.30)$$

$$\delta_{n-1} = \delta_n + \alpha_n \lambda_n^2 \sigma^2 \mu \Delta t_n. \qquad (4.31)$$

The sequential-auction equilibrium is thus more complex than the single-auction equilibrium found earlier. The constant terms capture the multiperiod linkage between the order strategy and price movements, and hence they form a difference equation system. While the same linear equilibrium prevails as before, the coefficients β_n in the order strategy and λ_n in the price strategy change every period.[5]

Of particular interest is how the informed trader chooses to strategically exploit his information across time. A key property of this equilibrium is that information is gradually incorporated into prices across time. Whereas in the single-period framework the informed trader chose his order so that prices in the next period reflected half of his information, now this is no longer optimal. Indeed, the variance now takes the form

$$\Sigma_n = (1 - \beta_n \lambda_n \Delta t_n)\Sigma_{n-1}. \qquad (4.32)$$

As the time periods in the model are shortened to approach a continuous auction (i.e., $\Delta t_n \to 0$), this smoothing behavior by the informed trader

---

5. While our focus here is on the sequential-auction outcome, the continuous-time version of Kyle's model has been extensively characterized by Back [1992]. That research characterizes the market maker's pricing rule and the informed trader's order strategy in more detail, but at some cost in technical complexity.

results in prices that have constant volatility.[6] As expected, the price path also has the property that prices follow a Martingale, and so prices are "efficient" in the sense that an uninformed observer's expectation of the future price is today's price. Kyle demonstrates that prices eventually reflect the informed trader's new information, with prices in the continuous auction framework incorporating all information.

One consequence of this equilibrium is that the informed trader profits more by continuously trading rather than by attempting to manipulate prices through some mixed strategy. Unlike in the sequential trade models, however, it is not the case that the informed trader trades the same amount every period. Because the coefficients in both his and the market maker's strategies change every period, his optimal trade size also moves. Indeed, it is this ability to vary the trade size that allows the trader to "hide" from the market maker. Because the informed trader is eventually "found" by the market maker, profits are bounded, and the return to information can be calculated.

In the sequential-auction model, the informed trader trades in a series of discrete call markets. As the interval between these markets goes to zero, trading behavior approaches that of a continuous market. A more formal analysis of trading in a continuous market is given by Back [1992]. He characterizes the equilibrium that arises with continuous trading, and in particular he determines the equilibrium pricing rule in a model allowing for more general distributions for asset value. Because Back's model is essentially the limit of the discrete-time Kyle model, properties derived in this continuous setting may provide insights into more general properties of the Kyle equilibrium.

Rather than work through the formidable mechanics of the model's continuous-time structure, it may be more useful to consider the general approach and its equilibrium results. In this model, trade occurs in the interval [0, 1]. At time 1 there is assumed to be public arrival of information and the asset value is known to be worth $\tilde{v}$. Informed traders in the market know $\tilde{v}$ at time 0. Uninformed traders do not know the realization of $\tilde{v}$, nor do the competitive risk neutral market makers.

The structure of the trading process is extremely important in this model. Uninformed trade, denoted Z, is assumed to follow a Brownian motion. There is a single informed trader, whose trades, denoted X, are assumed to

---

6. This constant volatility property is also a characteristic of a random walk. Hence, a prediction of the Kyle model is that security prices will, in fact, follow a random walk. While this behavior is theoretically consistent with "efficient" markets, its existence in actual markets is contentious. Lo and MacKinley [1988] reject the random walk specification, while Richardson and Smith [1991] reach a different conclusion.

be a semi-Martingale adapted to v and Z. This semi-Martingale property allows the trade process to exhibit jumps, although Back shows that in equilibrium such jumps do not occur. The risk neutral competitive market makers compete for the order flow $Y_t \equiv X_t + Z_t$.

In this model, the informed trader can infer the uninformed trades by continuously monitoring the order flow, and hence he can know what Z is before submitting his order. This ability to condition on the uninformed trades turns out, however, to be of no advantage to the informed trader. While in a discrete-time model it would be useful to simply offset the trades of the uninformed (set $X = -Z$), in a continuous-time model large orders introduce jumps into the order process. Since the uninformed orders do not have such jumps, this order behavior is suboptimal for the informed trader, as it reveals his trade and thus his information.

Equilibrium in this model involves finding a pricing rule P and an order strategy X such that given P, X yields the trader the highest utility over all trading, and given X, P (or more precisely, $P(Y_t, t)$) is rational for the market maker. Finding X requires solving the Bellman equation of the trader's optimization problem.[7] Back shows that if a solution to the Bellman equation for X exists, then optimality requires that the strategy X has two properties. First, X has continuous finite variation paths. Second, $P(Y, 1) = v$, a.s.: all information is incorporated into prices at the end of trading, almost surely.

These properties of X allow Back to characterize the optimal pricing rule by focusing on the underlying order flow. Back shows that, for the pricing rule P to be rational when X has continuous finite variation paths, the order flow (Y_t, t) must be a Martingale. If the order flow (Y_t, t) is a Martingale and X has continuous finite variation paths, then this dictates that the order flow (Y_t, t) must also be a Brownian motion. This is the key to the model, as if the uninformed orders Z follow Brownian motion and the total orders Y follow Brownian motion, then the informed trades X must have the same distribution as the uninformed trades Z.

This order process behavior explains why it is that setting the informed orders to simply offset the uninformed cannot be optimal. With the uninformed orders following a Brownian motion, there are no discrete jumps in the order process. The informed order flow must have the same distribution as the uninformed, and so it, too, cannot have discrete jumps. Back shows that consistent with this condition there may be many optimal trading strategies for the single informed trader.

---

7. This optimization is similar to that found in Ho and Stoll, where they also solve for the Bellman equation (see Chapter 2).

Given this order flow behavior, Back solves for the optimal pricing rule. The advantage of this approach is that Back finds closed-form solutions for the general problem, and not merely for the specific example considered by Kyle. Back shows that the optimal pricing rule will have the property that price changes are proportional to order sizes. If the asset value is normally distributed (as in Kyle), then Back shows that the pricing rule is the same linear one found in Kyle. For log-normally distributed asset values, prices follow a geometric Brownian motion, and the pricing rule has a different form but is still a function of the order quantity.

This continuous-time approach allows the equilibrium to be investigated in a number of interesting ways. For example, the Back model can consider the effects on the equilibrium of alternative liquidity trader order processes. If liquidity trades vary throughout the day (for example, less trading at midday), then the optimal strategy for the informed trader changes as well. Back shows that there is more informed trade, greater volatility, and more information transmitted when there is more liquidity trade than at times when liquidity trade is less. These results suggest a complexity to the informed trader's optimal order strategy not predicted by the discrete-time Kyle model.[8] This model also provides an interesting complement to the research on uninformed behavior that we investigate in the next chapter.

The Kyle model and its extensions thus provide an elegant way to characterize how a single informed trader optimally exploits his informational advantage and what this, in turn, implies for the price process. While the model does not capture the evolution of prices (or quotes) in response to individual trades that the sequential trade models do, it does allow the return to information to be explicitly calculated. In subsequent work, this will allow authors to incorporate equilibrium in the information market into their analysis of equilibrium in the securities market.

There are, of course, many aspects of strategic behavior not included in the Kyle [1985] model. One such aspect is order strategy, as in this model the single informed trader is not permitted to submit price-contingent orders. Given the batch nature of trading, a more natural characterization might be to trade via limit orders that allow the trader greater flexibility in the size of his trade. The Kyle [1985] model can be reformulated to include price-contingent orders, and in the one-shot game insider profits and information revelation remain unchanged. The general issue of the relationship of order strategy and the trading mechanism, however, remains an open question. We consider this in more detail later in this chapter.

---

8. Back [1993] also shows that, with continuous trading and asymmetric information, options can no longer be priced via simple arbitrage. This has important implications for option-pricing models.

A second important strategic issue is the effect on the equilibrium of multiple informed traders. Because the informed trader acts strategically, in equilibrium he makes positive profits. These positive profits, however, may induce other traders to become informed, so that in equilibrium the number of informed traders is endogenous. In Kyle's [1985] model with only one informed trader, this issue of endogenous information-based trading is not considered. If, however, there can be multiple informed traders, then whether the solution derived above remains an equilibrium is unclear. A related issue is the availability of information through nonprivate sources. If the amount of publicly available information can vary, then the value of private information will surely be affected. These issues suggest examining how information affects trading behavior when the informed trader is not a monopolist.

4.2 PRICE BEHAVIOR AND MULTIPLE INFORMED TRADERS

Allowing multiple informed traders introduces an important complexity into the analysis. If an informed trader is no longer a monopolist, then the actions of other informed traders will affect the price, and hence the return to private information. In rational expectations models with multiple competitive informed traders, this interdependence typically results in prices reflecting so much information that they become revealing. With no return to being informed, there is no incentive for traders to ever gather information in the first place, and the process by which information is incorporated into prices becomes questionable.

One might expect this difficulty could be overcome by simply allowing the informed traders in rational expectations models to act strategically. This, however, is not easily accomplished. The reason is that in the standard rational expectations equilibrium the actual trading mechanism, or design of the market, is never considered. Since traders are competitive, how orders affect the "terms of trade" is irrelevant since it does not affect their trading behavior. If traders act strategically, however, the actual trading mechanism does matter because it determines how trades affect prices, which, in turn, affects traders' order strategies.

Given a specific trading mechanism, it may be possible to calculate the effect on prices of traders' orders and hence initiate investigation of the effect of multiple informed traders on market behavior. This is the approach taken in Kyle [1984] and more recently in work by Foster and Viswanathan [1993] and Holden and Subrahmanyam [1992]. While the Kyle model is highly structured, it does explicitly incorporate multiple informed traders in a model in which prices are not revealing, and hence it provides a useful starting point for our discussion.

The Kyle model employs a simple three-date framework involving N speculators (or informed traders) and M market makers. The limiting case of $M = \infty$ corresponds to the competitive case, while smaller values of M allow the market makers to exert some market power. The model shares the same batch-trading approach of Kyle [1985], and it also requires that speculators must submit market orders prior to knowing the price at which they will trade. This timing convention is what will allow prices to not be revealing, as they would be in more conventional rational expectations models. One important difference between this model and the Kyle [1985] model is that trading takes place only at two dates. At the end of time 2, all contracts are assumed to liquidate, and hence the adjustment of prices to information over time cannot be addressed in this framework.

In this model, there are two sources of information, one private and the other public. The public signal is observed by all market participants, whereas the private signal is known only to the informed traders. The linear equilibrium framework also applies in this model, so that the informed traders' strategy is essentially the same. With multiple specula-tors, this strategy will depend on the specific number of informed traders, and this dependence, in turn, allows the effects of increasing (or decreasing) the number of informed traders to be analyzed. Because the model involves several highly stylized assumptions, it is perhaps more useful to consider the general implications of the approach rather than analyze its specific derivation.

If entry of informed traders is possible, then in equilibrium the profit to any trader of becoming informed must be equal to the cost of doing so. Consequently, the number of informed traders can be specified endoge-nously, and the effect this has on prices determined. One can think of informed trader endogeneity as having two effects on the profits of the informed. First, if more informed traders enter, then there are more potential traders to share in the surplus generated by the private informa-tion. Hence, the number of traders has a direct effect on per capita profit, with entry reducing any individual trader's return. A second, and potential-ly more important, effect is the influence of the number of traders on trading behavior. Since each informed trader will choose the profit-maximizing trade given the expected behavior of all other traders, the aggregate number of traders will affect the size of each individual trade. This raises the potential that the total amount of information-based trading will also change as the number of informed traders changes.

One way to investigate these issues is to consider the effect of this informed-trader endogeneity on the informativeness of prices. Suppose that we consider changing the amount of uninformed noise trading in a market. With n exogenously fixed, increasing the amount of noise (σ_μ^2) has no effect on prices because the informed traders (or trader, as in Kyle [1985]) simply increase their own trading to keep their relative effect the same. This results in increasing the overall profit of the n informed traders but has no effect on the level of prices. This is not true, however, if n is endogenous. Increasing noise trading increases the potential profits of informed traders, and this, in turn, induces greater entry. While existing informed traders alter their trade quantity to incorporate the effect of these additional informed traders, Kyle demonstrates that the overall result is an increase in the amount of informed trading. This causes prices to become more informative as the larger numbers of informed traders reveal more of their information by trading. In effect, the informed traders compete among themselves for the available profits and, in so doing, reduce the total available rents to be shared.

A related, albeit opposite, entry effect occurs if the amount of publicly available information increases. In this case, if n is fixed, then prices unambiguously reflect more information and are thus more "efficient." This reduces the profits to privately informed traders because part of their informational advantage is dissipated by the public disclosure of information. In n is endogenous, the increased informativeness of prices also induces some informed traders to leave, with the result that less of their private information becomes impounded into the price. Kyle provides a nice result that the increased informativeness of the public signal is enough to offset the decreased activity of the informed traders, leading to prices being more informative overall.

One aspect of these results that should be stressed is that they are derived in an environment of risk neutrality. In this model, as in Kyle [1985], all traders and the market maker are assumed to be risk neutral. This assumption greatly simplifies traders' behavior because only mean effects need be considered. If traders or the market maker care about variance, however, then their behavior may differ dramatically. In particular, if informed traders are risk averse, then the total scale of trading may affect each agent's decision, leading to very different effects when the number of informed traders is allowed to vary.

These risk aversion effects are the focus of research by Subrahmanyam [1991b]. Using the Kyle [1984] model, Subrahmanyam demonstrates that increasing the number of informed traders can actually *decrease* market liquidity if traders are risk averse. This result, the opposite of that predicted with risk neutral traders, arises because risk aversion changes trader behavior in two ways. First, risk aversion induces traders to trade less aggressively than if they were risk neutral. Second, the total number of traders now affects the overall aggregate risk tolerance of traders.

Subrahmanyam shows that these two effects result in the sensitivity of price to the order flow (the λ) being unimodal in the number of informed traders.[9] As the number of informed traders increases, λ initially increases, reflecting that risk averse traders trade less aggressively than do risk neutral ones. With more traders, however, the second aggregate risk tolerance effect prevails, and λ decreases. These dual effects dictate that while traders still "compete" with each other, for small numbers of informed traders prices can actually "worsen" from the point of view of reflecting underlying information. Thus competition between informed traders does not necessarily improve the market from the perspective of information revelation. We return to these price effects further in the next chapter when we investigate how changes in uninformed behavior affect market behavior.

In both the Kyle [1984] and [1985] models, therefore, risk neutral informed traders can strategically exploit private information to maximize their profit. What is significant about both models is that informed traders take account of their trades' effect on the "terms of trade" or, more simply, the market price. When the informed trader is an information "monopolist" as in Kyle [1985], the trader can control the flow of information so that the price path that emerges has constant volatility. When there are multiple informed traders, this control is not as great, and, not surprisingly, informed trading causes prices to reflect information sooner.

This latter property raises the important question of exactly how quickly this price adjustment occurs. If price adjustment is quite sensitive to the number of informed, then market prices may reach "full-information" efficient levels quite quickly. A concomitant effect will be that the return to information becomes small, leaving little incentive for traders to expend resources to gather new information. In this case, the intriguing results of the Kyle [1985] model on the role of volume, depth, and price behavior may no longer hold.

This issue of price adjustment with multiple informed traders is addressed by Holden and Subrahmanyam [1992] and by Foster and Viswanathan [1993]. Both papers employ variants of the Kyle [1985] model in which the number of informed traders is allowed to vary. The Foster and Viswanathan paper extends the Kyle model in a potentially important way by allowing the random variables to be elliptically distributed. In this framework, they

---

9. In general, $1/\lambda$ is the market depth, so that increases in market depth allowed greater order flow to be accommodated without affecting prices.

address several interesting questions, including the impact of multiple informed traders on price behavior. The Holden and Subrahmanyam paper retains the original Kyle structure, but solves the difference equation system when there are multiple informed traders. As this is related to our earlier discussion, we will focus on this latter paper.

Holden and Subrahmanyam (henceforth, HS) begin with the Kyle sequential auction framework but allow for M informed traders. Because there are multiple informed (and they each know how many there are), the conjectures each trader makes about the other informed traders' behavior affect the equilibrium outcome. In this model, each informed trader knows the same information and is identical in every way, and so it follows that each also conjectures the same thing. This greatly simplifies the solution because it allows any individual informed trader's decision problem to be formulated in a simple game.

HS demonstrate that there is a unique linear equilibrium in which, for constants α_n, β_n, λ_n, and Σ_n, the following holds for all auctions $n = 1, \ldots,$ N, and for all informed traders $m = 1, \ldots, M$:

$$
\begin{aligned}
\Delta x_n &= m\beta(v - p_{n-1})\Delta t_n, \\
\Delta p_n &= \lambda(\Delta x_n + \Delta u_n), \\
\Sigma_n &= \text{var}(v \mid \Delta x_1 + u_1, \ldots \Delta x_n + u_n), \\
E(\pi_n \mid p_1, p_2, \ldots, p_{n-1}, v) &= \alpha_{n-1}(v - p_{n-1})^2 + \delta_{n-1}
\end{aligned}
\tag{4.33}
$$

This equilibrium is essentially the same as in Kyle but differs in one fundamental way. With multiple traders, the explicit solution to the constants $(\alpha_n, \beta_n, \lambda_n,$ and $\Sigma_n)$ requires solving a series of difference equations, but now their equilibrium values depend explicitly on the number and expected trading behavior of the M informed traders. Consequently, each trader determines his optimal trading strategy based on his expectations of the others, and that, in turn, affects the behavior of prices in equilibrium. The exact solution to these constants is straightforward but messy, and rather than focus on their derivation, we consider their economic implications.

Perhaps the most interesting of these constants to consider are λ_n, the market depth parameter (or how much order flow affects price adjustment), and Σ_n, the measure of price efficiency (in the sense that it reflects the remaining variance of the distribution). Recall that in the Kyle model the single informed trader acted so as to keep λ_n essentially constant, while the Σ variable declined in a deterministic manner. HS demonstrate that this is not the case when informed traders act as imperfect competitors. With multiple informed traders, λ_n is larger in earlier periods than in the information monopolist case, and it falls rapidly in later periods. This reflects that informed traders are trading more aggressively in the early periods, causing more information to be revealed earlier. This, in turn, causes the Σ_n variable to decline sharply toward zero, as increasingly large amounts of information are impounded in the price. HS demonstrate that the greater the number of informed traders, the more rapidly λ_n and Σ_n fall.

More insight into this price adjustment process can be obtained by considering the limit behavior of the market as the number of trading intervals is increased. In particular, suppose that the time interval is $\Delta dt = 1/N$ and the number of informed traders is fixed. Then, in the limit as the number of trading intervals goes to infinity, HS demonstrate two interesting results. First, letting τ denote an arbitrary calendar cutoff time, they show that for the last auction (n') before any τ,

$$\lim \Sigma_{n'} = 0 \text{ and } \lim \lambda_{n'} = 0, \text{ as } N \to \infty. \tag{4.34}$$

This result can be interpreted as showing that as the number of auctions goes to infinity, the information is revealed in an arbitrarily small period. Hence, no matter when you chose the cutoff point τ, the information has already been revealed and the market depth (defined as $1/\lambda$) has gone to infinity. This means that, unlike in the Kyle framework, information is impounded into market prices almost immediately.

This intuition is confirmed by looking at the limit behavior of the first auction when the number of trading intervals goes to infinity. In particular, HS demonstrate that

$$\lim \beta_1 = \infty, \; \lim E_0[\Delta x_1 \mid v] = 0, \text{ and } \lim \lambda_1 = \infty, \text{ as } N \to \infty. \tag{4.35}$$

Now, the presence of private information in the first period causes market depth to be very small, reflecting that trade entails substantial risk of being information-based. In later periods, when the information has been largely incorporated into the market price, the depth parameter goes to infinity as the risk of informed trading is largely dissipated. This market depth behavior is similarly reflected in the strategy of the informed trader, as in the first auction the expected quantity of informed trades is now zero. This occurs because with λ low any trade by the informed in the first period has such a large effect on prices that it obliterates any return to the informed traders' information.

These results suggest that market prices reflect information quite differently when there are multiple informed traders. This multiple trader impact can be investigated directly by considering price behavior in the limit when the number of informed traders goes to infinity. Given a fixed number of trading intervals, HS show that, for the first auction,

$$\lim \Sigma_1 = 0, \lim E_0[\Delta x_1 \mid v] = \infty, \lim \lambda_1 = 0,$$

$$\text{and } \lim p_1 = v, \text{ as } M \to \infty. \tag{4.36}$$

Thus, as the number of informed traders goes to infinity, all information is revealed in the first trading interval, market depth and the expected quantity of informed trade go to infinity, and the price equals the true value.

That prices become fully revealing in the first period is an important result. Earlier we noted that in competitive rational expectations models, traders' behavior resulted in prices instantly reflecting true values. Holden and Subrahmanyam demonstrate that this same competitive rational expectations equilibrium also arises in a Kyle framework with multiple informed traders acting as imperfect competitors.[10] What generates this result is simply that as the number of informed agents increases, their optimal strategy becomes increasingly competitive. The noise trading that preserved the return to information with a single informed trader is now not enough to prevent the trades of the informed from dominating the order flow. And, as in the standard rational expectations models, price instantly reflects underlying information.

With prices reflecting full information, we confront the standard conundrum of how information gets into prices given that if prices are efficient, traders can receive no return on their information. One question that naturally arises, however, is whether the results demonstrated in this setting are merely artifacts of the specific trading arrangements analyzed. In particular, given a richer trading mechanism, could a nonrevealing equilibrium with strategic trading arise? Indeed, an important issue in all microstructure research is determining how the trading mechanism affects the behavior of security prices. This topic is the focus of Chapter 7, where we examine how alternative market structures and trading instruments affect market behavior. In the remainder of this chapter, we consider the more theoretical issue of how the trading mechanism affects the nature of equilibrium when informed traders act strategically.

---

10. This result is also demonstrated by Foster and Viswanathan [1993].

4.3 STRATEGIC BEHAVIOR AND THE TRADING MECHANISM

In standard rational expectations models, the actual trading mechanism is generally unmodeled, in large part because the focus of research is on determining properties of the equilibrium. By contrast, the market microstructure literature has focused on modeling the specifics of the trading process with an eye to understanding how market structures and organization affect the resulting equilibrium. While these approaches may seem divergent, this need not be the case if an invariant equilibrium will, in fact, arise from any (or at least a wide range of) trading mechanisms. What needs to be determined, therefore, is how the equilibrium generally analyzed in rational expectations models is actually ever attained.

One way to address this issue is to ask a simple question: Can I write a trading game (or mechanism) with N informed traders and get a rational expectations equilibrium for large enough N? If the answer is no, then the reasonableness of the entire rational expectations equilibrium is subject to question. If the answer is yes, then the issue of the trading mechanism may be of interest to students of market design, but need not be of interest to researchers investigating general issues of price behavior.

This is essentially the question posed by Blume and Easley [1990]. Using a game-theoretic approach, they demonstrate that, regardless of the number of traders, if any trader has information that he alone possesses, then there is no trading game or mechanism that will result in a rational expectations equilibrium for all standard economies.[11] The difficulty is that if a trader can be an "information monopolist," then the prices predicted by the rational expectations models are unattainable. Consequently, the equilibrium so extensively analyzed in the rational expectations literature cannot in general be expected to prevail. It is the case, however, that in specific examples it may be possible to obtain a rational expectations equilibrium. While these examples will be of limited generality, they may be important if the trading mechanism they employ is of interest in itself.

As discussed in the previous section, these trading mechanism issues become particularly important if the issue of strategic trader behavior is considered. These strategic issues in a rational expectations framework are the focus of yet another paper by Kyle [1989] and work by Rochet and Vila [1993] and by Jackson [1991].[12] Although the Kyle [1984, 1985] models

---

11. Note that this does not contradict the Holden and Subrahmanyam result, as they assume that all informed traders have the same information.

12. Bhattacharya and Spiegel [1991] consider these trading mechanism issues as well as more general issues relating to the optimality of linear order strategies.

allow strategic behavior, the specific trading mechanism employed does not allow traders to condition on the equilibrium price because the trader's order must be turned in before the market-clearing price is known. Kyle [1989] attempts to incorporate more complicated order strategies by allowing multiple informed traders to submit entire demand schedules. These schedules arise from traders' optimal strategies and can be viewed as isomorphic to price-contingent orders. The Rochet and Vila model is similar to that of Kyle [1989] but differs in that they consider a unique informed trader and a continuum of market makers.

The Kyle [1989] model returns to the more standard rational expectations framework by considering a one-period model in which traders submit demands to a central market. In this model, market clearing is handled by a Walrasian auctioneer who sets a single price. The market maker, or specialist, who sets bid and ask prices is not a feature of this model, as the auctioneer plays no role other than aggregating the submitted demand schedules to find a single, market-clearing price.

The model includes three types of participants: noise traders, uninformed traders, and informed speculators. The noise traders play a similar role as in previous models by trading an exogenous random quantity z, where z is assumed normally distributed with variance σ^2_z and mean 0. The uninformed traders and the speculators have more complex demands in that they are permitted to submit demand functions (as opposed to demands). Since such strategies are available in actual markets, this trading mechanism incorporates a realistic, and important, property of actual trading markets.

Each of the N speculators is assumed to receive a signal, i_n, of the underlying value of the asset v, where $i_n = v + \varepsilon_n$, with $\text{var}(v) = \tau_v^{-1}$ and $\text{var}(\varepsilon_n) = \tau_\varepsilon^{-1}$. All random variables are independently and normally distributed. Each speculator chooses a strategy or demand schedule, denoted $X_n(p, i_n)$, where p denotes the market price of the asset. These demands result from solving a maximization problem given the information each speculator has on the underlying asset. Similarly, each of the M uninformed traders chooses a trading strategy or demand schedule, denoted $Y_m(p)$. Since the uninformed do not receive private information, their behavior can only depend on price. The equilibrium in this model is a Nash equilibrium in trading strategies.

Unlike in previous microstructure models (but similar to rational expectations models), speculators are assumed to be risk averse and maximize a negative exponential utility function of the form

$$U_n(\pi_{In}) = -\exp(-\rho I \pi_{In}), \qquad (4.37)$$

where ρ_I denotes the risk aversion coefficient. Similarly, the uninformed maximize a utility function of the form

$$V_m(\pi_{Um}) = -\exp(-\rho U \pi_{Um}) \tag{4.38}$$

with ρ_U defining the risk aversion coefficient.

Equilibrium requires that markets clear and that traders can follow no other strategy that results in greater utility. If traders act competitively, then a competitive rational expectations equilibrium is defined as a price function $P(z, i_1, i_2, \ldots, i_n)$ and a set of strategies such that, for each $(z, i_1, i_2, \ldots, i_n)$,

$$\sum_{n=1}^{N} X_n(p, i_n) + \sum_{m=1}^{M} Y_m(p) + z = 0 \tag{4.39}$$

and

$$E\{U_n[(v-p)X_n(p, i_n)|p, i_n]\} \geq E\{U_n[(v-p)X_n'(p, i_n)|p, i_n]\} \tag{4.40}$$

$$E\{V_m[(v-p)Y_m(p)|p]\} \geq E\{V_m[(v-p)Y_m'(p)|p]\}, \tag{4.41}$$

where $X'(\bullet)$ and $Y'(\bullet)$ denote alternative strategies, and p is the value of the price function at $(z, i_1, i_2, \ldots, i_n)$.

If informed traders act strategically by taking account of the effect of their trades on the price, then an imperfectly competitive rational expectations equilibrium requires a price function $P(X, Y, z)$ and a set of strategies such that for each $(z, i_1, i_2, \ldots, i_n)$ markets clear and

$$E\{U_n[(v - p(X, Y, z))X_n(p, i_n)|p, i_n]\}$$
$$\geq E\{U_n[(v - p(X, Y, z))X_n'(p, i_n)|p, i_n]\} \tag{4.42a}$$

and

$$E\{V_m[(v - p(X, Y, z))Y_m(p)|p]\}$$
$$\geq E\{V_m[(v - p(X, Y, z))Y_m'(p)|p]\}, \tag{4.42b}$$

Notice that this equilibrium differs from the competitive outcome in that the informed traders specifically take account of their actions on the market price. While this may seem a subtle change, it has a number of important implications for the amount of information traders need to know. In particular, in a competitive rational expectations equilibrium, to determine their optimal strategies, traders are assumed to know their own preferences, the structure of the market, and the function translating information into prices. In the imperfect competitive equilibrium, traders must again know all this information, but in addition they must also know the function translating demands into prices as well as everybody's demand schedule. Moreover, the trader needs to know the exact number of traders N and M; changes in the number of either type will affect the equilibrium. Such extensive information requirements are difficult to reconcile with actual market characteristics.

As in any rational expectations model, the strategies traders expect to prevail must be the strategies that do prevail. Kyle demonstrates that under certain conditions there exists a symmetric linear equilibrium in which traders' strategies are given by

$$X_n(p, i_n) = \mu_I + \beta i_n + \gamma_I p, \quad Y_m(p) = \mu_U + \gamma_U p, \qquad (4.43)$$

where μ_I, μ_U, γ_I, γ_U, and β are coefficients determined in the equilibrium.

For this equilibrium to occur, there must be a sufficient number of speculators to ensure a reasonably "competitive" outcome. If not, then the assumption that noise traders' demands are price inelastic means that even a single informed trader makes infinite expected profits (as would a single uninformed speculator if he were the only nonpassive agent). With "enough" speculators, however, the informed essentially compete among themselves, so that this monopolistic outcome cannot occur. In this sense, this result is similar to that demonstrated in Kyle [1984].

An important property of this imperfectly competitive equilibrium is that prices are less informative than they are in a competitive rational expectations equilibrium. Because traders recognize the impact of their trades on the market price, they choose their trading strategy to incorporate this effect. This also has the important implication that informed traders do not "trade away" their informational advantage, because prices will now not reveal the underlying information to the uninformed. In this example with strategic behavior, therefore, the rational expectations equilibrium both exists and has the reasonable property that informed traders earn a return to information.[13]

---

13. An interesting question is how the equilibrium results of this model relate to those of the Kyle [1985]. Rochet and Vila [1994] show that if the Kyle [1989] model is specified with a unique insider and a large number of uninformed traders, then the equilibrium in Kyle [1989] is the same as in Kyle [1985] when the informed trader is permitted to condition on the noise trade when submitting his order. They interpret this as showing that the equilibrium in the "limit order" game is the same as that in the "market order" game.

From a microstructure perspective, this result is useful because it arises in a model in which the trading mechanism captures at least some features of actual markets. We will return to these issues of market structure and design in Chapter 7, with the equilibrium issues in rational expectations models discussed again in Chapter 6. One aspect of strategic behavior that we have not discussed, however, is the optimal strategy of uninformed traders. It is to this issue that we now turn our attention.

Appendix:
Rational Expectations Models

What happens when people with differential information decide to trade? This question, fundamental to many issues studied in the market microstructure literature, is the underlying issue addressed in the rational expectations literature. Beginning with a paper by Muth [1961], researchers have investigated how market prices are affected by traders' information, and how this, in turn, affects the information traders can infer from market prices. A fundamental insight of these rational expectational models is that along with clearing markets, prices also aggregate information. This dual role dictates that the behavior of security prices (and markets) may exhibit a complexity far beyond that predicted by simple models of asset behavior.

This appendix provides a brief review of the basic rational expectations framework. Because the rational expectations literature is voluminous and the issues involved complex, my focus here is limited to establishing only the most important properties of this approach. In particular, I first motivate the underlying issues by examining a simple graphical depiction of the trading process with differentially informed traders. I then define and analyze a simple rational expectations equilibrium, and I discuss some of the many important issues involved in the existence of such equilibria. The appendix concludes by outlining the basic rational expectations example typically used to address issues in security market behavior.

4.A.1 THE BASIC PROBLEM

Suppose we consider two traders who trade a single asset and money. One trader receives a signal, S, of the asset's true value; the signal can be either high or low, $S \, \varepsilon \, [H, L]$. The other trader is uninformed of any signal. To represent the trading desires of each trader, consider a simple Edgeworth box with the informed trader's origin at the upper right corner, the uninformed trader's origin at the lower left corner, and the endowment in the lower right corner. Equilibria can be found at the intersection of the trader's price-consumption curves. (A price-consumption curve represents the collection of bundles of goods that the trader would demand at various prices.)

Figure 4.A.1 presents such an Edgeworth box. Since the informed trader sees a signal of the asset's value, his price-consumption curves differ depending on the signal's value. Thus, his pc curve is pc_H if the signal is high, and it is pc_L if the signal is low. The uninformed trader sees no such

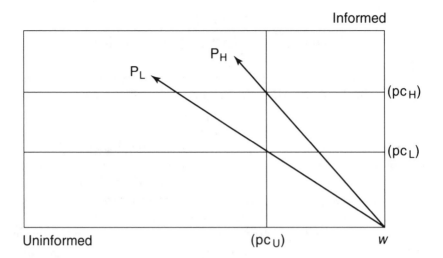

Figure 4.A.1 Price - Consumption Curves - The Naive Uniformed Trudar Case.

signal, and so he has a single pc curve. This is represented by the single vertical line, pc$_U$.[14]

The Walrasian equilibrium price is determined by the intersection of the traders' pc curves. Note that this is simply p_L if the signal was low and p_H if the signal was high. What is immediately apparent from the picture is that the uninformed trader is naive; once he sees that the price is, say, p_L, he should know that the signal must have been low. Had he known the signal was low, however, his demand would not be that depicted by pc$_U$. In this simple Walrasian market, however, this inference issue is ignored, suggesting that this is not the appropriate depiction of equilibrium when prices can convey information.

Incorporating this complexity into the trading problem requires recasting the problem in a different framework. Again, Let there be two traders, $i = 1$, 2, l goods, and let their endowments be denoted $w^i \in \Re^l+$. Let the signal each trader receives be defined as $s^i \in S^i$, where $S = S^1 \times S^2$ is the space of joint signals. Let utility for each trader be denoted by $u^i(x^i, s)$, where $w^i \in \Re^l +$ is the trader's portfolio. Hence, an agent's utility depends both on his allocation and on the joint signal.[15]

---

14. These curves are approximately price-consumption curves. They are accurate in the interior of the box, where equilibria will be found.

15. For example, suppose the assets will have eventual value $\tilde{v}$ where the distribution of $\tilde{v}$ given s is $f(\tilde{v}|s)$. Let utility of the portfolio x_i at eventual value v be $\hat{u}^{ii}(x^i, v)$. Then expected utility conditional on s is $\int \hat{u}^i(x^i, \tilde{v})f(\tilde{v}|s) d\tilde{v} \equiv \hat{u}^i(x^i, s)$. The utility function in the text is this expected utility.

Prices in this model play a dual role of market clearing and conveying information. Suppose the equilibrium price relation is given by $P(s)$. That is, $P(s)$ is the market-clearing price when joint signal s occurs. Given price p, traders can infer that $s \in P^{-1}(p)$ So at price p, each agent's decision problem can be written

$$\text{Max}^i \ E^i[u^i(x_i, s)|s^i, s \in P^{-1}(p)]\text{s.t.} \ p(x^i - w^i) = 0. \tag{4.44}$$

Solution of this problem results in a demand function for the asset, denoted $D^i(p, s^i, P(\bullet))$.

To find a rational expectations equilibrium, we must calculate the aggregate excess demand function and then find a price function that equates excess demand to zero for all signals. This excess demand function is

$$Z(p, s, P(\bullet)) = \sum_{i=1}^{2}(D^i(p, s^i, P(\bullet)) - w^i). \tag{4.45}$$

Given this setup, we now define a rational expectations equilibrium:

A rational expectations equilibrium (REE) is a price function $P(\bullet)$ such that $Z(p(s), s, P(\bullet)) = 0$ for each $s \in S$.

There are two important properties to note about this equilibrium . First, the equilibrium price satisfies its traditional market-clearing role by setting excess demands to zero. Second, the price function must accomplish such market-clearing for every signal. Moreover, it must be the case that the price function traders use in forming their demands is the actual price function that occurs in the market. In this sense, expectations are "correct" and traders' beliefs are rational.

A crucial question is, how do we ever find such a rational expectations equilibrium? In principle, such a task is daunting, since the mechanics of doing so far exceed the simple market-clearing approach traditionally taken. And, indeed, it may be the case that such an equilibrium cannot be found. These difficulties can be illustrated by returning to our Edgeworth box example.

If price can convey information, then the uninformed trader in a rational expectations equilibrium must recognize this property. Suppose that the informed trader has price-consumption curves as before, but now suppose that the uninformed trader also knows s. Then his price-consumption curves would differ depending on s. As Figure 4.A.2 shows, if the traders know that $s = L$, the market price will be p_L, while if they see $s = H$, the

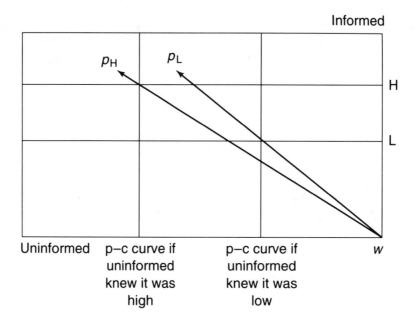

Figure 4.A.2 Price - Consumption Curves - The Revealing Case.

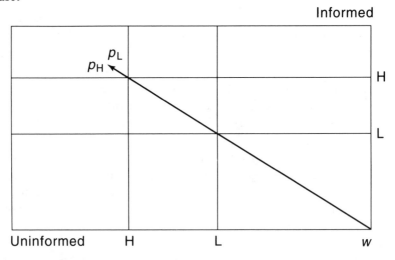

Figure 4.A.3 Price - Consumption Curve - The Nonrevealing Case.

market price will be p_H. This is, of course, an artificial full-information economy. It tells us, however, how to construct an REE.

Consider the price function $P(L) = p_L$ and $P(H) = p_H$. This is an REE. To see why, note that at price, say, p_L, the uninformed trader would infer that $s = L$, and so by the argument above, $p_L$would clear the market.

It can be the case, however, that such an outcome does not arise. Suppose instead that the price-consumption curves for the full-information economy are given as in Figure 4.A.3, where the artificial full-information pc's both intersect along the same budget line. If these are the full-information price-consumption curves, then it is not possible to infer the underlying state from the price. Consequently, a revealing rational expectations equilibrium cannot exist. Figure 4.A.1 shows that for this economy there is no nonrevealing REE. So no REE exists. This difficulty illustrates the fundamental problem in rational expectations models. For some economies there is no REE.

4.A.2 THE EXISTENCE OF RATIONAL EXPECTATIONS EQUILIBRIA

Given this difficulty, when can we expect a rational expectations equilibrium to exist? This issue has been a subject of extensive research, much of it focusing on the dimensionality of the signal space. There are four results in this literature that provide boundaries on the existence of equilibria in rational expectations models. As these conditions apply to most of the models used to address security market issues, it is useful to review these results.

First, if the signal set S is finite, then for a generic set of economies a rational expectations equilibrium exists and is revealing.[16] This result, demonstrated by Radner [1979], requires that any signal must take on specific values (such as high, low) and so does not apply to signals drawn from a normal distribution.

Second, let l denote the number of assets. Allen [1982] demonstrated that if $l - 1$ is greater than the dimension of S, then for a generic set of economies an REE exists and is revealing. What this result basically states is that if the number of relative prices (which is $l - 1$) exceeds the dimensionality of the signal space, then an REE does exist. An intuitive interpretation of this result is that if you have more prices than signals, then you have sufficient flexibility to both clear markets and aggregate information.

Third, Jordan and Radner [1982] proved that if $l - 1$ equals the dimension S, then there is an open set of economies with no rational

---

16. I will use the term *generic* loosely. Roughly it means for almost all. For precise definitions, see the papers referred to in this section.

expectations equilibrium. Here, the exact fit between prices and signals means that while it may be possible to find an equilibrium, it is not guaranteed. This result is important because it suggests a major difficulty that arises in many standard REE applications. In models with two assets (a risky asset and a risk-free asset) and a one-dimensional signal, the number of relative prices $(l - 1)$ equals the signal dimension. This result dictates that an equilibrium may not exist at all and hence suggests a fragility to the results found in such models. This also explains why the examples usually employed to demonstrate rational expectations equilibria are not easily generalizable.

Finally, Jordan [1982] provides the somewhat perverse result that if $l - 1 < S$, then there is a generic set of economies with REE and these equilibria can be chosen to be as close to revealing as desired. This nonintuitive result is perhaps best viewed as casting doubt on the entire concept of an REE, as the resulting price function in this case may possess such perverse properties that it is difficult to believe it would exist in any actual economy, or ever be learned by market participants if it did.

This latter problem highlights two additional issues in the rational expectations approach. In these models, individuals must know the pricing rule that provides equilibrium prices. How such knowledge actually comes about, however, is not specified. One possibility is that individuals learn this rule over time, and hence the REE can be viewed as the long-run steady state result. Research on learning (see Blume, Bray, and Easley [1982] for a survey), however, suggests that learning to form rational expectations is problematic.

A second difficulty in standard rational expectations models is the assumption of Walrasian equilibrium. Assuming that prices are set by a Walrasian auctioneer avoids the difficulty of specifying any actual trading mechanism. This simplicity, however, hides several important problems, among them being the assumption of competitive behavior. Blume and Easley [1990] show that unless restrictive informational conditions are met, there is no trading mechanism that can implement REEs for all classical economies. In the market microstructure literature, the market-clearing mechanism has been shown to have important effects on the behavior of both prices and traders, a complication virtually ignored in the REE literature.

These results on the existence of REEs illustrate why such models are both difficult to construct and difficult to interpret. The approach often taken to avoid these problems is to use a specific example of a trading environment that satisfies the conditions given above and permits the calculation of an REE. While this approach is both useful and tractable, it is also very special in the sense that any deviations in the environment will likely change the equilibrium, if it exists at all.

4.A.3 THE STANDARD RATIONAL EXPECTATIONS EXAMPLE

To conclude this appendix, we review the most widely used rational expectations framework for analyzing trading between differentially employed agents. This model, developed by Grossman and Stiglitz [1980], uses a simple two-asset economy in which all random variables are independent and are normally distributed. Agents hold a risk-free asset, M, and a risky asset, X. The price of the risky asset is denoted p, and the price of the risk-free asset is normalized to one.

The future value of the asset, v, is unknown and is normally distributed with mean φ and variance $1/\rho_v$. There are two traders in the economy, and one of the traders receives a signal of the asset value (the other does not). The signal, s, is normally distributed with mean v and variance $1/\rho_s$. Each agent begins with some endowment (M, X^i), where the level of X^i is a random variable that is normally distributed with mean 0 and variance $1/\rho_x$. The random aggregate endowment is $X = X^1 + X^2$. Agents maximize the utility of terminal wealth, where utility is defined by the negative exponential function $U(W) = -\exp(-W^i)$.

In this model, the signal dictates that the informed trader knows more than the uninformed trader. The uninformed, however, knows that the informed's trade will affect the price. Hence, if he knows the pricing rule, the uninformed trader can extract information about the informed's signal from the market price. To construct an equilibrium, suppose that the uninformed conjectures that this pricing rule has a particular linear form given by

$$p = \alpha\varphi + \beta s - \gamma X \qquad (4.46)$$

where the coefficient values are determined in the equilibrium. Thus the price function depends on the asset's prior expected value, the signal value, and the random aggregate endowment of the risky asset.

Given his signal, it follows that informed trader's posterior distribution on v is

$$N\left(\frac{\rho_v\varphi + \rho_s s}{\rho_v + \rho_s}, \frac{1}{\rho_v + \rho_s}\right) \qquad (4.47)$$

To construct the uninformed trader's posterior distribution on v, we need to describe how he uses the price observation to update his prior on v. An easy way to do this is to construct the observable (to the uninformed trader) random variable θ:

$$\theta = (p - \alpha\varphi)/\beta = s - (\gamma/\beta)X \qquad (4.48)$$

Using the right-hand side of the equation, we see that θ is distributed as $N(v, 1/\rho_s + (\gamma/\beta)^2(2/\rho_x))$. Defining the variance as $1/\rho_\theta$, the uninformed's posterior can be written

$$N\left(\frac{\rho_v\varphi + \rho_\theta\theta}{\rho_v + \rho_\theta}, \frac{1}{\rho_v + \rho_\theta}\right). \qquad (4.49)$$

What is important to note is that both the informed's posterior and the uninformed's posterior are still normal. Solving the maximization problem for each of their demands is then tractable and results in a demand function for the informed trader of

$$D^{\mathrm{I}} = \frac{E[V|s] - p}{\mathrm{var}[V|s]}, \qquad (4.50)$$

and for the uninformed trader of

$$D^{\mathrm{U}} = \frac{E[V|p, P(\cdot)] - p}{\mathrm{var}[V|p, P(\cdot)]}, \qquad (4.51)$$

These demands can easily be found by using the posterior distributions solved for earlier. Hence, the informed trader's demand is

$$D^{\mathrm{I}} = \frac{\frac{\rho_v\varphi + \rho_s s}{\rho_v + \rho_s} - p}{\frac{1}{\rho_v + \rho_s}} = \rho_v\varphi + \rho_s s - p(\rho_v + \rho_s), \qquad (4.52)$$

and the uninformed trader's demand is

$$D^{\mathrm{U}} = \rho_v\varphi + \rho_\theta\theta - p(\rho_v + \rho_\theta). \qquad (4.53)$$

The equilibrium price can be found equating demand to supply, i.e., $D^{\mathrm{I}} + D^{\mathrm{U}} = X$. This yields

$$p = \frac{2\rho_v\varphi + s[\rho_\theta + \rho_s] - X[1 + (\gamma/\beta)\rho_\theta]}{2\rho_v + \rho_s + \rho_\theta}. \tag{4.54}$$

Notice that an alternative way to write this is

$$p = \alpha\varphi + \beta s - \gamma X, \tag{4.55}$$

where

$$\alpha = \frac{2\rho_v}{2\rho_v + \rho_s + \rho_\theta},$$

$$\beta = \frac{\rho_\theta + \rho_s}{2\rho_v + \rho_s + \rho_\theta}, \tag{4.56}$$

$$\gamma = \frac{1 + (\gamma/\beta)\rho_\theta}{2\rho_v + \rho_s + \rho_\theta},$$

and $\rho_\theta = \rho_s + (\gamma/\beta)^2 2/\rho_x$.

In this equilibrium, therefore, the actual price will be linear in φ, s, and X, and the conjectured price will be the actual price. Traders' expectations are thus correct, and prices clear markets. Because of the noise induced by the random aggregate supply, the price now does not reveal the informed's signal to the uninformed trader.

5

Strategic Trader Models II: Uninformed Traders

The previous chapter demonstrated the important price effects that can arise when informed traders act strategically. An important restriction of these analyses, however, is that the uninformed traders are not permitted to act strategically. Instead, noise traders are assumed to transact every period for reasons exogenous to the model, an assumption also made in the sequential trade models. Yet, if it is profitable for an informed trader to time his trades, it must be profitable for an uninformed trader to do so as well. Moreover, if uninformed traders behave differently, then the optimal informed strategy may also change. The issue of uninformed strategic behavior, therefore, introduces a number of interesting dimensions into the analysis of market behavior.

Allowing uninformed traders to consider the impact and cost of their trades introduces a new level of complexity to the game analyzed by previous market microstructure researchers. In the strategic models discussed thus far, the game analyzed is between the market maker and the informed traders. In that game, the market maker attempts to learn the private information from the trade flow; the informed trader attempts to hide his trades and thus prolong his informational advantage and maximize his profits. The role of the uninformed traders is strictly passive. If the uninformed instead act strategically, then the game must be broadened to analyze their order strategy and the effect that it has on the informed traders' and market makers' strategies.

One reason for considering this aspect of the trading process is that it may allow the uninformed to reduce the losses they incur in trading. The uninformed, and their losses, are necessary in information-based microstructure models, as they generate the gains made by the informed. Nevertheless, it is troubling that the only role played by the uninformed is

129

that of being "taken" by the informed traders. Furthermore, in the models considered thus far, the extent to which the uninformed lose to informed traders is exogenous to the model; why such losses should be any particular level is left unspecified.

Allowing the uninformed to time their trades also introduces the possibility that uninformed trades could themselves have interesting price effects. In particular, if the uninformed attempt to "hide" from the informed traders, then patterns of trade may arise. Such trade patterns are characteristic of actual security trading, with several researchers (see Jain and Joh [1988]; French and Roll [1986]) empirically documenting both within and across day patterns. Given a passive role for the uninformed, it does not appear that strategic decisions by informed traders result in such variations in the timing and volume of trade. Moreover, in the microstructure models considered thus far, market makers play only a passive role by accommodating, rather than initiating, trades, and so their role in introducing price patterns is unclear. This suggests that, to understand trade patterns, the role of the uninformed must be specified in greater detail.

Numerous authors have addressed this issue of uninformed strategic behavior in a variety of contexts. Admati and Pfleiderer [1988, 1989] focus on the timing decisions of uninformed traders transacting within a single day. Foster and Viswanathan [1990] examine the interday strategic effects induced by varying levels of public and private information across trading days. Seppi [1990] analyzes the factors influencing a large uninformed trader's decision to trade blocks versus round lots. In these applications, the focus is on the ability of the uninformed to choose strategically either the composition or the timing of their orders. Spiegel and Subrahmanyam [1992] consider uninformed trading from a different point of view by specifying the trading decisions of risk averse uninformed hedgers. This one-period model does not investigate the intertemporal question of when to trade, but rather focuses on the more basic issue of why trade occurs.

One factor common to these papers is a reliance on a game-theoretic approach. While the strategic informed trader models in the previous section also draw on game theory, the issues that arise when multiple uninformed traders act strategically are more complex. As will be apparent, the equilibria in these models crucially depend on the strategy sets from which traders are allowed to select. In some cases, the tractable linear equilibrium so ubiquitous in strategic analyses no longer need exist. And, if it does exist, whether an equilibrium involves mixed strategies or can be restricted to more tractable pure strategies affects our ability to characterize the properties of security prices arising with strategic behavior.

Because the optimal behavior for the uninformed traders will depend on the decisions of other market participants, analyses of uninformed strategic behavior have generally adopted the basic modeling approach developed by Kyle. One issue that immediately arises in doing so, however, is the duration of the informeds' information. Since the optimal behavior of the uninformed depends at least partially on the behavior of the informed, whether the informed can delay trading is crucial to characterizing this behavior. The simplest specification is to assume that this information is short-lived, and hence intertemporal issues need not be considered. This is the approach taken by Admati and Pfleiderer [1988]. As their paper involves a variant of the Kyle [1984] model, it provides a convenient starting point for our discussion.

5.1 STRATEGIC BEHAVIOR AND UNINFORMED TRADERS

In Admati-Pfleiderer's [1988] model, uninformed liquidity traders are assumed to be of two types. There are nondiscretionary liquidity traders, who must transact a given amount at a specific time for reasons exogenous to the model. These traders are identical to the noise traders found in previous work, and they perform the same role of guaranteeing that a nontrivial equilibrium exists. There is a second group of uninformed traders, who also must trade an exogenously given amount, but they have some discretion with respect to the timing of their trades. These discretionary traders must satisfy their liquidity demands before the end of the trading day, but may choose when during the day to submit their order.

The trading day is divided into T intervals of time, and in each interval traders may submit orders to a competitive market maker. As in Kyle's model, orders are batched and the market maker sets a price after seeing the net order flow. The market maker is assumed to be risk neutral and competitive, and so prices reflect the expected value of the asset given the order flow. The underlying value of the asset at time T is given by

$$\tilde{V} = \overline{V} + \sum_{t=1}^{T} \tilde{\delta}_t, \tag{5.1}$$

where the $\tilde{\delta}_t$ are mean zero i.i.d. random variables that become public information at the beginning of each period. In each period t, there are assumed to be n_t traders who observe a private signal $\delta_{t+1} + \varepsilon_t$, where the variance of ε_t is given by φ_t. Hence, informed traders receive a noisy signal in period t of the public information that will be revealed at the start of period $t + 1$.

An important assumption is that this information is short-lived. The public information arriving at the beginning of the next period dictates that private information is valuable for only one trading interval. Consequently, informed traders have no choice but to trade on their information in the period they receive it. Given that they will be trading, the informed traders' only decision involves determining the order size to submit. The informed traders' decision problem is also simplified in that they need not consider the effects of their trade on next period's price. In effect, the informed face a one-period problem because the intertemporal impact of their actions is vitiated by the arrival of public information. This myopia, combined with the independence of the $\tilde{\delta}_t$ (the information increments each period), also dictates that the informed quantity traded in any one period is independent of the informed quantity traded in other periods. Hence, the intertemporal linkage between trades and information that was the focus of much prior research is not a property of this model. This informed order flow for period t is represented by

$$\tilde{X}_t = \sum_{i=1}^{n} \tilde{x}_t^i. \qquad (5.2)$$

The uninformed traders face a different strategic decision. The *discretionary* traders are assumed to face exogenous liquidity needs, and so the amount that trader j wishes to trade is exogenously given as $\tilde{Y}j$. Admati and Pfleiderer initially assume that uninformed traders cannot split trades between periods, so that when trader j trades, the trade size is $\tilde{Y}j$. The discretionary traders can choose when to trade, however, and so their strategic decision involves the timing of their order flow. Discretionary demand in period t can thus be described by

$$\sum_{j=1}^{m} \gamma_t^j \qquad (5.3)$$

where $\gamma j = Yj$ if the jth discretionary trader trades in period t, and is 0 otherwise.

The *nondiscretionary* order flow is assumed exogenous in each period and is given by $\tilde{z}_t$. Total liquidity trading in any period t is then simply the sum of the discretionary and nondiscretionary orders. As this is a Kyle model, in equilibrium the variance of uninformed trading influences the equilibrium strategies of the strategic players. This variance of total liquidity trading in period t is then given by

$$\psi_t \equiv var\left(\sum_{j=1}^{m} y_t^j + z_t\right). \tag{5.4}$$

This variance is determined endogenously since it depends on the strategic decisions of the discretionary traders as to when they will transact.

The total order flow in period t, denoted $\tilde{\omega}_t$, is given by

$$\tilde{\omega}_t = \sum_{i=1}^{n} \tilde{x}_t^i + \sum_{i=1}^{m} \tilde{y}_t^j + \tilde{z}_t. \tag{5.5}$$

The market maker observes this aggregated order flow and sets a single market-clearing price. Because the market maker is risk neutral and competitive, his period t price is equal to the expected value of the asset conditional on his prior information and the order flow received in period t. The assumption that $\tilde{\delta}_t$ is public information at the beginning of period t means that previous order flow has no information content. So the prior expected value of the asset in period t is $\bar{V} + \Sigma_{\tau = 1}^{t} \delta_\tau$.

Following Kyle, Admati and Pfleiderer assume that the market maker uses the linear pricing rule

$$P_t = \bar{V} + \sum_{\tau=1}^{t} \delta_\tau + \lambda \omega_t, \tag{5.6}$$

where ω_t is the total order flow in period t and λ is the effect of order flow on the market price. Since this order flow can include the trades of agents who know $\tilde{\delta}_{t+1}$, the market maker's order strategy reflects the impact of both public and private information.

Given that the market maker follows this pricing rule, optimal strategies for the informed traders and the uninformed discretionary traders can be determined. These strategies will depend on ψ_t, the variance of trades, which is determined jointly with the strategies in the equilibrium. For a given level of ψ_t, the optimal order strategy of informed trader i is given by

$$\tilde{X}_t = \beta_t^i \left(\tilde{\delta}_{t+1} + \tilde{\varepsilon}_t\right), \tag{5.7}$$

where

$$\beta_t^i = \sqrt{\frac{\Psi_t}{n_t \left[var\left(\tilde{\delta}_{t+1}\right) + \phi_t\right]}}. \tag{5.8}$$

The optimal informed order quantity $\tilde{X}_t$, therefore, depends on the number of informed traders, the variance of the uninformed order quantity, and the variance of the private information (the signal variance).

With informed traders pursuing this order strategy and for a given level of ψ_t, the equilibrium value of λ is given by

$$\lambda_t = \frac{\text{var}\left(\tilde{\delta}_{t+1}\right)}{n_t + 1} \sqrt{\frac{n_t}{\Psi_t\left[\text{var}\left(\tilde{\delta}_{t+1}\right) + \phi_t\right]}}. \tag{5.9}$$

There are two comparative statics properties of this solution that are particularly important. First, as was demonstrated in Kyle [1984], λ is decreasing in n, the number of informed traders. Hence, as n increases, order flow has less of an effect on prices. This effect occurs here because the informed essentially compete among themselves in submitting orders, thereby dissipating their advantage of being informational monopolists. Second, λ is also decreasing in ψ_t, the variance of total uninformed trades. This reflects the ability of deeper markets to accommodate informed trading with less effect on price. Since ψ is endogenous, discretionary liquidity traders can thus affect the behavior of prices through their strategic choices. This reflects a significant departure for the uninformed traders from the passive role of "sheep" found in earlier models.

Recall, however, that these comparative static results depend crucially on the assumption of risk neutrality for market participants. As we discussed in Section 4.2, Subrahmanyam [1991] shows that with informed trader risk aversion, λ need not be decreasing in n. Indeed, if λ were increasing in n, then this would imply that the terms of trade for the uninformed are *worse* when there are more informed traders than when there are less. This relation between λ and n will be important in characterizing the uninformed traders' timing decision. We will discuss this issue further later in this section.

The optimal behavior for an uninformed discretionary trader is determined by solving for the minimum cost trading period in which to transact. Since the uninformed lose to the informed, this cost depends on the price the market maker sets, which, in turn, depends on the amount of informed and uninformed trade. Here a crucial issue arises as to whether discretionary traders are permitted to act strategically or are constrained to be competitive. In particular, since there are a finite number of uninformed traders, where discretionary traders choose to trade will affect the terms of trade, which in this model is captured by the λ variable.

If discretionary traders act strategically, they should explicitly recognize that their trading affects λ. This means that discretionary traders should choose their optimal order strategy recognizing both that the λ's differ across trading periods *and* that their behavior affects the λ's. This is not permitted in the Admati and Pfleiderer analysis, nor is it a feature in the other strategic models typically employed to analyze trading behavior. Instead, discretionary traders are assumed to take the pricing rule (the λ's) as given, and hence they act competitively in making trade decisions. By taking the terms of trade as given, the discretionary traders' decision problem simply reduces to choosing to trade in the lowest cost period offered by the market maker.

This problem underscores the difficulty of applying game-theoretic techniques to market microstructure problems. If traders are truly to act strategically, then the resulting equilibrium must incorporate all strategic interactions such behavior engenders. Allowing strategic behavior, however, may result in mixed strategy equilibria that are consistent with a wide range of market conditions or involve complex nonlinear functional relationships that are difficult, if not impossible, to characterize. Restricting the strategic choices of the discretionary and the informed traders is one way to avoid these difficulties, but it raises the difficulty that the resulting equilibrium need not be robust to more complete behavioral specifications. Perhaps a more basic problem is that it is not really possible to apply game-theoretic equilibrium concepts in these settings because the underlying model is not really a game. Specifying a true game requires more endogeneity than is ever allowed in these market microstructure applications. With much of the structure exogenously imposed, the equilibrium in these models need not be the same as in more standard game theory approaches.

Given a linear pricing rule, the parameter values derived above, and the assumption that discretionary traders act competitively by taking the pricing rule as given, the lowest-cost period in which to trade is the one in which the variance of uninformed trade, ψ, is highest. It follows that to maximize ψ discretionary traders all select the same period in which to transact, inducing patterns in the distribution of trades.

One way to characterize this behavior is to note that discretionary traders do better by trading in a separating equilibrium than they do by trading in a pooling equilibrium. Hence, it is optimal for the discretionary traders to "clump" together in an attempt to separate their trades from the ill effects of the informed traders. Of course, discretionary traders cannot completely separate themselves from the informed traders because, by assumption, informed traders cannot time their trades and so are always present in the market. Moreover, in every period there must be some nondiscretionary uninformed traders active in the market, or else the trades (and hence information) of informed traders would instantly reveal their information to the market. Nonetheless, by banding together, discretionary traders increase the liquidity of the market and thereby reduce the losses they suffer to informed traders.

The strategic decisions of discretionary traders, in turn, affect the strategic choices of informed traders. Since the informed trader's optimal order quantity depends on the variance of total uninformed trade (i.e., ψ), it follows that informed trade quantity will also follow the pattern set by discretionary traders. In periods with greater discretionary trading, total informed trading will increase, and conversely, it will decrease in periods where discretionary trading is less.[1] The strategic decisions of informed traders thus serve to exaggerate the patterns introduced by the discretionary traders.

One interesting aspect of this informed trading behavior is its effect on price revelation. As was also true in Kyle's model, the amount of private information revealed by trading is the same across periods and is independent of the total variance of liquidity trading. Thus, though the variance of liquidity trading affects the trading of both discretionary and informed traders, the variance of price changes is constant across periods. This reflects the result that in equilibrium informed traders always adjust their order size to keep their relative share of the order flow constant. This result, of course, follows from assuming a fixed number of informed traders.

What is of more interest is what happens to trading patterns when informed trader entry is endogenous. Interestingly, the endogeneity of informed traders acts to intensify the presence of patterns. The reason is that as the number of informed traders increases they essentially compete with each other, causing prices to be less affected by the threat of information-based trading. In the earlier Kyle model, this is what led prices to reflect different variances as the effect of informed trading varied across periods. In this setting, periods with higher numbers of informed traders have smaller λ's, which in turn make them more attractive trading periods for discretionary traders.

The equilibrium derived here thus has the property that uninformed traders clump, informed traders follow, and trade patterns emerge. This provides an explanation for the observed trade patterns based on rational loss-minimizing behavior by the uninformed traders. What may be useful

---

1. Recall that the expected uninformed volume is zero, even in periods where discretionary traders trade. What matters here, as it did in Kyle, is the variance of trading, and hence greater discretionary participation induces larger trade variance.

to consider, however, is the robustness of this result. For example, an important assumption underlying the equilibrium derived here is the independence of trade between periods. Unlike in the sequential trade models or in Kyle [1985], trade in one period is not informative about trade in any subsequent period. This reflects the dual assumptions that informed traders' information lasts one period and that discretionary traders cannot split their trades between periods. In this setting, there is no endogenous learning problem for either the uninformed or market makers because there is nothing to be learned from market statistics; subsequent prices do not reflect the effects of previous order flows beyond public information.

This restriction greatly affects the nature of the equilibrium, and hence the qualitative predictions, that emerge from the model. For example, Admati and Pfleiderer consider a simple extension in which discretionary traders are permitted to split their trades across two periods. Two problems immediately arise in characterizing the solution. First, it is not clear that a pure-strategy equilibrium always exists, and even if it does, it is not generally possible to find a closed-form solution. Second, there is no way to guarantee that if we find an equilibrium, it is in fact the only equilibrium. Once discretionary traders are permitted to act strategically across periods, the potential for multiple equilibria becomes a major concern. We return to these equilibrium considerations in more detail in Section 5.3

The assumptions regarding the nature of information are also important. In the models considered thus far, informed traders receive homogeneous information. Admati and Pfleiderer provide a nice result that with heterogeneous information the effect of n, the number of informed traders, on λ may differ dramatically. In particular, the "positive" effect on price from competition between informed traders that arises when n increases need not hold. The reason is that with more informed traders the trading process now reveals more information, and this increased information effect overwhelms the increased competition effect. This can result in λ increasing in the number of informed traders, rather than decreasing. Consequently, the 'concentration" of trading results no longer need hold.

The optimality of clumping behavior thus appears to hinge largely on the behavior of λ, the price sensitivity to the order flow. Provided λ decreases with greater informed or uninformed trading, then discretionary traders benefit from trading together. If, however, λ can increase in the number of informed traders, then it is not apparent clumping occurs at all. Instead, changes in discretionary trading could induce changes in informed trading, which could *worsen* the terms of trade for the uninformed. But then it is not clear that such discretionary behavior would (or even could) actually exist in equilibrium. This suggests the need to specify the origins of discretionary behavior in more detail.

This is the issue addressed by Spiegel and Subrahmanyam [1992]. They depart from the exogenous uninformed trading assumptions of previous models by considering uninformed trading as arising to meet hedging demands. This focus on hedging motivations is reminiscent of more standard rational expectations analyses, but their analysis employs a variant of the one-period Kyle [1985] model.[2] In their model, the sensitivity of hedging demands to price variability can eliminate linear equilibria.

In the model, k risk neutral informed traders and n risk averse uninformed traders submit orders to a risk neutral, competitive market maker. Trading occurs at time 0 and liquidation of the asset occurs at time 1. At time 1, the asset will be worth $\tilde{V} = \bar{V} + \tilde{\delta}$, where $\bar{V}$ is known to all agents and $\tilde{\delta}$ represents an information innovation that is normally distributed as $N(0, \Psi)$. Informed trader i receives a signal $\tilde{\delta} + \varepsilon_i$, where the ε_i are i.i.d random variables with distribution $N(0, \varphi)$.

The uninformed traders in this model are risk averse and have negative exponential utility functions with a common absolute risk aversion coefficient of A. Each of the n uninformed traders has an endowment ω_j, $j = 1, \ldots, n$, where the ω_j are assumed independently normally distributed with mean 0 and variance σ_ω^2. As in Kyle, the market maker sees the net order flow and sets a single price. Let this price be denoted P, and let the order flow be denoted Q. Then, as in previous papers, we need to find a pricing strategy for the market maker and an order strategy for the informed traders such that prices are efficient and no other order strategy results in higher utility for the traders.

Suppose the market maker uses the (now familiar) linear pricing strategy

$$P = \bar{V} + \lambda Q. \tag{5.10}$$

Then informed traders use the linear order strategy

$$X^i = \beta\left(\delta + \varepsilon_i\right), \tag{5.11}$$

and uninformed traders use orders that are linear functions of their endowments, $\gamma\omega_i$. Spiegel and Subrahmanyam show that there is a linear equilibrium in which the constants β, λ, and γ have unique solutions provided that

$$A^2 n\sigma_\omega^2\left(\Psi + 2\phi\right)^2 > 4k\left(\Psi + \phi\right). \tag{5.12}$$

---

2. This hedging motivation was also developed in Glosten [1989], a paper we consider further in Chapter 6.

If this condition does not hold, then there cannot exist a linear equilibrium.

The condition implies that there exists a linear equilibrium only if the uninformed traders are not overwhelmed by the trading of informed traders. Hence, if there are many hedgers or their risk aversion (the A) or *ex ante* endowment variability (σ_ω^2) is high, then such an equilibrium might be expected to hold provided there are not too many informed traders. If this not the case, then the orders of informed traders dominate trading to such an extent that the market maker cannot set a zero expected profit price. In this case, the linear equilibrium breaks down. While a nonlinear equilibrium could exist, finding it is highly problematic.

If a linear equilibrium does exist, then its behavior need not be that of a standard Kyle model. Of particular importance is that λ need not have the monotonicity properties it has when uninformed trade is exogenous. Spiegel and Subrahmanyam show that λ is monotonically decreasing in A and σ_ω^2, but can be nonmonotonic in n (the number of uninformed), k (the number of informed), and φ (the signal variance). Thus, for some market parameterizations, adding liquidity traders to a market can cause the terms of trade to worsen, rather than improve as is the case in Kyle's analysis. This occurs because increasing n increases price variability, and this induces hedgers to scale back their trades. Counterbalancing this tendency is the beneficial effect on prices of more non-information-based trades. For some specifications, the first effect dominates, and λ can initially increase in n. Spiegel and Subrahmanyam also show that changing the number of uniformed traders can have virtually any effect on λ given particular market parameter settings.

These results underscore the fragility of equilibria in which trade concentration occurs. In Admati and Pfleiderer's model, increases in n and k unambiguously improve the terms of trade and so result in traders clumping together. While this may certainly occur, it is not guaranteed, and reasonable factors such as trader risk aversion or hedging demands can be enough to result in the opposite trade behavior occurring. Since trade patterns do arise in actual markets, perhaps at least some of these phenomena can be explained by discretionary trader behavior.

If clumping of trades does occur, an interesting and related question is, when will these trades take place? In actual markets, volume is heaviest early in the day and again before the close of trading. Given the independence assumptions in Admati and Pfleiderer's model, there is no reason why any specific period should be preferred to any other. Admati and Pfleiderer argue that if discretionary trade flows become informative over time, then discretionary traders are more likely to trade early in the day rather than later. Their intuition is that traders may benefit from trading before the extent of their participation is known to the market.

A similar earlier versus later story is considered in an analysis of interday trading patterns by Foster and Viswanathan [1990]. Their analysis involves a variant of the Kyle [1985] model in which trade occurs only once a day and information is 'lumpy.'' In this paper, the single informed trader's information can persist across more than one trading interval, allowing both informed and uninformed traders the potential to gain from timing their trades. If this occurs, then trading patterns may arise in the presence of long-lived information.

5.2 STRATEGIC BEHAVIOR AND LONG-LIVED INFORMATION

The basic issue considered in Foster and Viswanathan is the trade pattern arising when the informational advantage of the informed trader deteriorates across time. Their model uses the basic structure of the continuous-auction Kyle [1985] model, where trade takes place in a finite number of discrete periods. These periods are assumed to be a day, and so there is essentially only one trading period a day. There is a single, risk neutral informed trader who receives a private information signal every day. There is also a noisy public signal available to all traders at the close of trading each day. Because trading does not take place on weekends, the informed trader, who continues to receive signals over the weekend, enters trading on Monday with a large informational advantage over uninformed traders.

If uninformed traders are not permitted to time their trades, then the behavior of the single informed trader is essentially that predicted by Kyle. Foster and Viswanathan focus on a linear equilibrium, and so the informed trader's optimal strategy can be calculated in the same manner as in Kyle. If the public signal provides no information, then the informed trader chooses her order quantity to release the same amount of information each day and thus equate the variance of price changes across days. If the public signal is informative, however, the value of the informed trader's information declines across time, causing her to accelerate her trades. This results in the sensitivity of prices to the trade flow, the λ variable, declining monotonically across the week, which, in turn, causes the variance of price changes to similarly decline across the week.

What drives this result is the imbalance of information at the start of the trading week. Because informed traders have more information on Mondays, they begin the week with a greater informational advantage. If the single informed trader trades simply on a day-by-day basis, then there would be large price effects on Monday because the market maker knows that more of the order flow is information-related. This makes it optimal for the informed trader to delay her trades, but the availability of public information limits the extent to which this can be done.

Obviously, if the pattern of private information did not have this "lumplike" characteristic, then such trading patterns need not arise. For example, if no information of any kind were available on weekends, then no informational imbalance would occur, and trade patterns would be the same across days. An equally important assumption is that uninformed liquidity demand does not accumulate over the weekend; so there can be no liquidity imbalance on Monday to offset this informational imbalance.

Given that there is more private information on Mondays, it follows that uninformed traders might prefer to delay their trades and transact when the terms of trade are more favorable. As in Admati and Pfleiderer [1988], Foster and Viswanathan assume that there are both discretionary and nondiscretionary uninformed traders, and that their behavior is limited in several dimensions. Discretionary traders are allowed to delay their trades for at most one calendar day. Hence, in this model a discretionary trader may postpone trading from Monday to Tuesday, but not from Friday to Monday or from Monday to later in the week. Discretionary traders are also not permitted to split trades across trading days, nor can they skip trading altogether if market prices seem unreasonable. All discretionary traders follow the same rule, either all delaying or all staying.

These assumptions are needed to restrict the equilibrium to the linear pure-strategy case, but they highlight the difficulty in analyzing these strategic problems. With long-lived information, allowing the discretionary traders to split their orders essentially allows them to learn more from the order flow (and thus, by extension, about the asset's true value) than the market maker. In particular, the uninformed trader is more informed in the second period since he knows what his orders were in the first period. This creates the difficulty of dual types of informed traders, and the problem becomes intractable.[3]

As is also true in Admati and Pfleiderer, the uninformed discretionary traders act competitively in choosing when to trade. One difference between the two models is that since Foster and Viswanathan have only a single informed trader, the dissipative effect on information arising with multiple informed traders is not a feature of this model Hence, even if discretionary traders are able to delay trading, if there is no public signal then the single informed trader simply adjusts her trading volume to offset the discretionary effects. In this case, the behavior of the uninformed only

---

3. I am particularly grateful to S. Viswanathan for his comments on this point.

affects the profit of the informed trader and, with entry precluded, there is no pattern in security prices and variances.

When there is a public signal however, the informed trader cannot offset the uninformeds' order flow behavior, and patterns emerge. Indeed, Foster and Viswanathan show that multiple equilibria are possible, with single or dual periods of trade concentration being feasible outcomes. This demonstration that multiple equilibria prevail is an interesting and important contribution of the model. In strategic analyses, it is often the case that there is not a single equilibria. This difficulty makes it problematic to ascribe policy implications, and it may reflect the difficulty that in some strategic models virtually everything can be an equilibrium. This issue of the robustness of strategic models is discussed further later in the chapter.

If there are multiple equilibria, then the question arises whether the equilibrium solutions share any common properties. Foster and Viswanathan show that in each equilibrium, Monday volume is always lowest because the uninformed delay trading to avoid the informed trader's large informational edge. Similarly, the variance of returns on Mondays differs from other days because of this differential trading behavior. Foster and Viswanathan argue that this trading behavior may explain the daily variance differences empirically found by French and Roll [1986].

In both the Admati-Pfleiderer and Foster-Viswanathan models, therefore, the ability of uninformed traders to delay trades introduces patterns in trade behavior. What appears to be needed in both models is some impediment that restricts the informed trader from offsetting the effects of the uninformed. As we have discussed, while it is possible to show that such results hold, their generality is constrained by the specific structure required to retain the tractable, linear structure needed to characterize equilibrium.

While these models provide predictions about variance and volume effects, another interesting empirical finding is that patterns exist in security returns. For example, Harris [1986] shows that there are intraday patterns in security returns, and that these patterns differ across days of the week. Further, numerous researchers have found puzzling interday patterns such as the "weekend" effect. In the theoretical models considered here, however, there need be no systematic difference in returns, because the informed are just as likely to know good news as they are to know bad news. Hence, while price variances differ, expected returns do not. Similarly, since the uninformeds' trades are not connected with information, they, too, can have no effect on returns. To develop patterns in returns, there must be some difference between the buy and sell sides of the market that is not symmetric with respect to information. One possibility is that it is connected with the price-setting behavior of the market maker. We now consider this issue in more detail.

5.3 STRATEGIC BEHAVIOR AND SECURITY RETURNS

The problem of analyzing patterns in trade returns is straightforward: If security prices follow a Martingale, then the expected return is always zero.[4] Predictable patterns in returns are precluded because that would require predictable differences in expected returns, and that is inconsistent with the Martingale property. In both the sequential trade models and strategic trader models, security prices are Martingales, and so it is not immediately obvious how to address return issues in either framework.

That the Martingale property should prove to be an impediment points out an interesting difficulty in the modeling of microstructure phenomena. In particular, a property generally ascribed to security markets is that they are efficient. While the actual meaning of this is increasingly subject to debate, one somewhat less contentious version of efficiency is that traders cannot systematically make returns simply by watching the market. Such behavior is ruled out if the price process is a Martingale, and hence from the point of view of market efficiency, this property is desirable.

From other perspectives, however, this property poses difficulties. For example, in the sequential trade model of Glosten and Milgrom, the Bayesian adjustment process that results in prices being Martingales precludes anything other than individual trades from affecting prices. Thus, if one wanted to look for patterns based on aggregation of trades, for example, a simple sequential trade model would not be applicable. And, as the papers in the previous section demonstrated, in the Kyle model, where trades are always aggregated, return patterns do not arise.

One possible modeling approach to alleviate this is to consider price behavior in a call market where the market maker sets prices before the beginning of trading. This approach was taken by O'Hara and Oldfield [1986] (see Chapter 2 for discussion) in modeling how the market maker sets prices given both market orders and limit orders. A multiperiod analysis using such a construction is found in the work of Easley and O'Hara [1987b], who analyze the effects of trade volume on the market maker's pricing problem.[5] The advantage of this approach is that it allows actual order imbalances to have real effects in the model. The disadvantage is that

---

4. The interest rate is implicitly assumed to be zero in these models. They could be modified to incorporate a nonzero return on the risk-free asset, and then prices adjusted for this return would follow a Martingale.

5. In Easley and O'Hara [1987b], traders may submit at most one order per trading period and the overall volume of buys and sells provides a signal to the market maker of where the informed traders are transacting. Although the actual orders submitted could (and, indeed, usually would) result in a gain or loss to the market maker, his expected profit was zero. They use the model to address issues relating to the speed of price adjustment and market efficiency. A later version of this paper is Easley and O'Hara [1992b].

this structure is not actually found in any market setting, although one might argue that foreign exchange markets, where quotes are honored up to very large trade sizes, approximate this market structure.

In addressing the issue of varying security market returns, Admati and Pfleiderer [1989] employ a call market construction to analyze how the relative and absolute numbers of buys and sells could affect return patterns. Their analysis considers both the cases of competitive market makers and a monopolistic market maker, and as the intuition is similar, we focus on the competitive scenario. Admati and Pfleiderer consider a T period model in which a risky asset pays a liquidating dividend at time T of

$$\tilde{F} = \overline{F} + \sum_{t=1}^{T} \tilde{\delta}_t, \tag{5.13}$$

where for $t = 1, 2, \ldots, T$, the δ_t are assumed to be i.i.d. random variables with zero mean. The δ_t are assumed to be public information before the start of period t, and so the expected value of the asset at time t given public information is

$$\tilde{V}_t = \overline{F} + \sum_{\tau=1}^{t} \tilde{\delta}_\tau. \tag{5.14}$$

Trading takes place through M risk neutral market makers, who quote bid and ask prices. Each market maker is assumed willing to transact all orders received in any period t at the bid and ask prices he sets for time t. Rather than consider these prices per se, Admati and Pfleiderer focus on the bid and ask commissions, which they define as the deviations of price from the expected value. For any market maker j, the ask commission a_t^j and the bid commission b_t^j are defined as

$$a_t^j = A_t^j - \tilde{V}_t, \tag{5.15}$$

$$b_t^j = \tilde{V}_t - B_t^j, \tag{5.16}$$

where Aj and Bj are respectively the bid and ask prices in period t. These commissions can be thought of as the spread the market maker sets on each side of the market at any time t.

In this model it is assumed that at time 1 each trader knows every commission that will be charged in all future trading periods. One way to guarantee this is to assume that at time t each market maker posts the bid and ask commissions at which he will trade in each period t in all future periods. Note, however, that this is not the same as posting the bid and ask prices. Bid and ask prices depend upon the expected value of the asset at any time t, and that, in turn, depends on the realizations of the δ_t up to time t. It is not possible to know at time 1 what this expectation will be in the future, and so it is not possible to know what the bid and ask prices will be. Thus, although future trading prices cannot be known, Admati and Pfleiderer assume that future commissions can be known.

There are three types of traders in the market: informed traders, nondiscretionary liquidity traders, and discretionary liquidity traders. As in the earlier Admati and Pfleiderer analysis, an informed trader is assumed to observe in period t the information innovation $\tilde{\delta}_{t+1}$. Private information again only lasts one trading period, and so the issue of informed traders delaying trades is not relevant. The assumption of short-lived information also means that interperiod issues need not be considered. In this model, the number of informed traders is allowed to vary on a period-by-period basis, with the number of potentially informed traders in any period being a random variable with mean $I > 0$. It is assumed that any potential informed trader has a probability φ of becoming informed, so that the expected number of informed traders in any period t is φI.

The trading decision of an informed trader depends upon the market makers' prices and the informed traders' information. In particular, an informed trader will buy in period t if and only if $E(\tilde{F} \mid V_t, \delta_{t+1}) = V_{t+1} > A_t$. From (5.15), this is equivalent to the informed trader buying whenever $\delta_{t+1} > a_t^j$. Similar reasoning shows the informed trader wishes to sell if $-\delta_{t+1} > b_t^j$. If these conditions do not hold, then the trader simply does not trade. Notice that at these prices a risk neutral informed trader would want to submit an infinite number of orders, since this would result in infinite profit. To prevent this, much as in the sequential trade models, a trader is permitted in any trading period to buy one unit of stock, to sell one unit, or to not trade.

The uninformed traders include both *discretionary* and *nondiscretionary* traders. The nondiscretionary uninformed traders are assumed to trade in a specific period t. The discretionary traders are allowed to choose the period in which they trade, which can be in the interval $[T', T'']$. All liquidity traders are assumed to have a reservation "price," which is identically and independently distributed across traders. The reservation price, denoted $\tilde{z}^v$, is defined in terms of the bid and ask commissions, so that the *nondiscretionary* liquidity buyer submits an order at time t if and only if $a_t < \tilde{z}^v$ and a seller submits an order if and only if $\tilde{z}^v > b_t$. *Discretionary* liquidity traders submit a buy order in period t if and only if (1) $a_t < \tilde{z}^v$ and (2) a_t is the smallest trading commission over the trading interval $[T', T'']$, with the equivalent also holding for a discretionary liquidity seller.

Defining the uninformed traders' decisions in terms of trading commissions rather than prices reveals an interesting feature of this model. Traders are assumed to care not about the actual price of the asset they are buying or selling but only about the commissions they are paying. Hence, it might be that if the asset price were actually 46 and the commission 1 a trader would not buy, but he would do so if the price were 49 and the commission 1/2. The reason for this construction is that if the discretionary trader who cares about prices is to choose a period in which to transact, he must have expectations about the trading prices in each trade period. This would result in a much more complex analysis. Since commissions can be set independently of the asset's value, this problem can be avoided, but it does require the uninformed to pursue an unusual objective.[6] We return to these issues later in discussing the equilibrium of the model.

The numbers of nondiscretionary liquidity buyers and sellers in period t are i.i.d. random variables with mean $N > 0$, while the numbers of discretionary liquidity buyers and sellers are i.i.d. random variables with mean $D > 0$. Let a^* be the lowest ask commission over the period $[T', T'']$ and b^* the lowest bid commission. Market makers post trading commission schedules at time 1, and so the expected number of uninformed buyers in any period $t \in [T', T'']$ is

$$
L_t^A = \begin{cases} N + D / \tau^A & \text{if } a_t = a^*, \\ N & \text{otherwise,} \end{cases}
\tag{5.17}
$$

where τ^A is the number of periods in $[T', T'']$ in which $a_t = a^*$.[7] A similar expression can be derived for the expected number of uninformed sellers.

In a competitive market, the commissions each market maker quotes must provide zero expected profit. As in previous models, this involves offsetting expected losses to the informed with expected gains from the uninformed. The expected gains from each uninformed buyer are given by

$$
G(a_t) \equiv a_t \Pr\{\tilde{z}^v > a_t\},
\tag{5.18}
$$

---

6. Since the price is the expected value, this is equivalent to the uninformed preferring to minimize transaction costs given that they will buy the asset at a fair price.

7. Note that this is not correct if the market makers post prices on a period-by-period basis. If they did, then the actual number of discretionary traders who had traded before would be relevant for determining the expected number of such traders in period t, and hence the trading periods would be linked together. This is similar to the difficulties discussed in Admati and Pfleiderer [1988] when uninformed traders could split their trades.

where the Pr(•) term is the probability that a potential liquidity buyer trades given the ask quote and his reservation price. A related equation captures the expected loss to each informed trader. Admati and Pfleiderer define the function ψ by

$$\Psi(a_t) \equiv \Pr\left\{\tilde{\delta}_t > a_t\right\}\left[E\left(\delta_t | \tilde{\delta}_t > a_t\right) - a_t\right], \tag{5.19}$$

which gives the informed trader's expected profit (and hence the market maker's expected loss) from trading at the ask price. Admati and Pfleiderer then demonstrate that for any commission x, the function $\Psi(x)$ is decreasing in x. Consequently, the market maker's expected loss to an informed trader is decreasing in the commission he charges.

Given the expected numbers of traders in each trading period and the expected gains and losses, the market makers' equilibrium commission structure can be examined. Admati and Pfleiderer demonstrate that if $-\varphi I\Psi(x) + (N + D)G(x) > 0$, then discretionary liquidity buyers strictly prefer to concentrate their trading in one period and discretionary sellers strictly prefer to concentrate their buying. The reason for this is straightforward: with more uninformed trading, the commission can be lower because there are more gains to offset the losses to the informed. Hence, if all the uninformed clump together, they can improve their terms of trade and thus pay the lowest commission. Note that in this chosen period there is more expected informed trade because the lower commission raises the probability that $\delta_t > a_t$. Since, however, each informed trader can only trade one unit and, at this point, the total number of informed is exogenous, this increased informed trading cannot negate the advantages of clumping for the uninformed.

While this suggests that buys and sells will be concentrated, this concentration may take place at any time in the trading day. Moreover, it is possible that buyers and sellers may choose the same period in which to trade, leading to an increase in volume in that period but no trading imbalance. Since the focus of this paper is on return effects, it is also important to consider how these trading decisions affect security prices. Admati and Pfleiderer define an average transaction price as

$$\tilde{P}_t = \tilde{V}_t + \frac{\tilde{\omega}_t^a a_t + \tilde{\omega}_t^b b_t}{\tilde{\omega}_t^a + \tilde{\omega}_t^b} \tag{5.20}$$

where $\tilde{\omega}_t^a$ and $\tilde{\omega}_t^b$ are the number of buys and sells, respectively, and their sum is the total order flow. Note that no trade ever actually occurs at this price; all buys take place at a_t and all sells at b_t. Hence this "average" price essentially captures imbalances that arise from different volumes of buys and sells.

Given that discretionary uninformed traders trade together, it follows that the transaction pattern may induce biases in this transaction-weighted average price. Since this price is a function of the bid and ask commissions, Admati and Pfleiderer show that if the discretionary buyers and sellers choose the same period in which to transact, then $E(\tilde{P}_t \mid \tilde{V}_t) = \tilde{V}_t$ and $E(\tilde{P}_t - \tilde{P}_{t-1}) = 0$. This follows because the buying and selling of the uninformed is symmetric, so that the average "bias" in prices is zero. With price equal to the expected value, it follows that the expected change between this period's price and the next period's price is also zero.

If there are to be patterns in mean returns, therefore, it cannot simply be due to uninformed buyers and sellers trading together. If uninformed buyers and sellers choose to trade in different periods, however, then the average transaction price will, by definition, not equal the expected value. In the period in which buyers predominate, the average price exceeds $\tilde{V}_t$, and since the discretionary buyers will have then all transacted, it follows that in the next period the average price must be lower. Conversely, in the period where sellers predominate, the average price is biased downward, so that the next period's expected average price will be higher. If returns are measured with weighted average transaction prices, therefore, patterns arise if buyers and sellers choose different times to transact.

The analysis suggests that such an equilibrium is possible. To attribute mean return effects to trader behavior, however, what is needed is a demonstration that such time-separable trading will be an equilibrium or, better still, the only equilibrium. Admati and Pfleiderer argue that this will occur if the number of informed traders is endogenous.

For the number of informed traders to be endogenous, there must be some cost to becoming informed, or otherwise all traders would choose to do so. Let $c(\varphi_t)$ be the cost to any trader of having a probability φ_t of becoming informed in period t. In equilibrium it must be the case the number of informed traders is such that the gains from being informed are just equal to the cost of becoming informed. Note that this endogeneity must be done on a period-by-period basis. If the trader were informed for all periods, then in some later periods the market maker's zero expected profit condition might require prices to be set so that no trading at all could occur.

Since an informed trader is equally likely to learn good or bad news, it follows that the expected gains to being informed depend on both the bid and the ask commission. Finding an equilibrium when the number of informed is endogenous is thus quite complex; the commissions the market maker sets depend on the number of informed traders, but this number, in turn, depends on the market maker's commissions. Admati and Pfleiderer do not establish that such an equilibrium exists. Instead, they argue that in such an equilibrium it must be the case that the market maker sets commissions such that the discretionary buyers trade in one period and the discretionary sellers in another.

To understand why this is so, consider the problem facing the competitive market makers. Suppose there are three trading periods and that market maker A sets the following commissions:

$$
\begin{array}{ccc}
\text{period 1} & \text{period 2} & \text{period 3} \\
a = 1 & a = .6 & a = 1 \\
b = 1 & b = .6 & b = 1
\end{array}
\tag{5.21}
$$

With both bid and ask commissions lowest in period 2, all discretionary traders will trade at that time. This added uninformed trading is what allows the market maker to set the lower commissions at time 2. The lower commissions also make it more profitable to be informed in period 2, however, so that more informed traders will also transact then. For these commissions to be an equilibrium it must be the case that the losses to these informed traders must equal the gains from the uninformed traders.

Suppose there is another market maker B, who now considers setting commissions as follows:

$$
\begin{array}{ccc}
\text{period 1} & \text{period 2} & \text{period 3} \\
a = 1 & a = 1 & a = .5 \\
b = 1 & b = 1 & b = 1
\end{array}
\tag{5.22}
$$

Since his ask price is lower in period 3, it follows that discretionary uninformed buyers will move to period 3. His higher bid in period 3, however, means that uninformed sellers will remain in period 2. The informed traders' profit increases from buying at the lower ask in period 3, but it is not guaranteed that they will receive good news. Hence, while the number of informed in period 3 will be larger than in period 1, it will be strictly less than the number of informed in period 2, all of whom will be trading with market maker A. This cannot be an equilibrium, however, because A will lose money at his posted prices, while B will make money.

Market maker A could react to this situation by setting the following commissions:

$$
\begin{array}{ccc}
\text{period 1} & \text{period 2} & \text{period 3} \\
a = 1 & a = 1 & a = 1 \\
b = 1 & b = .5 & b = 1
\end{array} \qquad (5.23)
$$

In this case, the market makers will have tacitly divided the market so that all discretionary buyers trade with B and all sellers with A. This, in turn, will result in a preponderance of buying in period 3 and a preponderance of selling in period 2. If such an equilibrium did prevail, then the resulting trade patterns could explain the observed return variability in the market. We conclude this chapter with a brief discussion of these equilibrium issues.

5.4 THE ROBUSTNESS OF STRATEGIC MODELS

While the outcome argued by Admati and Pfleiderer seems economically plausible, it need not be the equilibrium that actually occurs. Indeed, it may be that numerous other economically plausible equilibria could occur, or that no equilibrium at all will arise. The problem is that to characterize the actual equilibrium one would need to know not only the equilibrium concept being applied, but also the specific game being played. In this application, however, neither the game nor the equilibrium concept is specified, leaving the question of equilibrium uncertain.

This problem highlights a major difficulty in applying strategic models to market microstructure issues. To formally model the underlying game in a market requires specifying the rules of the game, the players, their strategy sets, and their payoffs. Moreover, if these are to be games of incomplete information, then the role of nature (and nature's moves) must also be carefully delineated. In most microstructure settings, such a specification would be a formidable task, if it were possible at all. Formally analyzing an incomplete information n-period game with M market makers, I informed traders, N liquidity traders, and D discretionary traders, for example, would be virtually impossible. Without such a specification, however, determining the equilibrium outcome of the game becomes problematic.

A second difficulty arises with respect to the equilibrium concept. Exactly how the players' beliefs and strategies are tied together is crucial for determining the resulting equilibrium. There need not be a single way to account for this, however, and consequently different equilibrium concepts can apply. For example, many games employ a Bayes-Nash equilibrium concept, in which each individual's strategy is a best response given the other individuals' strategies, and each trader's expectations about these strategies are correct. Such an equilibrium concept is employed in the Kyle model, for example. There are also various refinements of this equilibrium concept, however, as well as alternative equilibrium concepts that could be used (see Fudenberg and Tirole [1991]).

While this need not preclude the use of a game theory approach to microstructure problems, it does require extreme caution in interpreting the results. In particular, the common difficulty of multiple equilibria in game-theoretic analyses suggests that policy implications drawn from such an application may be particularly fragile, if not altogether misleading. Moreover, the ability to ever attain the proposed equilibrium in any actual market setting may also be a serious concern. Nonetheless, as the models in this chapter have demonstrated, strategic models of trader behavior can provide substantial insight and intuition into the trading process, and hence they may be useful in the analysis of specific problems.

6

Information and the Price Process

In the three previous chapters we examined the general market microstructure modeling approaches used to analyze the effect of information on security prices. In both the sequential trade framework and the batch strategic trading models, new information becomes impounded into prices as a result of the trading behavior of informed and uninformed traders. A characteristic of both approaches is that this price adjustment is not instantaneous. Because prices are conditional expected values, the price at each point reflects all publicly available information, but not necessarily all private information. Consequently, until prices adjust to the new-information value, informed traders earn a return to their information and prices are only semi-strong-form efficient.

In this chapter we turn our attention to the question of how prices adjust to new information over time. In both microstructure paradigms, prices eventually converge to new-information values, but, since this adjustment takes place in the limit, the actual adjustment time can be infinite. To understand how prices become "efficient," we need to know more about the process by which this adjustment occurs. Moreover, since different market structures can affect this adjustment, understanding how the price process behaves may provide insight into how markets should be structured and regulated. We consider these structure issues in more detail in Chapters 7, 8, and 9.

Examining the process of price adjustment requires focusing on how prices change across time. Since the specialist is responsible for setting market-clearing prices, this requires understanding how the specialist and other uninformed participants learn from observing market information. In the models discussed in the previous three chapters, as well as in actual security markets, what is actually observable can differ in fundamental ways. Individual trades, for example, are not publicly observable in batch systems, but are observable in continuous auctions. Similarly, the sequence of trades and their timing may be observable in some trading systems but not in others. This suggests that characterizing the price adjustment process requires a careful analysis of how information generated by the trading process is related to information on the underlying asset value.

As a starting point, we consider the simplest version of this problem by analyzing the information revealed by the price sequence. If prices are not fully revealing, then the sequence of prices may provide information that individual prices do not. Consequently, the adjustment of prices to information may involve drawing inferences from the price process itself to determine what the new full-information value should be. This inference process has been largely studied in rational expectations batch-style models, and we first consider the adjustment issue in this framework. In subsequent sections, we consider the effects of volume and time on the price adjustment process.

The limited scope of our discussion in this chapter should be stressed. Investigations of price adjustment in rational expectations models are multitudinous, and it is beyond our focus here to consider such work. What is of interest for us is how in a market setting traders can infer information from market parameters. In subsequent chapters, we extend this focus to considering how the market structure itself affects the available information.

6.1 INFORMATION AND THE SEQUENCE OF PRICES

In rational expectations models, a fundamental issue is the existence of a revealing rational expectations equilibrium. As noted by Grossman and Stiglitz [1980], if traders act competitively, their trades can result in prices impounding so much information that, in equilibrium, the price "reveals" all private information to uninformed traders. In this case, the issue of price adjustment is moot; prices instantly adjust to full-information values and markets are full-information efficient.

In actual markets, such instantaneous adjustment is rarely observed. While uninformed traders recognize that prices are related to information, it may be difficult to isolate the pure information effects on security prices from the more transitory liquidity effects. Moreover, even the effects of information are rarely pristine. While some traders may acquire information, it is not always obvious how that information relates to the ultimate value of the firm (or to its securities) and hence not immediately apparent how unbiased (or even how valuable) the information is. These difficulties imply that simple models of price adjustment may yield little insight into the behavior of actual asset markets.

What underlies the difficulty in characterizing the price adjustment process is that price movements depend on how market participants learn from market information, and this, in turn, depends on myriad factors such as traders' risk preferences and endowments, the nature and extent of uncertainty, and even the market structure itself. In the simplest models, where the only uncertainty is the value of the informed trader's private signal, uninformed traders can draw sufficient inference from just one price observation to learn the "truth." In more complete models (and presumably in actual market settings) this learning problem is more complex, making the link between market information and the asset value less apparent.

If an equilibrium exists and it is not revealing, traders can glean some, but not all, information from a single price. If they watch a sequence of prices, however, then traders have both the information conveyed by more observations as well as any information conveyed by the increments in prices. In effect, traders can follow or "chart" the pattern of prices to learn any underlying information. Such technical analysis of market data is widespread in markets, with elaborate trading strategies devised to respond to the appearance of a "head and shoulders" in the data, or to some more mundane movement in a moving average of prices.[1] But why such patterns should be, or even how they could be, valuable is unclear. And even the fundamental question of what traders could learn from such market data has not been resolved.

Rather than focus on this general question, which surely goes far beyond the issues generally addressed in market microstructure, our focus will be on the more limited question of the information contained in specific pieces of market data. A natural starting point is the information content of price sequences. In the models considered in previous chapters, the price sequence per se plays little role. The specialist in a sequential trade model sets each price equal to the conditional expected value, and the movement between prices reflects only the updating of the market maker's posterior beliefs. Similarly, in a Kyle framework the market maker learns nothing from the movement of prices that is not already in his information set. In these models, the adjustment of prices cannot depend on any information generated by the price movement, because prices are not a source of information to the market maker.

An alternative framework that does capture an informative role for the price sequence is the "noisy" rational expectations approach. Such models

---

1. The study of patterns in market data underlies the recent development of neural nets to predict stock market returns. Thus, while technical analysis has a long history, the role of trade patterns may be increasingly important given the increased ability to analyze real-time data.

have been used to address a wide variety of issues, with the informational role of the price sequence (and, by extension, technical analysis) in price adjustment the focus of research by Brown and Jennings [1989] and Grundy and McNichols [1989].[2] While both papers address the same issue, their approaches differ in an interesting, and fundamental, way; so it is useful to consider both approaches in detail. To economize on notation, we consider a general framework and then distinguish the features special to each approach.

In a noisy rational expectations framework, prices are affected both by private information and by supply uncertainty. Information affects prices because some (or even all) traders are assumed to receive a private signal of the asset's true value. This signal may be the "truth" or it, too, may contain noise that interferes with agents knowing with certainty the actual value. Supply uncertainty is incorporated to capture transitory effects on price that are not related to information. This supply uncertainty can be introduced in several ways, but its role is always the same: with multiple sources of uncertainty, traders cannot immediately sort out the information effects on price from the supply effects on price.

Brown and Jennings [1989] consider a standard rational expectations framework in which there is an exogenously given random supply of the asset. While they consider a three-period model, the intuition of their approach can be captured in a simpler two-period framework. Let i agents trade a risky asset and a riskless asset in time periods 1 and 2. There are $i = 1, 2, . ., N$ agents, with the limiting case of $N = \infty$ being the case analyzed. Prior to the start of time 1, traders receive some endowment, ω_i, of the riskless asset. Trading occurs at times 1 and 2, and at the end of time 2 the risky asset pays a liquidating dividend Ψ. Traders' common prior beliefs about Ψ are given by $N(\Psi_0, 1/\rho_0)$. As is standard in rational expectation models, all random variables (i.e., asset supplies, signals, and payoffs) are assumed to be independently distributed normal random variables.

Each trader maximizes the negative exponential utility function

$$U\left(W_i\right) = -\exp\left[-W_i\right], \tag{6.1}$$

where W_i is the trader i's wealth and, for simplicity, I have set the risk aversion coefficient to 1. In a multiperiod model, wealth depends on asset demands and consumption decisions in both periods 1 and 2, and these decisions, in turn, affect each other. Unfortunately, the general solution for

---

2. Noisy rational expectations models are developed by Grossman and Stiglitz [1980], Hellwig [1980], and Diamond and Verrecchia [1981].

such a problem is quite complex; a simplification employed by Brown and Jennings (and most researchers in this area) is to focus on "myopic" behavior. With myopic behavior, traders focus only on the immediate period, and so decisions are independent across periods. This effectively ignores any interperiod linkages but does allows the problem to be analyzed tractably.

At time 1, each trader is assumed to receive a signal, y_i, of the liquidating dividend

$$y_i = \Psi + \tilde{\varepsilon}_i \qquad (6.2)$$

where $\tilde{\varepsilon}_i$ is distributed as $N(0. s_i)$. In the limit economy, $\sum_{i=1}^{N} \left(y_i \big/ N \right) \rightarrow \Psi$ with probability one, and so the aggregated signal of all traders is an unbiased estimate of the true value.

While traders' demands arise from utility maximization problems, the asset supply is assumed to be an exogenous random variable X, with per capita supply given by $X/N = x$ for all N. Equilibrium requires that supply equals demand, and so denoting each trader's demand by d_i and considering per capita values, this dictates that

$$x = \sum_{i=1}^{N} d_i/N. \qquad (6.3)$$

The exact nature of these demands, d_i, depends on traders' information sets. Given information set H^i, each trader conjectures a form for the equilibrium price function, and based on this price function, the traders determine their demands. In a rational expectations equilibrium, the price conjecture is correct and per capita demand equals per capita supply.

The price function traders are assumed to conjecture at time 1 is the linear relation

$$p = \alpha \Psi_0 + \beta \sum_{i=1}^{N} \left(y_i \big/ N \right) - \gamma x, \qquad (6.4)$$

where α, β, and γ are coefficients determined in the equilibrium. Hence, the price is assumed to be a function of the asset's liquidating value, the traders' signals, and the aggregate supply. As discussed in the Appendix to Chapter 3, the assumptions of negative exponential utility functions and normally distributed random variables dictate that traders' demands are given by the function

$$d_i = \frac{E\left[\Psi|H^i\right] - p}{\text{var}\left[\Psi|H^i\right]}. \tag{6.5}$$

As demand involves conditional expectations, the form of traders' information sets affects the equilibrium.

Suppose that traders know only their own signal and the equilibrium price p, so that $H^i = (y_i, p)$. Brown and Jennings demonstrate that in equilibrium neither the time 1 nor time 2 price alone is revealing, and so uninformed traders simply watching the price are unable to infer the private signal value. In a two-period model, however, traders can observe the sequence of prices. Brown and Jennings show that under very general conditions the combination of p_1 and p_2 is *jointly* fully revealing. Hence, the sequence of prices provides information that individual prices cannot.

This joint revelation provides a rationale for technical analysis. In this model, prices are not efficient because neither the time 1 nor time 2 price is a sufficient statistic for market information. Since price does not impound all available information, traders who track prices know more than traders who simply know the current market price. This suggests that the sequence of prices provides information to traders, and hence it affects the adjustment of prices to full-information values.

A similar conclusion arises in the work of Grundy and McNichols [1989]. They also employ a noisy rational expectations framework, but they do not assume exogenous supply uncertainty. Instead, in their model the i traders, $i = 1, \ldots, N$, each receive random endowments, ε_i, of the underlying asset, and the total asset supply, X, depends on these endowments. The endowments are assumed to be identically and independently normally distributed random variables, with distribution $N(\mu_x, \sigma_x^2 N)$. Grundy and McNichols consider the limiting case where $N = \infty$. Because the variance of the endowments depends on the number of traders N, in this limiting case traders cannot infer any useful information from their endowments. Without such an infinite variance, endowments would be correlated with per capita supply, and characterizing the resulting equilibrium becomes extremely difficult, if not altogether intractable.

In this model, each trader also gets a signal

$$\tilde{Y}_t^i = \tilde{\psi} + \tilde{\omega}_t + \varepsilon_t^i, \tag{6.6}$$

where $\tilde{\psi}$ is the payoff from the risky asset, $\tilde{\omega}_t$ is a common error term (with variance σ_ω^2), and ε_t^i is an idiosyncratic error term (with variance σ_ε^2). This error structure means that no trader "knows" the true value, and that even all traders together do not have sufficient information to determine the underlying true asset value.

Equilibrium in the model requires finding price conjectures resulting in traders' demands such that supply equals demand, and the price conjectured is the price that prevails. As in Grundy and McNichols, traders maximize negative exponential utility functions defined on wealth, and the price functions are assumed to be linear in signals and supply. This conjectured price function in the first period is given by

$$P_1 = \alpha_1 + \beta_1 \overline{Y} + \gamma_1 X, \tag{6.7}$$

where α, β, and γ are determined in the equilibrium, and $\overline{Y}$ is defined by

$$\overline{Y} = \lim_{N \to \infty} \sum_{i=1}^{N} \frac{Y_i}{N} = \tilde{\psi} + \tilde{\omega}_t. \tag{6.8}$$

The price conjectured in the second period is defined similarly.

Grundy and McNichols now consider the equilibrium prevailing in each period of the model. Perhaps the most interesting case is when there is no additional endowment given to traders at the beginning of period 2. In this case, traders have the opportunity to exchange claims at time 1 at some price p_1, and since there is no new uncertainty introduced at time 2, it is not obvious why additional trade occurs at time 2. Grundy and McNichols demonstrate that there are multiple equilibria in the model, and in some equilibria, first-period prices are not revealing and no further trader occurs. Such a "no-trade" equilibrium is consistent with the results of Milgrom and Stokey [1982]. Grundy and McNichols also consider the case where there is an interim supply shock and provide conditions under which the "no-trade" equilibrium results of Milgrom and Stokey do not hold. As these topics are not specifically related to the price adjustment questions considered here, we do not consider them further, but their results on this topic are of great importance for the general question of trade in rational expectations models.

Of perhaps more interest is that there are other equilibria in which trade does occur at time 2. In these equilibria, traders learn the underlying information based on the combination of time 1 and time 2 prices. In effect, traders use the two price observations to solve for the two unknowns: supply uncertainty and private information. Thus, as in Brown and Jennings, the sequence of two prices reveals information that individual prices cannot. What is also true in this model, however, is that a third trading price is irrelevant, as all information is revealed by two observations.

Only if there are multiple sources of uncertainty could analysis of longer series of prices be useful.

From the perspective of price adjustment, these two analyses demonstrate that the movement of prices to full-information values need not be automatic. With asymmetric information, prices play a dual role of market clearing and information aggregation. This latter role dictates that the sequence of prices can be informative beyond the information provided by the individual prices themselves. In this adjustment process, uninformed traders learn from watching market data, and this learning is what allows price to ultimately reflect information. These analyses thus provide one explanation for the pervasive use of technical analysis in markets that are supposedly efficient.

While the Grundy-McNichols and Brown-Jennings models focus on the informational role of prices, other market variables may also be informative. For example, volume may be correlated with useful information on the underlying value process since it subsumes information from aggregate trading demands. The role of time and, in particular, the time between trades may also affect the adjustment process. In the next two sections we address the relation of these variables to price adjustment.

6.2 THE VOLUME CRITIQUE

One market variable long thought to be a factor in price adjustment is trading volume. Indeed, an oft-cited adage is, "It takes volume to move prices," and, not surprisingly, much research has investigated this link (Karpoff [1987] provides an excellent survey of work in this area; more recent work is discussed in Stickel and Verrecchia [1993]). In general, empirical research has identified a strong link between volume and the absolute value of price changes. Empirical researchers have also established some asymmetric patterns to volume and the direction of price changes, although the generality of these results is subject to debate.[3]

While the empirical link between price movements and volume appears strong, it is not obvious why this should be so. In general, theoretical research provides no definitive answer. In the accounting literature, numerous researchers (for example Verrecchia [1981] and Kim and Verrecchia [1991]) have modeled the link between public information announcements and volume. The concern here is to explain why prices do

---

3. For example, it is alleged that volume is larger when prices move up than when they move down. Several researchers have exploited the idea of short sale constraints to explain this asymmetric behavior. The price-volume relationship in futures markets is also not the same as it is in equity markets. Karpoff [1987] discusses these issues in more detail.

not instantly adjust to publicly available information and why volume appears to increase around the announcement of public information. In the Kim and Verrecchia [1991] analysis, this change in volume is proportional to the precision of the public information signal and is decreasing in the amount of preannouncement public and private information.

In the microstructure literature in which private information is the concern, however, the price-volume link is less clear. In the Kyle [1985] model, for example, trading volume is not a factor in the price adjustment process. The reason is that the informed trader always adjusts his order amount to keep his relative fraction of trades the same. Consequently, the price path is independent of the scale of trading volume, and the empirical link between price movements and volume is not present. In the sequential trade models, a similar difficulty arises in evaluating the role of volume. Since the probability of trading with an informed trader is constant across time, the total amount of trade causes prices to change, but the volume per se does not affect the movement at any time. In effect, the market maker does not use volume as a signal of any underlying information because all relevant information is contained in the individual trades.

One reason it is difficult to evaluate the link of price and volume is that it is not obvious what information volume, in itself, provides to the market. Just as traders can learn by watching prices, it seems likely they could learn by watching volume. In the extreme case, it is possible that volume alone could reveal underlying information, with prices playing a redundant information role. A more likely scenario is that the combination of price and volume could provide information to the market in much the same way that the sequence of prices revealed information, as discussed in the previous section.

Numerous researchers have examined this informational role by analyzing how volume matters in a noisy rational expectations framework (see, for example, Pfleiderer [1984]; Wang [1994]; Campbell, Grossman, and Wang [1991]; Blume, Easley, and O'Hara [1994]; a somewhat different framework is used in Harris and Raviv [1993]). There are two general approaches in this rational expectations-based literature. One approach analyzes the volume that emerges when traders with different information signals transact. This provides correlations between volume and variables such as trader heterogeneity, and it allows explicit characterizations of the link between price changes and volume. The second approach focuses on the information inherent in the volume statistic, and what traders can learn from observing volume.

The first approach is exemplified by Wang [1994], who examines how factors such as dividend information and private investment opportunities affect the price-volume relation. In Wang's model, some traders are better informed of a risky asset's dividend process and the returns on private investment opportunities. These latter opportunities allow trading for liquidity-based reasons, while the former capture the familiar information-based motive. There are also the uninformed (or more precisely, less well-informed traders) who receive a noisy signal of the dividend process and who are not allowed access to private investment opportunities. This latter restriction means that only informed traders face hedging needs, and it is these hedging-related trades that allow uninformed investors to trade without facing a certain loss.

In this model, volume is decreasing in the amount of the informational asymmetry. If the risk of information-based trading is too high, then uninformed traders opt not to trade given that there is little chance of not losing to the informed traders. This risk of information-based trading also dictates that volume and the absolute value of excess returns are positively correlated, reflecting the price movement necessary to induce uninformed traders to take the other side of the trade. An interesting feature of this model is that volume is also positively correlated with the arrival of public information. Thus, as in Kim and Verrecchia [1991], public information stimulates trading. In the Wang model, this occurs because public information affects different investors in different ways. The greater the asymmetry between traders' information, the greater the trading volume. This provides one explanation for the puzzling increase in volume around predictable events such as earnings announcements.

In this model, as in other standard rational expectations analyses, volume emerges as the result of traders' optimal demands, but it does not play any role other than market clearing. In particular, traders do not extract information from volume, nor do they use any of the correlations implied in volume in forming their demands. A second approach to studying volume focuses on the learning problem that arises when traders can condition on the information contained in volume. In particular, it is standard in rational expectations models to allow traders to condition on the market price in forming demands. If traders know the price, however, it seems almost axiomatic that they also know other market information such as volume or at least their own demands. Blume, Easley, and O'Hara [1994] analyze this learning problem and demonstrate how the volume statistic itself affects the adjustment of prices to information. As this relates to the approaches we have discussed thus far in this chapter, we first consider this learning approach to studying volume.

As a starting point, it is useful to consider how allowing traders to condition on greater market information affects the conclusions of the

Brown-Jennings and Grundy-McNichols price adjustment analyses.[4] Perhaps the easiest variable for traders to include in their information set is their own trade. Since demands involve conditional expectations with respect to information sets, each trader's information set H^i now includes their signal value, the price, and their own demand, denoted d_i; so $H^i = (y_i, p, d_i)$. In the Brown and Jennings framework, it is easy to demonstrate that allowing traders to condition on their own net trade results in multiple equilibria. These multiple equilibria arise in an interesting way. In particular, if traders conjecture that price is *not revealing*, then, as before, in equilibrium traders' conjectures are correct, prices are not revealing, and the role of technical analysis, or the sequence effect of prices, remains. Paradoxically, if traders conjecture that prices are *revealing*, then their conjecture is also correct, and the equilibrium involves no role for technical analysis.

The explanation for this divergence lies in the effect of traders' conjectures on their demands. If traders expect the price to be revealing, then the solution of the demand equation (6.5) reveals that each trader's optimal demand depends not on his private signal, but on the average signal. But with individual signals playing no role, all demands are the same, and in equilibrium the price, as conjectured, is revealing. Since a single price observation reveals all information, the price sequence is irrelevant for price adjustment, and the role of technical analysis becomes less apparent.[5]

If traders can condition on market volume, then whether the price sequence is informative depends on how supply uncertainty is modeled in the noisy rational expectations framework. In the random exogenous supply model (as typified by Brown and Jennings), allowing traders to condition on volume results in an equilibrium in which price reveals all information to the uninformed. This occurs because in any equilibrium, demand must equal supply, and allowing traders to condition on volume and the direction of their trade (either buying or selling) essentially allows them to know the exogenous supply. If supply is known, however, the only uncertainty is the private information, and this single unknown can be revealed by a single market price.

If the supply uncertainty is modeled in the Grundy and McNichols random endowment framework, however, this revealing equilibrium does not arise. The reason is that volume per se provides no information at all. In

---

4. This discussion is drawn from Blume, Easley, and O'Hara [1994], which contains a more technical derivation of the conclusions drawn here.

5. This multiple equilibria difficulty arising from traders using the information in their own trade was demonstrated for the general case by Jordan [1982].

the limit economy, volume can have no information content because the expectation of even per capita volume is infinite. In particular, in the Grundy-McNichols framework (with no second-period endowment shock), expected per capita volume, v, at time 1 is simply[6]

$$v = \frac{1}{2} E\left[\left|d_i - x_i\right|\right].$$ (6.9)

The variance of the endowment x_i is infinite (recall that the definition of the variance is $\sigma_x^2 N$, where N is infinite), and so taking expectations results in v being infinite as well. Considering the economy at some point other than in the limit results in volume not being infinite, but then, with finite endowment variances, traders can draw inferences from their endowments, leading to the same revealing equilibrium problem noted earlier.

The difficulty with volume in the noisy rational expectations framework, therefore, is that it provides either too much information or none at all. Because volume is correlated with the underlying supply uncertainty, the information it provides relates only to the exogenously introduced randomness and not to the asset's true value. A second difficulty is how traders use whatever information they glean from volume. Suppose that conditioning only on prices, traders do not learn the asset's true value (i.e., the equilibrium is not revealing). Now suppose that conditioning on price and volume together, the equilibrium is revealing, and so presumably volume is providing useful information to traders. If, however, the equilibrium is revealing, then traders all know the same thing, and then their demands must be identical. So volume could tell them nothing! In essence, if there is information in volume, its use vitiates its value, rendering volume useless in affecting the price adjustment process.

This difficulty arises because of the contemporaneous linkages required in rational expectations analyses. In rational expectations models, traders use the information contained in their current trade to determine that trade. Thus, traders use the price (and volume) at which the trade executes to determine the trade they make. If traders use this contemporaneous information to form demands, however, then the simultaneity of the process can vitiate any information the trade may have. This difficulty led

---

6. Expected per capita volume at time 2 is not the same because there is no interim endowment shock, and hence volume will be finite. It is this second-period volume that Grundy and McNichols discuss in their paper.

Hellwig [1982] to suggest allowing traders to use past rather than contemporaneous data in forming their conditional expectations. Since in actual markets technical analysis involves past rather than contemporaneous data, this approach seems particularly well suited to address this issue.

Blume, Easley, and O'Hara [1994] use such a framework to investigate how traders learn by watching both price and volume data. In their model, traders maximize negative exponential utility functions of the form discussed earlier. There is a risky asset and a riskless asset, and the eventual value of the risky asset, Ψ, is a random variable, which is assumed normally distributed with mean Ψ_0 and variance $1/\rho_0$. Traders receive zero endowments of the risky asset, and there is no exogenous supply uncertainty. As in the Brown-Jennings and Grundy-McNichols models, there are N traders, with the analysis done for the case of $N = \infty$.

Each trader in the model receives an informative signal every period. The traders are divided into two groups, with $N_I = \mu N$ of the traders in one group and $N_U = (1 - \mu)N$ in the other. The traders in each group receive signals from a common distribution, but there are different distributions for the two groups. Each trader in group 1 receives a signal at date *t*:

$$y_t^i = \psi + \omega_t + e_t^i, \qquad (6.10)$$

where ω_t is a common error distributed as $N(0, 1/\rho_\omega)$, and e_t^i is an idiosyncratic error distributed as $N(0, 1/\rho_t^1)$. The precision ρ_t^1 is a random variable, and so the "quality" of group 1's information varies over time. Similarly, each trader in group 2 also receives a signal of the form given in equation (6.10), but the distribution of their idiosyncratic error is $N(0, 1/\rho^2)$, and so the precision of group 2's signal does not vary with time.

This information structure is complex: both the level and the quality of signals are unknown to the market. Each trader knows his own signal and has a common prior on the asset value and the signal distributions. The traders in group 1 know at time *t* the precision of their signal, but traders in group 2 do not know ρ_t^1. Since there is also a common error (ω_t) in the signals, this creates a complex learning problem for the agents. Conditional on ω_t, each signal y_t^i is distributed as $N(\theta_t, 1/\rho_t^1)$ for traders in group 1 and $N(\theta_t, 1/\rho^2)$ for traders in group 2, where $\theta_t = \psi + \omega_t$. By the Strong Law of Large Numbers, the mean signal in each group converges almost surely to θ_t, the true value plus common error.

Each trader chooses his demand to maximize expected utility and, as in Brown and Jennings, traders are assumed to do so on a period-by-period basis (i.e., they are myopic). Summing first-period demands results in an equilibrium price for the large economy ($N = \infty$) of

$$p_1 = \frac{\rho_0 \psi_0 + \left[\mu \rho_1^{s1} + (1 - \mu)\rho^{s2}\right]\theta_1}{\rho_0 + \left[\mu \rho_1^{s1} + (1 - \mu)\rho^{s2}\right]} \tag{6.11}$$

where $\rho_1{}^{s1}$ is the signal variance, defined by $\rho_1{}^{s1} = \rho_\omega \rho_t{}^1 / (\rho_\omega + \rho_t{}^1)$ and similarly for $\rho^{s2} = \rho_\omega \rho^2 / (\rho_\omega + \rho^2)$.

This equilibrium price is not revealing. Because traders in group 2 do not know the signal precision ρ_1^{s1}, they cannot determine the signal value τ_1 from the equilibrium price. In effect, group 2 traders face the problem that there is one equation with two unknowns. Traders in group 1 do know ρ_1^{s1}, and so they can infer θ_1, which is everything that can be known about the underlying asset.

With price not revealing, group 2 traders have an incentive to look for additional information, and hence they could look to volume. Volume is found by summing up the absolute value of demands at price p_1 and dividing by 2. As it is more useful to consider per capita volume, this is given by

$$V_1 = \frac{1}{2N} \left[\sum_{i=1}^{N_I} \left| \rho_0 \left(\psi_0 - p_1\right) + \rho_1^{s1} \left(y_i^1 - p_1\right) \right| \right.$$
$$\left. + \sum_{i=N_I+1}^{N} \left| \rho_0 \left(\psi_0 - p_1\right) + \rho^{s2} \left(y_i^1 - p_1\right) \right| \right], \tag{6.12}$$

where the first term is simply the demands of group 1 traders, and the second term, of group 2 traders.

This definition reveals an immediate problem in analyzing the properties of volume. Because of the absolute values, volume is not normally distributed, and so the multivariate normal structure typically used to characterize the behavior of random variables in this type of model cannot be employed. To characterize how traders learn from volume, however, we must know how traders interpret the information in volume, and this entails understanding its statistical properties. Blume, Easley, and O'Hara (BEO) show that the volume statistic can be represented as

$$V_1 = \frac{\mu}{2} \left[2 \frac{\rho_1^{s1}}{\left(\rho_1^1\right)^{1/2}} \phi \left(\frac{\delta^1 (\rho_1^1)^{1/2}}{\rho_1^{s1}} \right) \right.$$

$$\left. + \delta^1 \left[\Phi \left(\frac{\delta^1 (\rho_1^1)^{1/2}}{\rho_1^{s1}} \right) - \phi \left(\frac{-\delta^1 (\rho_1^1)^{1/2}}{\rho_1^{s1}} \right) \right] \right],$$

$$+ \frac{1-\mu}{2} \left[2 \frac{\rho^{s2}}{(\rho^2)^{1/2}} \phi \left(\frac{\delta^2 (\rho^2)^{1/2}}{\rho^{s2}} \right) \right. \tag{6.13}$$

$$\left. + \delta^2 \left[\Phi \left(\frac{\delta^2 (\rho^2)^{1/2}}{\rho^{s2}} \right) - \phi \left(\frac{-\delta^2 (\rho^2)^{1/2}}{\rho^{s2}} \right) \right] \right]$$

where ϕ is the standard normal density, Φ is the standard normal cumulative distribution function, and $\delta^i = \rho_0 (\psi_0 - p_1) + \rho^{si}(\theta_1 - p_1)$. This volume statistic is clearly complex and does not lend itself to any simple intuitive explanation. Nonetheless, with its statistical properties defined, volume can be used by traders to update their beliefs.

With the price and volume statistic now specified, the question of interest is, what do traders know? BEO demonstrate that given the price, volume conveys information about signal quality, ρ_1^1, which can then be used to make inferences about the asset value θ_1. In particular, for any price p_1, per capita volume is increasing in the precision of group 1's signal if the signal precision exceeds the common error precision, and it is decreasing otherwise. Intuitively, this result reflects the differing effects of information quality on trading volume. If signal quality is low, i.e., ρ_1^1 near 0, then traders in group 1 receive very dispersed signals and place little confidence in them. At the extreme value of $\rho_1^1 = 0$, the only equilibrium has a volume of 0. Conversely, when signal quality is high, group 1 traders signals are all highly correlated, and so they do not trade with each other. The only trade that occurs is between traders in the two groups. This suggests that low volume may be as indicative of new information as high volume is.

In equilibrium, BEO demonstrate that for a fixed precision, volume is strictly convex (or V-shaped) in price. Moreover, the steepness and dispersion of the V-shape depend on the quality and dispersion of the underlying information. These theoretical results accord well with the observed empirical relation of price and volume (see Gallant, Rossi, and Tauchen [1992]), and they suggest the explanation for the price-volume link may be found in the quality and quantity of traders' information. The divergent behavior of volume before event dates may thus be explicable by the differing information available at that time.

In this model, therefore, volume provides traders with the ability to sort out the effects of the quality of information from the direction of information effects impounded in price. A trader observing only a high price cannot determine whether price is high because of a high average-quality signal or an average signal with high quality. Volume picks up signal quality in a way independent from price because volume is not normally distributed. This dictates that a trader watching only prices cannot learn as much as a trader watching prices and volume, and so it provides the justification for technical analysis of market data.

Volume's role in the price adjustment process, therefore, is to facilitate learning of the underlying uncertainty. An important feature of this model, however, is the common error in the information. If price and volume together revealed the true value Ψ (as would occur without the common error), then higher volume need not necessarily accompany the absolute value of price changes: whatever volume arose would be sufficient to move prices to full-information values. With even informed traders unsure of the true Ψ, however, large volume generally accompanies large price changes.

One way to interpret these results is that market statistics in general provide information to uninformed market participants. Although price and volume are perhaps the most obvious of these market statistics, the parameters of the order flow may also play a role in the adjustment process. In particular, while traders can obviously learn from the orders they observe transact, there may also be information in the lack of trade. To address this issue, we consider how time itself affects the movement of prices.

6.3 THE ROLE OF TIME IN PRICE ADJUSTMENT

In the microstructure models considered thus far, time does not play a role. In the Kyle framework, for example, trades are batched so that when individual orders arrive is not relevant (or even known) to the market maker. Similarly, in the sequential trade models, orders arrive in some probabilistic fashion that is independent of any time parameters. In these models, the timing of trades is irrelevant for price behavior because time itself has no information content.

This specification makes sense if time is exogenous to the price process. If, however, time can be correlated with any factor related to the asset price, then the presence or absence of trade provides information to market participants. This correlation could arise from characteristics particular to the trading mechanism or it could reflect properties of the underlying information process. In either case, if market participants can learn from watching the timing of trades, then the adjustment of prices to information will also depend on time.

This notion of time as a signal is developed in research by Diamond and Verrecchia [1987] and Easley and O'Hara [1992a]. Diamond and Verrecchia consider whether market short sale constraints affect the propensity to trade and thereby introduce asymmetries into the speed of price adjustment to good and bad news. Easley and O'Hara pursue the idea that timing of trades is related to the existence of new information. While the motivations and results in these papers differ, both analyses focus on what market participants can learn from the timing and sequence of trade. As Diamond and Verrecchia analyze a variant of the Glosten-Milgrom model, we begin our discussion by considering their approach.[7]

If traders are unable to transact in certain states of the world, then observing an absence of trade may indicate the underlying state. This is the intuition behind Diamond and Verrecchia's [1987] analysis of short sale constraints and price behavior. In actual security markets, short sale constraints take various forms. In some markets, short sales are strictly prohibited or are permitted only when prices are rising (for example, the "uptick" rule found on the NYSE). Short sales can also be affected by "proceeds" constraints, which limit a short seller's ability to receive the proceeds until after a short sale is reversed. Such proceeds constraints clearly raise the cost of short selling and, to the extent they affect traders' order decisions, affect the behavior of prices.

Diamond and Verrecchia capture trading costs by assuming that all traders fall into one of three categories. Some fraction of the trader population, c_1, face no costs associated with short sales, some fraction c_2 are "proceeds constrained," and the remaining fraction c_3 are prohibited from short selling altogether. Because traders face different costs, their willingness or ability to trade may also differ, and this in turn imparts information content to the presence or absence of trade.

In this sequential trade model, the trading day is divided into $t = 1, 2, \ldots, T$ trading intervals. As in Glosten and Milgrom, a competitive market maker sets bid and ask prices at each time t equal to conditional expected values given the type of trade and all publicly available

---

7. If time is a factor in price adjustment, then any model of this phenomenon must incorporate the time between trades in an explicit manner. In particular, it must be the case that "no-trade" intervals are observable to market participants. The batch-style rational expectations models obliterate such information and so are not appropriate for this question. Because the sequential trade models do permit a trade-by-trade analysis, this framework provides a reasonable venue to address the role of time.

information. Some traders, a fraction α, receive an equally probable signal, low or high, of the asset's true value. The other fraction $(1 - α)$ of traders do not receive a signal, and these uninformed traders are assumed to trade for exogenous liquidity reasons.

At each time t, a trader is randomly selected from the total population of traders and given the opportunity to trade. Diamond and Verrecchia assume that with probability γ the trader would potentially like to transact, and with probability $1 - γ$ the trader does not want to trade. These probabilities are exogenously given, and so the trade decision is not correlated with information on the asset's true value. If a trader is selected to trade, he may either want to buy one unit, sell one unit, or not trade at all. Note that the decision to sell may also involve a decision to short the stock. If the trader does not own the stock, then selling the stock by definition involves a short sale.

The *ability* to short sell, however, differs with the costs traders face. Consider first the decision faced by an informed trader. If he learns good news, short sale constraints are irrelevant as the trader always wishes to buy. If, however, he learns bad news, he will wish to sell or short sell depending on whether the trader already owns the stock. Suppose that he does not own the stock. For traders who face no costs or are proceeds constrained (i.e., are in fraction c_1 or c_2), shorting is optimal, as any delay in receiving the profit is assumed to be of lesser consequence than forgoing the trading opportunity completely. If the trader is prohibited from short selling (i.e., is in c_3), then he does not sell the stock.

An uninformed trader faces a similar decision problem. If he experiences a positive liquidity shock, he sells the stock if he already owns it. If he does not own it, then he shorts if he is faces no constraints (i.e., is in c_1). Since the uninformed trader needs liquidity, he will not short if he is proceeds constrained nor, of course, will he short if short sales are prohibited. An uninformed trader in either fraction c_2 or c_3 of the population, therefore, will not trade when his turn to transact arrives.

This trading behavior means that an absence of trade can occur for three reasons. First, the trader selected to trade simply does not want to transact. This decision is independent of information on the asset's value, and so there is no information content to the absence of trade arising for this reason. Second, an absence of trade can occur if an uninformed trader facing positive liquidity demands is unable to short sell because of constraints. Again, this decision is not information-related and so also provides no information to the market. Finally, a trader informed of bad news may be unable to trade if short sales are prohibited. In this case, observing a no-trade outcome may signal that there is bad news about the value of the asset.

Traders watching the market can compute the probability that any no-trade interval is actually a signal of bad news and can adjust their beliefs accordingly. Such a computation follows directly from Bayes Rule. The change in beliefs means that the movement of prices across time will also be affected by the no-trade outcome. How to measure such a dynamic effect, however, is not immediately obvious. In the limit, prices will have adjusted to full information whether there are short sale constraints or not. But presumably how long this takes is of both practical and policy importance.

What is needed is a measure of the speed with which the stochastic process of prices impounds information. In the Appendix of Chapter 3, we used an entropy approach to measure differences in the speed of adjustment. The intuition with that approach is that prices (and beliefs) are converging (at least) exponentially, with the specific rate calculated from the entropy measure. Diamond and Verrecchia employ a different approach in which first passage times give the length of time before the price process is approximately efficient. Their approach, the first in market microstructure literature to measure directly the speed of adjustment, provides a tractable means of comparing the behavior of stochastic processes.[8]

The first passage time approach essentially involves calculating the number of expected trading intervals N before the market maker's price(s) crosses a prespecified bound. Let P_H and P_L denote these upper and lower bounds, and let $\tilde{N}$ be a random variable representing the number of periods before a bound is passed. Let P_t denote the probability that the true state of nature is $v = 1$, and let $1 - P_t$ denote the probability that the true state is $v = 0$. Then the odds ratio, $P_t /(1 - P_t)$, captures the relative belief at time t of the asset value. The evolution of the odds ratio when A is observed is given by

$$\frac{P_t}{1 - P_t} = \frac{P_{t-1}}{1 - P_{t-1}} \frac{q_{v=1}^A}{q_{v=0}^A} \tag{6.14}$$

where the q terms give the probability of observing action A (a buy, sale, or no trade) given the true value of v.

To find the first passage time, let $\Psi = P_H /(1 - P_H)$ and $\Phi = P_L /(1 - P_L)$, and so $\log \Psi$ and $\log \Phi$ denote the possible values of the posterior log odds ratio. Define the variables

---

8. Glosten and Milgrom provide a rough measure of the speed of adjustment by showing that price convergence is related to the square root of the number of transactions.

$$\Lambda_N = \frac{P_N}{1 - P_N} \tag{6.15}$$

and

$$Z^A = \log\left(\frac{q_{v=1}^A}{q_{v=0}^A}\right) \tag{6.16}$$

What must be determined is when Λ_N crosses either Ψ or Φ; when that occurs, the market maker's beliefs (and thus prices) will be said to be within an acceptable range of being fully informed. This can be found by using Wald's Lemma, which states that

$$E[\tilde{N}] = \frac{E[\log(\tilde{\Lambda}_N)]}{E[\tilde{Z}]}, \tag{6.17}$$

and so calculating the first passage time essentially involves looking at how fast beliefs are changing relative to the information in the trade flow. Using the upper and lower bounds, it follows that

$$E[\log(\Lambda_N)|v = 0] = \frac{1 - \Phi}{\Psi - \Phi}\log \Psi + \frac{\Psi - 1}{\Psi - \Phi}\log \Phi \tag{6.18}$$

and

$$E[\log(\Lambda_N)|v = 1] = \frac{\Psi(1 - \Phi)}{\Psi - \Phi}\log \Psi + \frac{\Phi(\Psi - 1)}{\Psi - \Phi}\log \Phi. \tag{6.19}$$

The expected value of Z is simply given by

$$E[Z] = \sum_A q_v^A \log\left(\frac{q_{v=1}^A}{q_{v=0}^A}\right), \tag{6.20}$$

where q_v^A represents the probability of observing action A conditional on state v. The first passage time is then simply found by using equations (6.18)-(6.20) to solve equation (6.17).

This first passage time approach is clearly related to the entropy approach discussed earlier in that both use the log of the posterior likelihood ratio of beliefs (prices). The quicker these beliefs converge to the true value, the faster the rate of price adjustment will be in the entropy approach, and the sooner the exogenous bound is reached in the first passage approach. Since the first passage time approach measures the time until the price process first crosses the bound, the approaches can differ if the process exhibits large variability. In this case, prices could "cross back" over the boundary and become less than full-information efficient. This has no effect on the first passage time, but clearly does affect the actual time it takes prices to converge to the true value. The entropy approach is not affected by this switching, and so it provides a more robust (but approximately identical) measure of this speed of price adjustment.

Using this first passage time approach, Diamond and Verrecchia show that prohibiting short sales slows the adjustment of prices to new information, with the adjustment to bad news being particularly affected. If short sales are only subject to a proceeds constraint, however, the opposite effect occurs: prices adjust faster to information. The reason is that now an absence of trade only occurs for noninformation reasons since informed traders continue to short sell. This increases the information content of sales while removing any information content of no-trade intervals.

If short sale restrictions do affect informed trader's behavior, then this model suggest two results on the relation of time and price behavior. First, observing an absence of trade is a signal of bad news. This has the empirical implication that both bid and ask prices should fall following an interval of no trade to incorporate this bad news potential. Second, because prices adjust more slowly to information, prices are "less efficient" in markets with short sale constraints in that it takes them longer to reflect full-information values.[9]

What allows these differential effects to occur are the exogenously imposed short sale constraints and traders' presumed inability to avoid them. In this model, as in most sequential trade models, the composition of trade is determined solely by the parameters of the trader population. If all traders face identical constraints, then such a framework seems at least reasonable, if not necessarily realistic. If traders face different constraints, however, then it may be that both their trading behavior and their

---

9. Empirical researchers have investigated this hypothesis by examining how markets with and without options adjust to information (see, for example, Jennings and Starks [1985]). The notion here is that options replace the inability to short sell and thereby should increase efficiency. An interesting question, not yet addressed by researchers, is how the ability to trade index options (or futures) affects this speed of adjustment.

representation in the trader population are affected. For example, traders who do not face any short sale constraints clearly profit more from trading than those who do. If the number of informed traders were endogenous, then one might expect the number of informed to differ across markets depending on the extent of the constraints. A more serious concern is that traders who do not face constraints might be expected to trade more frequently or to transact larger amounts. In this case, the change in trading intensity may offset any decrease in trading occasioned by short sale prohibitions.[10] To the extent that these constraints affect trader behavior, however, the absence of trade affects price behavior.

A different explanation of the role of time is given by Easley and O'Hara [1992a]. In their model, traders learn from both trade and the lack of trade because each may be correlated with properties of the underlying information structure. In particular, while trades provide signals of the *direction* of any new information, the lack of trade provides a signal of the *existence* of any new information. This latter effect is referred to as "event uncertainty" and reflects the difficulty that uninformed traders face in even knowing whether new information exists.

In the standard sequential trade framework used by Glosten and Milgrom [1985], event uncertainty does not arise, because an information event is assumed to have occurred. Time plays no role because any interval of no trade can by definition have no information content. If information events are not certain, however, then whether trade occurs at all may provide a signal to the market. This suggests that intervals between trades may have information content, and so time per se is not exogenous to the price process.

To develop this concept, Easley and O'Hara consider a variant of their [1987] model in which information events occur with probability $\alpha > 0$. If an information event occurs, some traders receive a signal, Ψ, of the asset's value, while the other traders and the market maker do not. The signal can take on two values, L and H, with respective probabilities $\delta > 0$ and $1 - \delta > 0$.

Trade arises from uninformed and/or informed traders. We assume that the informed are risk neutral and trade to maximize expected profits. Since the informed may trade with greater intensity than the uninformed, if an

---

10. A parallel problem is the difficulty introduced by differential tax rates. If some traders are tax-exempt, for example, then their comparative advantage is to take trades that have unfavorable tax effects, such as purchasing stocks before they go ex dividend. In this case, the price should be set by the marginal trader, who will clearly not be one paying the full tax. In this setting, short sale constraints can be viewed analogously as a "tax" that is borne by some traders but not by others.

information event occurs, then the market maker expects the fraction of trades made by the informed to be μ (trades from the uninformed being $1 -$ μ). Because there is the added uncertainty over whether new information even exists, it is possible in this model to consider the realistic possibility that if an information event occurs, then all trades in fact come from informed traders (i.e., $μ = 1$).

The uninformed traders are of two types. Some uninformed are assumed to trade for exogenous liquidity reasons (i.e., are "noise" traders). The other uninformed traders are assumed to have demands that reflect more complex motivations such as price sensitivity or individual-specific trading rules. These demands mean that an uninformed trader may prefer not to trade at the market maker's posted quotes, and this provides the potential for no-trading intervals. For the uninformed as a whole, a fraction γ are assumed to be potential sellers and $1 - γ$ to be potential buyers. If at time t an uninformed buyer (seller) checks the quote, the probability that he will trade is $ε^B > 0$ ($ε^S > 0$).

The trading day is divided into discrete intervals of time, $t = 1, 2, . . ., T$, with each interval long enough to accommodate at most one trade. Each trader wishing to trade approaches the market maker and, if there are multiple traders who wish to transact, a queue forms. At each time t, the market maker quotes bid and ask prices and the first trader in line checks the quotes. The trader then decides to buy one unit of the asset, to sell one unit, or not to trade at all. If the trader wishes to trade further, he rejoins the queue. The market maker then has the opportunity to set new bid and ask prices for period $t + 1$, the next trader checks the quote, and trading begins anew.

Given this market structure, it may be that no trade actually occurs in some time intervals. Since an informed trader always transacts if the price is not at the full-information level, such a no-trade outcome only occurs when an uninformed trader checks the quotes and decides not to trade. If there has been an information event, this happens with probability $(1 - μ)[γ(1 - ε^S) + (1 - γ)(1 - ε^B)]$. If, however, there has been no information event, then all traders are uninformed, and so the probability of a no-trade outcome rises to $γ(1 - ε^S) + (1 - γ)(1 - ε^B)$. It is this divergence in probabilities that imparts information content to the absence of trading.

An interesting question is, how does a no-trade outcome, or an absence of trade, affect the market maker's prices? Easley and O'Hara demonstrate that if there is no trade at time t, then the market maker raises the probability he attaches to no information event and lowers the probabilities he attaches to a low signal or a high signal having occurred. Since only actual trades give useful information on the direction of any signal, the market maker keeps the relative probability of high and low signals the same, but lowers their absolute amount.

Given these changes in beliefs, it follows that following a no-trade outcome, the market maker changes trading prices for period $t + 1$. Since the market maker now believes the overall risk of trading with an informed trader is lower, he moves the quotes closer to the prior expected value of the asset, V^*. If the bid and ask prices were above V^* at time t, prices fall; if they were below V^*, prices rise. This price movement dictates that the spread is affected as well. With prices collapsing toward V^*, the spread narrows following the absence of trade.

These price and spread effects can be contrasted with the predictions of Diamond and Verrecchia. There, an absence of trade is construed as "bad" news because of its correlation with constraints on informed trading on the basis of bad news. The response of the market maker then is to unambiguously move prices down and to increase his spread. Here, an absence of trade indicates that information-based trading is less likely. What happens to prices at time $t + 1$ depends on where they were at time t, but the effect is to lower the spread due to the decreased risk of loss to informed traders.

These price effects due to the absence of trade mean that time is no longer exogenous to the price process. This has a number of important implications. First, the sequence of trades and no trades affects the behavior of prices. Second, the level of volume up to time t now affects where prices go at time $t + 1$. Third, volume affects the speed of price adjustment to new information, with prices in markets having large average volume being "less efficient" in that they adjust slower to full-information values. Fourth, empirical investigations using transaction data will be biased because examining only transaction prices ignores the information content contained in the nontrading intervals.

Volume effects arise in this model because the greater the volume, the less frequent no-trade outcomes are, and thus the more likely it is that new information exists. Uninformed market participants attempting to learn from the trade sequence draw different inferences from different levels of volume, causing prices at time $t + 1$ to differ depending on the volume to that point. Note that this is not the case in the standard sequential trade approach where new information is assumed to exist. There, volume is irrelevant for prices at $t + 1$ because volume provides no information beyond that conveyed by individual trades. Hence, as in the models discussed in the previous section, in this model traders learn from volume because volume is related to the underlying information structure.

The model suggest two effects of volume on price adjustment. From a cross-sectional perspective, markets with higher "normal" trading volume will adjust to information more slowly, reflecting the reduced trade information content found in more liquid markets. Second, unexpected volume will affect the time series of prices. Since unexpected volume implies the existence of new information, this model suggests the refined adage that 'unexpected volume moves prices." These unexpected volume effects are investigated (and confirmed) in empirical research by Lee, Mucklow, and Ready [1993].

The implications of the role of time in affecting price behavior are also important for empirical researchers. In this model, transaction prices are Martingales, but they are not Markov. This means that simply knowing the sequence of prices is not a sufficient statistic for all market information. If a researcher examines only transaction prices, then how prices move at time $t + 1$ is not independent of *all* preceding transactions. This difficulty arises because the series of transaction prices can be thought of as being formed by an optional sampling of the underlying true price process where the draw of a transaction is not uncorrelated with the underlying stochastic process of prices. Since informed traders are more likely to trade than uninformed traders, trades are more likely when there has been an information event. Thus, sampling of the underlying value process is higher when there is new information.

This sampling problem will also affect the variance structure of prices, causing the "true" variance to be inversely correlated with volume and imparting an upward bias to variances computed from transaction data. Just as volume affected price movements, expected volume also affects the variance, causing volatility to behave differently when there is unexpected volume.[11]

While the analyses in this section suggest that time is not exogenous to the price process, how much time matters and the significance and extent of the bias it imparts to market behavior are not known. The importance of time is ultimately an empirical question, and this has recently been addressed in empirical work by Hasbrouck [1989] and Hausman, Lo, and MacKinley [1992]. Their results suggest that time may matter, but it is not yet clear how much.

If time can affect market behavior, then how markets are structured may also be important. For example, in call markets time can play little role because individual trades are irrelevant. Similarly, if traders can preplace orders via limit orders or other trading strategies, then the information

---

11. The effect of unexpected volume on volatility is investigated empirically by Finucane and Diz [1993].

content of a sequence of trades can be dramatically affected. In the next three chapters, we turn our attention to these market structure issues.

7

Market Viability and Stability

The market microstructure analyses considered in the previous four chapters analyze a wide variety of issues related to the behavior of security prices in the presence of asymmetric information. While the specific models and applications differ, every microstructure analysis requires some specification of the underlying trading mechanism. In the models considered thus far, there have been two general mechanisms considered. The sequential trade models employ a framework in which market makers quote bid and ask prices, and a single trade transacts at the quoted price. Alternatively, in the strategic rational expectations-based models of Kyle, there are no bid and ask prices and orders are batched together to transact at a single market-clearing price.

While these depictions of the trading process clearly differ in the timing of trades, they share several characteristics. For example, most microstructure analyses consider a competitive environment in which market makers set asset prices equal to the asset's conditional expected value. It also is typically the case that traders are allowed to submit only simple buy or sell orders and cannot enter more complicated contingent orders. With only market orders, there is also no "book" of unfilled orders and no difference in the order flow information available to traders.

Each of these trading mechanism features is realistic in that there are actual markets exhibiting such characteristics. For example, the New York Stock Exchange uses a call auction to begin trading and a continuous auction to clear trades throughout the day.[1] The Paris Bourse switched in 1986 from clearing trades in a daily call market to a continuous structure.

---

1. This is the general NYSE trading mechanism. For inactive stocks, however, there may be no opening call.

The Toronto CATS system results (theoretically, at least) in all traders knowing the same trade information.

It is also the case, however, that many market structures are far more complex. The single specialist clearing trades on the NYSE may have monopoly power, which distorts prices from competitive levels. Traders may employ alternative order forms that change the timing and potentially the information content of their trades. Market makers who observe the order flow may learn more than floor brokers who observe only prices. Electronic clearing systems such as SOFFEX (the Swiss Options and Futures Exchange) or Globex may remove the specialist completely from the price-setting process. If the decisions of market participants are not independent of the specific trading mechanism used, then how markets are structured is clearly important for understanding the behavior of security prices.

In this chapter we investigate these issues by considering how market structure affects viability and stability. Our focus here is on understanding how various characteristics of the trading mechanism affect the transmission of information into prices. There are several reasons this is important. One reason is to provide insight into how institutional features affect agents' abilities to learn private information. Since the efficiency of the market depends on this learning process, understanding the role of specific institutional features may provide insight into the process by which prices become efficient. A second, more applied, reason for studying the trading mechanism is to develop an understanding of why some institutional arrangements dominate in some market settings and not in others. The diversity of trading mechanisms found in securities markets may reflect historical factors, or it may result from more effective trading mechanisms prevailing over time. Without an understanding of the role played by the trading mechanism, it is impossible to determine which explanation is correct. A third, and related, issue concerns the link between the trading mechanism and the stability and performance of the market. These stability issues have taken on increased importance in light of the market crash of 1987 and the subsequent proposed changes to the market.

Because the research examining market structure and performance is extensive, our discussion must, of necessity, be incomplete. In this and in the following two chapters, we focus on some (but certainly not all) of the critical issues in market structure. In this chapter, our focus is on market viability, and in particular on the design features that promote market stability. In the next chapter, we continue our investigation of market structure effects by considering more broadly defined issues relating to liquidity and the relationships between markets. Finally, in Chapter 9, we consider the effect of specific trading mechanism features on market performance.

As a starting point for our investigation, we consider the fundamental issue of how market design can affect the viability of the market in the presence of asymmetric information. Market design issues have taken on increasing importance for a number of reasons, not the least of which are the proliferation of European and Asian security markets and the development of new, fully automated trading systems. As new markets develop, the question of market viability is fundamental to their success and to the continued success of existing markets, and hence we analyze the microstructure research on this issue.

We then examine how the types of orders permitted in a trading mechanism affect market performance. In virtually all the models considered thus far, only market orders are permitted. Yet alternative orders are widely found, and some trading venues (for example, electronic order mechanisms) allow only limit orders, with market orders excluded. How such orders affect the price-setting behavior of the market is clearly a question of importance. A related issue is whether characteristics of the trading mechanism can affect market stability. We conclude our discussion of market structure in this chapter by examining the policy implications relating to stability.

7.1 INFORMATION AND MARKET VIABILITY

In the models considered thus far, the threat of information-based trading results in prices incorporating a "premium" to protect the market maker from the risk of trading with an informed trader. Glosten and Milgrom [1985] noted, however, that if information problems are too severe, there need be no market-clearing price at which trades can occur. This difficulty, a variant of the market-for-lemons problem first identified by Akerlof [1970], arises because a high enough threat of information-based trading may induce many or even all uninformed traders to leave the market, resulting in a sure loss to any trader (or market maker) on the other side of the trade. With no price able to clear the market (or, more precisely, no spread large enough to permit the market maker to break even), the only option is a trading halt in which the market ceases to function.

While it is true that trading halts do actually occur, it is not a usual occurrence in securities markets. What is not immediately obvious, however, is what prevents such information-induced difficulties from arising more frequently. One possible answer lies in the design of the trading mechanism. If there are features of the trading mechanism that alleviate the pricing problem induced by asymmetric information, then the market may be more robust than a simple asymmetric information analysis would imply.

Glosten [1989] argues that the monopoly position of the specialist provides such stability. An interesting feature of the NYSE and many other exchanges is that there is only a single specialist in each stock. This monopoly position of the specialist may be tempered by competition with floor brokers, limit order traders, and others, but it remains the case that the specialist may have some market power in light of his unique position. In most market settings, such monopoly power benefits the holder but generally reduces social welfare from what it would be if the market were competitive. If there is asymmetric information, however, Glosten argues that under some circumstances social welfare may actually be greater when there is a monopolistic, rather than a competitive, specialist.

The intuition underlying this result is that a monopolistic price setter need not be concerned with the profit arising from any individual trade, but rather may set prices that *on average* maximize profits. A feature of the competitive models examined thus far is that the market maker sets trade prices equal to the conditional expected value of the asset given that particular trade. Consequently, the expected profit on each and every trade is zero. Glosten considers the idea that a monopolistic specialist could instead choose a schedule of prices that results in an expected loss on some trades but an expected gain on others. This pricing strategy could allow the market to remain open when it would not be able to under a competitive pricing framework.

In Glosten's model this averaging takes place across trade sizes.[2] In this one-period model, risk averse traders receive a noisy signal of the asset's true value and choose their trade size to maximize their expected utility of wealth. The analysis employs a variant of the standard normal distributions-based example found in rational expectations models (see the Appendix to Chapter 4 for more details). In this model, risk averse traders transact shares with a risk neutral market maker. Because traders receive both endowments of the risky asset and informative signals of the asset's value, their motivations for trade are more complex than in standard microstructure models.

A trader's utility is given by the negative exponential utility function $U(y) = -\exp(-\rho y)$, where $\rho > 0$ is the risk aversion coefficient and y is the trader's wealth. The payoff on the security, X, is normally distributed with mean m and precision π_X, or $N(m, 1/\pi_X)$. Each trader also starts with an

---

2. Other researchers (for example, Gammill [1989] and Leach and Madhavan [1993]) have pursued similar averaging ideas with respect to intertemporal behavior.

endowment of cash, given by W_0, and receives an endowment of the risky asset, W, which is distributed as $N(0, 1/\pi_W)$. The trader sees a noisy signal, S, of the asset's payoff, where $S = X + \varepsilon$, and ε is distributed as $N(0, 1/\pi_S)$. The random variables X, W, and ε are assumed to be independent.

In this model, as in standard rational expectations analyses, transactions arise for two reasons. A trader receiving new information may trade to exploit his informational advantage and thereby profit on any price discrepancy. A trader may also transact, however, because of portfolio reasons related to the endowment shock he receives. This latter reason is not information-based, and it is this liquidity motive that makes trade possible.

The market maker is assumed to be risk neutral and can be in one of two regimes, competitive or monopolistic. If the market maker is competitive, he sets the price for each trade equal to the expected value of the asset given a trade of size Q, or $P(Q) = E[X/Q]$. This conditional expectation pricing rule corresponds to the standard pricing assumption made in most microstructure models. Alternatively, if the market maker is a monopolist, he selects a pricing schedule P_m to satisfy $P_m(\bullet) \in \arg \max E[P(Q)Q - XQ]$, where $Q = Q(S, W)$ is the trader's optimal demand given pricing schedule $P(Q)$.

The trader's decision problem is to choose Q to maximize the expected utility of wealth, where, in the competitive case, wealth is given by $W_0 - P(Q)Q + (W + Q)X$. Given the assumptions of normally distributed random variables and a negative exponential utility function, this is equivalent to maximizing the certainty equivalent, or

$$
\begin{aligned}
CE(W, S, Q, P(Q)) &= E[W] - .5\,\rho\,\mathrm{var}(W) \\
&= W_0 - P(Q)Q + (W + Q)E[X \mid S] \\
&\quad - .5\rho(W + Q)^2\,\mathrm{var}(X \mid S).
\end{aligned} \tag{7.1}
$$

Since the trader does not know X but sees only a noisy signal of its value ($S = X + \varepsilon$), he must determine the expected value of X given his signal. This calculation follows from the now-familiar application of Bayes Rule. As demonstrated in the Appendix to Chapter 3, for normally distributed random variables, this updating is simply the prior mean times its precision plus the signal times its precision over the sum of the precisions, or

$$
E[X|S] = (\pi_X m + \pi_S S)/(\pi_S + \pi_X). \tag{7.2}
$$

The investor's decision problem provides a first-order condition, which can be rearranged to yield

$$[P'(Q)Q + P(Q) - m](\pi_S + \pi_X)/\pi_S + \rho Q/\pi_S = S - (\rho W/\pi_S) - m. \quad (7.3)$$

In the competitive case, the market maker must set the trade price equal to the asset's expected value given the trade. This involves a somewhat complicated inference problem because the trades themselves partially depend on noisy signals. To characterize this learning problem, notice that the left-hand side of equation (7.3) contains only observable variables, while the right-hand side contains the unobserved variables $S - (\rho W/\pi_S)$ and the known mean m. Earlier, in our discussion of the Kyle model in Chapter 4, we solved the market maker's decision problem by defining a variable composed of unobservable variables but whose distribution the market maker could calculate. We can apply the same approach here to characterize the market maker's learning problem. Define the random variable $Z = S - (\rho W/\pi_S)$. Then a market maker observing an incoming order of size Q can calculate the left-hand side of the above equation. This is equal to $Z - m$, however, and the market maker knows both m and that

$$Z = S - (\rho W/\pi_S) = X + \varepsilon - (\rho W/\pi_S). \quad (7.4)$$

Hence, observing Q essentially provides the market maker a noisy signal of X.

To set his optimal price, the market maker simply uses Bayes Rule to find the expected value of X given Z, or

$$E[X \mid Z] = (\pi_X m + \pi_Z Z)/(\pi_Z + \pi_X). \quad (7.5)$$

Glosten shows that in the competitive case any differentiable pricing schedule will satisfy

$$P(Q) = m + \left(\frac{\rho \pi_W \pi_S}{N}\right)\left(\frac{Q}{2\alpha - 1}\right) + K[\text{sign}(Q)]|Q|^\gamma, \quad (7.6)$$

where

$$N = \rho^2 \pi_X + \pi_W \pi_S(\pi_S + \pi_X) \quad (7.7)$$

and

$$\alpha = \frac{\rho^2 \pi x}{N}, \neq .5, \gamma = \frac{\alpha}{1 - \alpha}. \tag{7.8}$$

There are two important properties of this solution to note. First, the pricing rule is upward sloping. This means that large trades transact at "worse" prices. The slope of the price schedule also means that there is some welfare loss associated with the risk of information-based trading. Since some traders transact for portfolio-rebalancing reasons, the greater the slope, the more costly it is for them to achieve their optimal holdings. If there were no informational trading, then the price schedule could be flat, allowing traders to move costlessly to their desired holdings. With prices increasing in trade size, however, traders cannot achieve the optimal position, and Glosten demonstrates that *ex ante* utility is strictly less with asymmetric information than it is with symmetric information.

A second interesting property of this solution is that for a differential equilibrium to even exist, it must be the case that $\alpha > .5$. Since α is a function of the traders' risk aversion and the precision of random variables, this condition essentially requires that the risk of informed trading is not so large as to overwhelm the market maker's ability to set market-clearing 'break-even" prices. If α does not meet this condition, there can be no market-clearing price, trading is halted, and the market shuts down.[3]

This failure of the market reflects the difficulty that, with prices set to conditional expected values on every trade, there may be no price that results in zero expected profit for the market maker. Suppose, however, that the market maker could set prices based on the *average* expected profit across trade sizes, rather than on a trade-by-trade basis. Since this would allow gains on some trades making up for losses on others, this strategy is only feasible if the specialist has sufficient market power to retain the profitable trades. Such market power is consistent with the pricing position of a monopolist specialist.

If the market maker is a monopolist, then his decision problem changes to choosing a price function $P(\bullet)$ to solve

$$\max E[R(z) - XQ(z)], \tag{7.9}$$

---

3. This "no-trade" outcome arises because the threat of informed trading is simply too large to sustain the market. This problem has long been recognized in the rational expectations literature, particularly in the work of Milgrom and Stokey [1982] and, as discussed in Chapter 6, Grundy and McNichols [1989]. An extensive characterization of when this "no-trade" outcome will occur in a Walrasian framework is given in Bhattacharya and Spiegel [1991].

subject to

$$CE[W, S, Q(z), R(z)] \geq CE[W, S, Q(z'), R(z')], \quad \text{for all } z', \qquad (7.10)$$

where CE denotes the certainty equivalent defined in equation (7.1), z is Z normalized to have zero mean and unit variance, $R(z)$ and $Q(z)$ are functions representing revenue and order quantity, respectively, and z and z' are strategies, with z equal to $[S - (\rho W/\pi_S) - m]/\sigma_z$. The constraint reflects the incentive compatibility requirement that the quantity the market maker believes a trader will select to trade at price p is, in fact, the quantity the trader selected.

Assuming differentiability of the relevant functions, Glosten proves that there exists a monopolistic pricing schedule such that the market does not shut down. With this pricing strategy, the specialist quotes prices such that he *loses money* for large trades but *makes money* on small trades. In this model, normality dictates that extreme trades (i.e. large Q) are unusual, and so the market maker can use the greater frequency of little trades to more than offset his losses. Of course, these higher prices for small trades mean trades are made at worse prices than would occur if a competitive dealer were willing to make the trade. From the perspective of an uninformed trader, this is clearly undesirable. But since the competitive market need not always exist, these higher monopolistic prices at least allow trade to occur. When the market would otherwise fail, Glosten demonstrates that welfare will be higher in a monopolistic market than it is in a competitive setting.

An interesting feature of this pricing strategy is that the market maker continues to make large trades even though they result in an expected loss. One might expect that a better strategy is simply to set prices for large trades so high as to make no trades at all. The difficulty with this reasoning can be seen by considering a simple discrete example.

Suppose that there are two types of uninformed traders, big and little. Big traders buy (or sell) 5 units, while little traders transact 1 unit.[4] Let there be four big uninformed traders and one informed trader (for now, the number of little uninformed traders is unimportant). Let the value of the asset, V, lie in the interval $[0, 4]$, with unconditional mean 2. Suppose that the informed trader knows the true value of the asset is 4. Since the informed trader knows good news, he wants to buy; so we first consider the market maker's ask price decision.

---

4. For simplicity, we assume that large uninformed traders either trade the large quantity or do not trade at all. This corresponds to assuming that large institutional investors do not wish to hold small quantities of assets, perhaps because of fixed management costs.

If the market maker is competitive, he sets the big trade price so that the expected losses to the informed trader, assuming he trades the large amount, equal the expected gains from the uninformed big traders. Since, given that a trader wants to trade the large size there is a one in five chance he in informed, it is easy to demonstrate that the big trade price must be set at 2.4. At that price, the informed trader makes a profit of 8 and the market maker breaks even. If the market maker now sets a small trade price of 2, the informed trader continues to trade the large amount, and so the market maker makes zero expected profit on each trade size.

Now suppose the large uninformed traders are price sensitive. If one large uninformed trader will not transact at any price above 2.3, then the equilibrium above is not feasible. With three uninformed large traders, the large trade price must be 2.5. If, however, this is above another large trader's reservation price, then the price must rise to 2.67, and so on until it can be the case that all uninformed traders leave and the large trade price goes to 4. This is not a feasible price, however, because once the large trade price passes 3.6, the informed trader shifts to trading the small quantity. Hence, the large trade market ceases to exist.

With the informed trader now trading the small quantity, the small trade price cannot remain at 2. If the little uninformed traders also have elastic demands, then as in the large trade market it may be that there is no price at which trades can clear. In this case, the market fails, and no trades occur. Hence, setting a high price for large trades cannot solve the underlying difficulty; since informed traders will choose the profit-maximizing quantity, any equilibrium will have informed traders in the market.

In the discrete competitive example above, it will always be the case that, if an equilibrium exists, the losses on the large trade just equal the gains on the small trades. In Glosten's continuous monopolistic model, however, it is possible to choose small and large trade prices so that the profit from the more elastic small trades overwhelms the loss on the large informed trade. The optimal pricing strategy for the specialist is then to keep the informed trader trading the large quantity. Hence, the market maker sets prices so that he loses money on the large trade but makes money on the small trades. This average pricing policy works because the specialist uses his monopoly power to have some trades essentially subsidize others. The result from a market stability standpoint is an improvement in traders' utility because the market remains viable.

That a monopolistic specialist can improve the stability of the market highlights the important role that the trading mechanism plays in overcoming the underlying difficulty introduced by asymmetric information. A question that naturally arises, however, is whether such a monopoly structure is the only mechanism to solve the problem. Madhavan [1992] demonstrates that another solution may be to organize trading as a call market. Since a call market is used to begin trading each morning on the NYSE and is the primary trading mechanism on several other exchanges, the role of such a trading mechanism is clearly important. Moreover, intriguing empirical research by Amihud and Mendelson [1987] suggests that the behavior of prices in a call market differs in important ways from price behavior in a continuous market.[5]

Madhavan's analysis involves comparing the behavior of competitive, quote-driven (or continuous) market mechanisms and competitive, order-driven market mechanisms in the presence of asymmetric information. The focus in the paper is on measuring the performance of various market structures, and as such we discuss this research in more detail in Chapter 9. For our purposes here, we consider a special case of the analysis where the order-driven mechanism is restricted to periodic clearing.

The analysis considers how the viability of the quote-driven mechanism of the market maker contrasts with a periodic order-driven (or call market) mechanism. The model of the quote-driven market is virtually identical to that in Glosten, and the optimal pricing policy for the specialist is the same as that derived above. As in Glosten, if the risk of informed trading is too great, there are no prices the dealer can quote that meet the zero expected profit condition, and the market fails.

If trades could be cleared in a call market, then Madhavan shows that this market failure outcome need not occur. In a call market, orders are batched together at a point in time and clear at a single price, and so there is no price schedule or "quote" as there is in a continuous market. Because traders have no 'quote' to hit, it follows that they do not know the actual trading price when they submit their orders. If traders are rational, however, they have expectations over the price and in equilibrium those expectations will be correct.[6] This results in adjusting the amount of liquidity-based trading so that the market still operates though the underlying asymmetric information problem remains. In effect, the order flow averages out the information effects so that a price can be set to clear the market.

---

5. In particular, Amihud and Mendleson show that the variance differs if measured on an open-to-open basis than on a close-to-close basis. They attribute this difference to the different trading mechanism employed at the open. Stoll and Whaley [1990] empirically investigate this behavior and conclude that NYSE opening practices can explain the observed price behavior.

6. An interesting aspect of the Madhavan model is that traders can submit demand schedules as opposed to the simple market orders typically considered. If traders have rational expectations, their optimal limit order is essentially a market order because they will, in fact, know the market-clearing price.

One might expect that this greater stability of the call market would lead to its clear dominance as a trading mechanism. As Madhavan demonstrates, however, this stability may come at a cost. For infrequently traded stocks, the lack of continuous prices impedes the price discovery process, and this results in prices potentially being less efficient and information gathering more expensive. Moreover, if there is a cost to providing a trading mechanism, then Madhavan's model suggests that the quote-driven system can only be sustained with a monopolistic price setter, while the continuous trading framework allows for multiple market makers.

In both the Glosten and Madhavan analyses, therefore, the trading mechanism is not irrelevant to the performance of the market. Because asymmetric information introduces distortions into the behavior of prices, it may be that the standard competitive mechanism is not robust if information problems are severe. These difficulties can be overcome by pricing so as to profit on an average basis rather than on an individual trade basis. The average basis can be across trade sizes as in the Glosten monopolistic framework, or across trades as a whole as in the Madhavan call market framework.

This averaging behavior, however, introduces a new and potentially critical impediment to market stability. If the market (or market maker) is pricing trades on average, then some trades are trading at "worse" prices than they would if priced individually. Suppose that a competing trading mechanism could be structured that would handle only these "overpriced" trades. Then even pricing these trades *on average* would result in a "better" price for those buyers and sellers, and one might expect such orders to flow to the competing exchange. Once, however, these orders depart the initial trading venue, the original average prices are no longer viable, and prices must rise to reflect the new trade composition. This, in turn, gives even more impetus for traders to move elsewhere, prices deteriorate further, and the average pricing equilibrium breaks down.

Such an unraveling of the equilibrium dictates that average pricing is only feasible under very restrictive conditions. In effect, the initial "pooling" equilibrium cannot be sustained if a subset of the underlying market can be separated out and priced accordingly. This problem is the subject of extensive analysis in the insurance literature (see, for example, Wilson [1977]). In insurance markets, the ability to segment risks means that the good risks always have an incentive to shift to contracts restricted only to them. Whether an equilibrium can exist in this new segmented structure is problematic. If risk quality is continuously distributed, for example, there need be no sustainable equilibrium at all.

In the microstructure context considered here, this suggests that the stability provided by average pricing mechanisms may be illusory. In the mechanisms analyzed by Glosten and Madhavan, liquidity traders pay a higher price than they would if they could trade separately from traders acting on information, suggesting that attempts to "cream-skim" such traders to other exchanges could be successful. If that occurs, however, then the stability of the original trading mechanism need not remain. Such equilibrium issues are considered in more detail by Glosten [1991b].

The development of active "third market" providers suggests that just such an outcome may be occurring. By restricting orders to small amounts (600 shares) and by offering to match the best bid or offer, third market participants such as Madoff Securities can extract the small, presumably uninformed, order flow away from the NYSE monopoly specialist by paying retail brokers for their order flow. Similarly, electronic clearing networks such as Instinet and POSIT can attract large uninformed institutional traders if the structure of their trading mechanisms provides a 'better deal" for executing the large orders such traders enter. The trading network of Steve Weunch and the Arizona Stock Exchange represents yet another mechanism designed to attract uninformed order flow.[7]

There is some evidence that such alternative mechanisms are succeeding in diverting order flow away from the single-clearing exchange mechanism. For example, in the first half of 1993, POSIT cleared an average of 5 to 6 million shares a day, with over 7 million shares a day trading in November 1993. Instinet volume is not publicly available, but is believed to be around 400,000 shares per day. The NYSE estimates that in 1993 as much as 20 percent of total volume and 35 percent of small trade volume (i.e., less than 2,100 shares) is now diverted to third party providers. With the order flow segmented, the behavior of security prices need not be that predicted by models of a single market-clearing agent.

Such a segmented market equilibrium raises intriguing, and important, questions about the stability and performance of the overall market. One such question is the effect of market segmentation on market liquidity, an issue addressed in more detail in the next chapter. But questions such as how segmented markets affect price discovery, or the welfare implications of alternative market settings remain unanswered.[8] Indeed, whether such a

---

7. Lee [1991] provides an interesting empirical analysis of the effects of the Cincinnati Exchange on market prices. McInish and Wood [1991] also provide empirical analysis of the effects of third market trades.

8. A particularly intriguing policy question relates to the ownership of the price quotes. If a competing exchange offers to match the best bid or offer on the NYSE at the time an order executes, then it is essentially free-riding on the price discovery function of the NYSE. In the absence of those quotes, it is not clear such a competing exchange could remain competitive. But, as part of a National Market System (which was mandated by Congress) quote and price

separating equilibrium is even sustainable is not immediately obvious. It seems likely that, in the absence of some transaction cost, excluded traders could mimic the trading behavior of included traders and thereby reintroduce a pooling equilibrium. These issues will undoubtedly remain important topics for future research.

While our discussion has focused on the viability of alternative market organizations, there are also interesting stability issues related to the design of trading mechanisms. In particular, if traders have the ability to place contingent orders, then they have the ability to adapt the trading mechanism to their own demands. This raises the interesting specter that order form alone can introduce price effects into securities markets. We consider this issue in the next section.

7.2   ORDER FORM AND PRICE BEHAVIOR

In actual security markets, a wide variety of order types can be found. The familiar market order to buy or sell one round lot at the prevailing price is certainly the mainstay of trading, but orders contingent on a variety of conditions abound. "Market-at-close" orders, for example, allow traders to specify the time that their order transacts. If the time of day issues addressed by Admati and Pfleiderer [1988, 1989] are important, then such orders provide one mechanism for traders to time their trades. Other orders such as "Fill-or-Kill" or "Immediate or Cancel" orders allow traders to control the quantity or execution of their trades. By far the most common alternative order forms, however, are price-contingent orders. It is to these orders and to their effects on the market that we now turn our attention.

Orders contingent on price can take many forms. The most common price-contingent orders are limit orders specifying a price and a quantity at which the trade is to transact. Since a limit order to trade at the current price is equivalent to a market order, feasible limit orders must specify prices outside the range of the current quote. With prices above the current ask and below the current bid, limit orders await the movement of prices to become active. If a limit order executes, it allows the trader to receive a better price than he would have submitting a market order. Since execution is not guaranteed (prices can always move the wrong way), one way to view limit orders is that they guarantee a price but not a quantity, while market orders guarantee a quantity but not a price.[9]

---

information are to be freely available. These issues are addressed in more detail in Mulherin, Netter, and Overdahl [1990].

9. This is not entirely accurate, because prices may move through limit orders, causing the limit to transact at a price other than that specified. Similarly, market orders may not transact

A similar, albeit opposite, price-contingent order is a stop order. A stop order also specifies a price and a quantity, but its price is "worse" than the current quote. Stop orders are typically used to sell stock when prices are falling, and so submitting a stop order allows a trader to put a "floor" under the value of his holdings.[10] Like all contingent orders, however, stop orders are not guaranteed to trade precisely at their specified prices; if prices fall through a stop, the order will execute at the first available price, which may be considerably below its stated price.[11] Because of this price insurance function, stop orders are closely related to (and may be used in) portfolio insurance strategies.

One important difference between stop orders and limit orders lies in their relation to the direction of order flow. Stop loss orders transact when the market is falling. Since these are sell orders, stops essentially take liquidity from the market and provide impetus to any downward market movement. Conversely, limit orders trade on the opposite side of the market. If the market is rising, the upward price movement triggers limit orders to sell; if the market is falling, the downward movement triggers limit orders to buy. Limit orders thus provide liquidity to the market and therefore are frequently characterized as competing with the market maker.

Because price-contingent orders depend on market movements, they are held in a "book" until they become active. The effect of a book on market behavior was addressed by several researchers in models with symmetric information. As discussed in Chapter 2, Cohen, Maier, Schwartz, and Whitcomb [1981] examined how limit orders affected the order strategies of traders in their gravitational pull model. O'Hara and Oldfield [1986] characterized the dealer's pricing problem given the known limit orders and the unknown market orders.

More recently, attention has shifted to the role of the book in a world of asymmetric information. Rock [1991] examines the interaction between the market maker and limit order traders. Easley and O'Hara [1991] analyze the

---

immediately if there are a flood of orders delivered to the market at one time. See also Harris and Hasbrouck [1993].

10. Stop orders to buy stock do exist but are used infrequently. The vast majority of stop orders are stop loss orders to sell stock. Our discussion in this section focuses on these sell-side orders.

11. There are actually two different types of stop orders available to traders. The commonly used stop loss orders are similar to market orders in that they are orders to sell whenever the market price reaches the order's specified level. Since these orders transact at the next available price, they may transact at prices below their specified level. There are also stop loss limit orders, which are orders to sell only at the specified price. If prices fall through these stops, therefore, the order is canceled rather than filled at the best available price. Because these orders provide a rather strange (and limited) type of insurance, they are rarely used. Our discussion focuses on the more usual stop loss (market) orders.

effect that allowing a book of stop orders has on price behavior and the stability of the market. In these analyses, the book of limit orders affects the behavior of the market even though the book *per se* contains no information on the value of the asset being traded.

Rock's analysis focuses on the adverse selection problem facing traders who submit limit orders. As noted earlier, limit orders can be viewed as "competing" with the market maker in that they take the other side of submitted market orders. Since a limit order is submitted at a price "off the quote," it follows that a limit order trader receives a better price if his order executes than he would receive trading at the market maker's quoted prices. One difficulty the limit order trader faces, however, is uncertainty over when the trade will execute. Because the limit order remains on the book until the price moves to the order's specified level, the limit order trader faces the risk that the value of the asset may have changed since the order was placed. In this case, the limit order will transact at a price that leaves the trader with a negative expected profit. This expected loss arises because the market maker can set his prices conditional on the trade size but the limit order trader cannot. This results in an adverse selection problem because, if the market maker is risk neutral, the only trades the limit order trader will participate in are those that lose money.

This situation is most likely to arise when a large market order transacts. The problem is that as orders execute, market participants update their beliefs on the asset's true value. Following a large sell order, the market maker lowers his expectation of the asset's value to reflect the risk that large orders are more likely the result of information-based trading. This can cause his quoted price for a large sale to fall below that of orders on the book, thereby allowing the limit orders rather than the market maker to clear the trade. Since the limit orders then transact at a price above the asset's new expected value, the limit order trader has an expected loss on the trade. Indeed, given this adverse selection problem, the optimal strategy for a limit order trader is not to trade at all, and the book would simply not exist.

Rock suggests that one factor alleviating this problem is the inventory exposure of the market maker. Rock considers a two-date (one-period) model in which limit orders are submitted at time 0, a single trade occurs at time 1, and the asset then liquidates at some random value $\tilde{v}$. In this model, the market maker is assumed risk averse, while limit order traders are assumed risk neutral. This divergence in risk preferences is clearly ad hoc and is, in fact, the opposite of the risk preference assumptions used by Glosten and by Madhavan in the previous section. A justification for the specification is that the single market maker must always stand ready to buy or sell, while the multiple limit order traders need only transact if it suits them. Since this allows limit order traders better control of their inventory, for inventory positions close to their desired level, even risk averse traders would be approximately risk neutral. Whether this is an accurate risk specification is debatable, but it is the case that Rock's results hinge on risk-bearing limitations on the part of the market maker.

Traders in this market are assumed able to submit limit orders or market orders. An important assumption is that limit orders are submitted *only* by uninformed traders, while market orders are entered by both informed and uninformed traders. This dichotomy in order behavior means that the book can be analyzed independently of any information on the value of the asset. Rock justifies this assumption by appealing to the delayed execution feature of limit orders; if informed traders have short-lived information, then the immediate liquidity of a market order is surely preferable. In a one-trade model like that considered here, this is certainly reasonable. Whether it holds in a dynamic setting is not so obvious. This issue of the information content of the book is discussed further later in this chapter.

With limit order traders uninformed and risk neutral, it follows that they will submit a limit order provided the order's expected profit, given that it transacts, is at least zero. This determination is not simple, however, as the expected profit on any order depends on both the market maker's optimal strategy and on the structure of the book. Because any trade may be jointly filled by the market maker and by orders from the book, how much the market maker takes depends on the price he quotes and on the number and distribution of orders on the book. This means, however, the market maker must know the orders on the book to set prices, and the limit order traders must know the market maker's pricing schedule to submit their orders. The book and the pricing schedule must therefore be determined simultaneously, and all market participants must have complete information on the structure of the book and on the market maker's inventory position.

These information requirements impose a severe restriction on the applicability of the model to many exchange settings. While the Toronto CATS system is generally transparent, a more common arrangement in markets is that the information on the book is unknown to at least some market participants. To the extent that markets are not transparent, this pricing problem becomes exceedingly complex. Moreover, it is not enough that traders know the orders; they must know how the market marker will price given the orders they submit. Such a simultaneous structure is typical of many rational expectations analyses, although a rational expectations framework is not specifically analyzed here.

As the market maker is risk averse, the price he quotes for any market sell order of trade size s, denoted $P(s)$, must leave him at least indifferent between paying that price or not trading at all. Letting y_0 be the specialist's endowment of cash and $z_0 =$ endowment of stock, then $w_0 = y_0 + z_0$ is the specialist's initial wealth where the initial price of the stock is normalized to one. Denote by $Q(p)$ the set of all limit orders to buy on the book at price p or above. Then the zero gain in expected utility condition requires that the price the specialist sets to buy stock, $p(s)$, be such that

$$E\left[U\left(y_0 + z_0\tilde{v} + \left(s - Q(p(s))\right)\left(\tilde{v} - p(s)\right)\right) \mid \tilde{s} = s\right] = E[U(w_0) \mid \tilde{s} = s].$$
(7.11)

The order strategy for the uninformed limit order traders also depends on the market maker's pricing strategy $P(s)$ because it affects how much of an incoming order will be taken by the book. Define $\Sigma_+(b)$ to be the set of market sell orders that cause a bid at price b to be triggered. Then $E[\tilde{v} \mid s \, \varepsilon \, \Sigma_+(b)]$ is the expected value a limit buyer receives given that his trade executes. A limit buy order will exist at price b, therefore, if and only if

$$b = E\left[\tilde{v} \mid s \in \Sigma_+(b)\right].$$
(7.12)

The actual order strategy pursued by a limit order trader is quite complex because of this triggering set $\Sigma_+(b)$. In particular, consider an existing limit order at some price b and, for the sake of argument, suppose it is the first limit order submitted at that price. The limit order could be triggered by a market order to sell a single share, but it could also be triggered by a market order to sell 10,000 shares (or any amount in between). If only the first case could occur, then a risk neutral limit order trader could set his limit price equal to the expected value of the stock given that someone wanted to sell one unit, a pricing decision we have already extensively characterized. But what of the second event? Certainly the price the limit order trader might want to trade against a block will differ from that of a single trade, but the limit order trader does not know exactly what this block size will be. His optimal price must incorporate all possible triggering trade prices, and hence it reflects an *average* price given that a trade occurs. Furthermore, his optimal price must also reflect the market maker's strategy since this, too, affects when his limit order transacts.

One way to characterize the equilibrium in this model is that it is a shared outcome between the market maker and the limit order traders. Specifically, if the unit of trade is made sufficiently small, then over some range the book can be thought of as approximately continuous. If s^* is a market order that begins its execution matched against some orders on the book and is cleaned up by the specialist at a price $p(s^*)$, then the price posted by the market maker is virtually the same as the price posted by the marginal limit order trader.

Rock argues that if the specialist's price schedule is continuous, then any limit trader who actually participates in s^* would also participate in any trade larger than s^*. Consequently, from equation (7.12) it follows that the triggering set for any limit order is $[s \mid s \geq s^*]$, which implies that the marginal limit order trader determines his bid such that $E[v \mid s \geq s^*] = v(s^*)$. Since the market maker takes the last piece of the trade, his price is equal to that of the marginal limit order trader, or $P(s^*) = v(s^*)$.

The actual pricing function the specialist sets may be quite complex, as it depends on both his risk preferences and inventory position. Some insights into its properties may be gained by considering how the market maker determines the price for a trade s^* given that the book takes an arbitrary quantity, x, and that his inventory position is small. Let $\pi(s, x)$ be the price the specialist would name in response to the market order s if he knew the book would absorb x shares of the order. From equations (7.11) and (7.12) any market sell order in which the book participates is priced by the specialist at $V(s)$, and so the amount the book takes can be found by equating $\pi(s, x)$ to $v(s)$ and solving for x.

Rock shows that the solution for x, denoted $x(s)$, has intervals in which the book takes a negative share of the trade. As this is impossible, the interpretation is that such orders simply do not exist, and the book essentially has a hole. Rock shows that this interval is for prices close to the small trade expected value, so that for small trades the specialist alone fills the order. For larger trades, the price moves out of this interval, limit orders exist, and the order is jointly filled by the specialist and the book. Since there are no limit orders entered at prices close to the specialist's small trade quotes, this model captures the notion of the spread as being a "hole in the book."

An interesting issue in this model is how the equilibrium is affected by the specialist's inventory. As the specialist's holding of stock increases, the increased inventory risk causes his quotes to fall. Because the specialist clears all small trades, this effectively *worsens* the terms of trade for small sellers. With the specialist less willing to absorb inventory, the book of limit orders deepens because the reduced role of the specialist lessens the adverse selection problem faced by limit order traders. Limit order traders are assumed able to know the market maker's prices (and inventory position) when they submit orders, and so the change in the market maker's inventory *increases* the optimal order position of the limit order traders. While small trade prices suffer, large trade prices do not and may even improve because a larger share of the order is taken by the risk neutral limit order traders.

This suggests that the book of limit orders can improve prices available to some traders by increasing the liquidity of the market. That this improvement occurs only when the specialist faces inventory problems, however, reveals some important characteristics of this model. If the market maker were risk neutral instead of risk averse, such an improvement would not arise because limit order traders could never provide any benefits over those already provided by the market maker. Indeed, this specialist risk aversion suggests that were there no market maker at all, all traders would do better provided the limit order traders could specify a price schedule related to quantity rather than simply to price. Because orders can be "batched" and limit orders cannot be made contingent on quantity, limit order traders lose out to any price-setting agent who can avoid such aggregation problems.

While Rock's one-period model focuses on the batching that occurs within trades, limit order traders face similar problems due to their inability to avoid price movements across trades. As trades change prices throughout the day, limit orders may be triggered because of the market maker's unwillingness to take additional inventory or by changes in the expected value of the stock. This latter effect necessitates that limit order traders must continuously monitor the market, or submit orders sufficiently "out of the money" to avoid this problem.

This highlights what has commonly been termed the "free option" property of limit orders. Because the limit order trader precommits to buying or selling at a particular price, he or she has in effect written an option at the specified strike price. As market prices change, this option can move in or out of the money, exposing the writer to the risk of the option being exercised at his expense. Stoll [1990] gives an example of this occurring in the Intermarket Trading System. With ITS, a dealer in Cincinnati can post quotes in an NYSE-listed stock that will automatically execute. If a floor trader in New York sees a large block in the stock or learns of any other event that might lower the price on the NYSE, he can send a sell order to Cincinnati and 'pick off' the dealer before he has a chance to change his quote.[12]

This option property of price quotes was noted by Copeland and Galai [1983], but it takes on particular importance for understanding the nature of the book and, by extension, the operation of any automated clearing system. Because the value of the option is directly related to the size of the contract, the risk to limit order traders of placing a large order can be onerous. Consequently, few traders submit large limit orders, preferring instead to work any intended trade via a series of small market orders. Only if the

---

12. Stoll [1990] provides an excellent discussion of market structure issues, including a detailed discussion of the free option problem. More discussion of what exactly these options are can be found in Copeland and Galai, and in our discussion of that paper is Chapter 2.

market can be continually monitored is the risk of the free option reduced, but this in turn imposes monitoring costs on the limit order trader. One solution is a system of more complex orders, an issue addressed in a series of an interesting working paper by Black [1991]. We return to this issue in the next chapter, but, for our discussion here, the free option problem suggests that a multiperiod model incorporating both the market maker and limit order traders will be extremely complex.

A related difficulty in modeling the book is the issue of market transparency. In Rock's model, traders know not only the complete structure of the book, but the market maker's inventory position as well. Neither condition is likely to hold in actual markets. To the extent the market maker has private information (about either order flows or his own inventory), he can exert market power on pricing. This both greatly complicates the traders' order strategy and renders obsolete our convenient (and tractable) assumptions of competitive behavior. Similarly, the optimal order strategy for a limit order trader may differ dramatically depending upon what order information is available to the market. Rock avoids these order strategy complications by assuming complete information, but this issue of the information content of the market maker's inventory position is clearly an interesting question for future research.

A different perspective on the role of the book is offered by Easley and O'Hara [1991], who analyze the effect of stop orders on market behavior. In their model, the market maker is assumed to be risk neutral, and so the inventory considerations so prominent in Rock's model are not an issue. Moreover, since stop orders *take* liquidity from the market, the free option problem does not arise in this model. Instead, Easley and O'Hara focus on how the ability to trade via an alternative order form affects the informativeness of the order flow and how this, in turn, affects the adjustment and stability of market prices across time. Because traders may have differential knowledge over the book's contents, this analysis considers how information on the order flow itself affects the performance and efficiency of the market.

In this multiperiod sequential trade model, traders are permitted to submit either market orders or stop orders. There is a single, risk neutral competitive specialist, who receives all orders and quotes bid and ask prices. An important difference between this model and Rock's is that only the market maker knows the actual composition of the book. Other traders know that the book exists and they have expectations about its size and structure. These expectations are assumed to be rational.

Some traders receive a private signal of the asset's true value, while the remaining traders and the market maker do not. As in all sequential trade models, a trader is selected to trade according to his probabilistic representation in the trader population. A fraction μ of orders received are from informed traders, while the fraction $1 - \mu$ are from uninformed traders. The trader so selected may then enter an order to trade one unit of the asset.

An important question to consider is, what type of order will a trader submit? Since stop orders can be submitted only at a "worse" price than the current quote, for a given trade an informed trader profits more by transacting at the better price offered by the market order.[13] In this model, as in all sequential trade models, traders are assumed able to submit only one order at a time, and so it follows that the informed trader submits a market order rather than a stop order. This myopia on the part of informed traders, while optimal in a sequential trade framework, need not hold in a model specifically incorporating strategic behavior. If it doesn't, then the book would also have information content, and determining its effects would be a formidable task. As yet, such dynamic behavior with alternative order strategies has not been solved.

If a trader is uninformed, then whether he prefers a stop order or a market order depends on his reasons for trading. If he does submit a stop order, however, it cannot be because he expects to piggyback or "front run" on an informed order. This follows because at the time a stop order is submitted, it has a zero expected return; if it executes, it trades at the conditional expected value of the asset, and if it doesn't execute, its return is zero. This suggests that any stop orders submitted are from uninformed traders, and their composition is unrelated to private information on the underlying value of the asset. This results in the book being composed only of uninformed orders.

Despite this lack of information content, the existence of stop orders can have large effects on market behavior. One effect may be on the composition of the order flow as some traders shift from using market orders to using stop orders. By placing a stop order, uninformed traders gain priority to sell at a given price, and this removes any need to submit a market sell order. A second effect may be to induce traders to enter the market who would not otherwise have traded. For example, if the ability to enter insurance-type trading arrangements is attractive (as has been alleged in the case of portfolio insurance), such an inducement effect could occur. Easley and O'Hara capture these effects by defining η to be the fraction of

---

13. If the trader could submit multiple orders at every trading opportunity, then there might be some dynamic trading strategy that makes use of stop orders. In actual security markets, however, most widely used stop order strategies (such as basic portfolio insurance schemes) are not information-related, and so it may still be the case that the information content of stop orders is fairly small.

uninformed who do not participate in the market if there is no book ($0 \leq \eta \leq 1$).[14]

In this model, the trading day begins with an initial book. Orders come into the book throughout the day, and orders are removed from the book as they execute. To begin trading, the market maker must determine his initial bid and ask quotes. Because the market maker knows the structure of the book, it would be tempting (and profitable) to set low prices and essentially "pick off" stop orders on the book. This, however, takes advantage of stop order traders, and so exchange trading protocol requires that stops only be triggered by market trades and not by the market maker simply moving prices. This requires the first trade to be a market order, and hence the market maker's initial pricing problem is to set prices equal to conditional expected values given that the trade is either a market sell order or a market buy order.

Although the initial trade is known to be a market order, provided that $\eta < 1$ the market maker will not set the same bid and ask prices as he would if there were no book. The reason is that while stop orders *per se* are not information-related, the diversion of orders from markets to stops means the remaining market order flow is now more likely to come from informed traders. With the order flow more informative, the market maker responds by setting a lower bid price, a higher ask price, and thus a larger initial spread.

For subsequent trades, the book itself may become involved as the movement of prices triggers orders. Because the market maker knows which orders are stops and that they are not information-related, he does not change his beliefs following an executed stop order, and hence he does not change his prices. Following an executed market order, however, the market maker adjusts prices *more* than he would in the absence of a book because of the market order's now greater information content. In this setting, individual stop orders do not affect security prices, but the aggregate collection of stop orders does. The effect of a book, therefore, is to change the stochastic process of prices.

That prices change in response to a book of price-contingent orders even though those orders are not correlated with the underlying value of the asset reveals the important role played by the trading mechanism in the price adjustment process. While prices are now different, however, it is not immediately obvious whether this is beneficial. Moreover, as prices adjust, the effects on the market become even more difficult to compare.

---

14. If $\eta = 1$, then introducing a book simply adds traders to the market but does not change the behavior of existing traders. For $\eta < 1$, some traders shift from using markets to using stops. As this is a more interesting outcome, the analysis focuses on this case.

Evaluating these alternative market arrangements requires comparing the resulting *stochastic processes* of prices.

In the previous chapter, we encountered a similar problem in the context of price adjustment issues. In that setting, we considered the Diamond and Verrecchia [1987] approach of computing first passage times for the price process to reach some prespecified bound around the true value. In this paper, Easley and O'Hara develop a related approach by using entropy measures to capture the speed of adjustment.

Suppose that informed traders receive either high (H) or low (L) signals. Let $p^L = (p^L(B), p^L(S))$ be the probability of observing a market buy, B, or a market sell, S, when the signal is low. Define p^H similarly. Then the speed of convergence of market prices will be affected by the entropy of p^H relative to p^L, defined by[15]

$$I_{p^L}\left(p^H\right) = p^L(B) \log\left(\frac{p^L(B)}{p^H(B)}\right) + p^L(S) \log\left(\frac{p^L(S)}{p^H(S)}\right). \tag{7.13}$$

One way to interpret this entropy measure is as a distance measure. If signals do not affect trading decisions, then the probabilities are equal, and the entropy of p^H relative to p^L is zero. Alternatively, if these probabilities are very different, then the relative entropy is large. The entropy of p^H relative to p^L reflects the information content of trades. When the entropy is large, trades are very informative; when it is zero, trades do not carry information about the signal. Since the entropy measure involves the log of the ratio of the low to high signal probabilities, it is clearly related to the log ratio approach Diamond and Verrecchia use to determine first passage times. An advantage of the entropy measure is that it allows explicit calculation of the speed of adjustment.

Easley and O'Hara demonstrate that prices in the model converge almost surely to their strong-form efficient value exponentially at a rate equal to the relative entropy between p^H and p^L. Moreover, given some general conditions on the existence of stop orders, allowing a book of stop orders increases relative entropy and so increases the rate of convergence of prices. Hence, in markets with stop orders, prices are *more efficient* in that they converge faster to full-information values. If efficiency (in this sense) is a desirable property in securities markets, then allowing stop orders improves the performance of the market.

One interesting aspect of this price behavior is the divergence between initial prices and subsequent prices. Introducing a book results in worse initial prices and larger spreads than occurs without a book, but subsequent

---

15. This entropy approach is discussed in more detail in the Appendix to Chapter 3.

prices adjust more rapidly. Thus, there is a trade-off: *small spreads with slow adjustment* versus *large spreads with faster adjustment*. This suggests that how trading mechanisms should be designed is not altogether obvious: properties viewed as desirable may be accompanied by characteristics viewed as undesirable.[16] This observation was first raised by Fisher Black is his provocative [1989] article on the role of noise in security markets. We return to this issue of market characteristics and market efficiency shortly.

In the analysis above, the market maker is assumed to know the structure of the book and whether any individual trade is a stop order or a market order. This is accurate if the only price-contingent orders are stop orders held on the book. In actual markets, however, traders may pursue more complex portfolio insurance strategies that do not explicitly involve the book. Consequently, the market maker may not know the extent of any price-contingent orders, or even whether any individual order is a market order or a stop order.

This order type uncertainty can be modeled by assuming that prices are set by floor brokers rather than by a market maker. Floor brokers are similar to the market maker in that they are risk neutral and competitive, but differ in their access to order flow information. In this framework, orders are kept in a central computer and are brought to the floor for execution. Each floor broker knows whether an order is a buy or sell, but not whether it is a market order or a stop order. Since brokers do not know the book, they must form expectations of its size and structure.

As in the market maker system, each broker must determine his initial bid and ask quotes. Since the first order will again be a market order, this first trade problem is the same as that of the market maker, except that it is the expected size of the book that enters the broker's decision problem rather than the actual size. Easley and O'Hara demonstrate that, while uncertainty over the size and structure of the book can cause broker prices to differ from those in a market maker system, provided brokers have rational expectations these initial prices are unbiased.

Where the broker and market maker systems differ more fundamentally is in the behavior of subsequent prices. As trade progresses through the day, price-contingent orders may be triggered. Now, however, brokers do not know which orders are which, and so they will adjust prices following every trade, and not just after market orders. In comparison with the market maker system, prices move more after stop orders, but less after market

---

16. Leach and Madhavan [1993] find a similar spread-speed trade-off in their analysis of price discovery activities by the market maker. In their model, larger spreads decrease uninformed traders' willingness to trade, causing the remaining order flow to be more informative, and convergence to occur more quickly.

orders. This change again raises questions as to which is the more desirable process.

Unfortunately, comparing these stochastic processes is not straightforward because the price paths differ depending on the specific trade sequence, and neither a first passage technique nor an entropy approach can be applied. The processes do, however, differ in a quantifiable way in variability. Easley and O'Hara demonstrate that if at date t the market maker and the floor brokers have the same beliefs, then the conditional variance of the market maker's quotes is *greater* than the conditional variance of the floor broker's quotes.

That prices are more variable in a market maker system in which price-contingent orders are known than in a floor broker system in which orders are not known is an interesting result. While this higher variance might seem undesirable, it does not necessarily imply that the floor broker system is "better." Relative to the floor broker system, the market maker's prices are more efficient in that the information they are based on is no coarser at each date and is finer at some date. The relative stability of the floor broker system is thus purchased at the cost of less efficiency in prices.

This suggests an interesting trade-off for policy makers to consider. If the goal of market design is price efficiency, then the market maker system seems more desirable. Although initial prices are worse, information is more quickly impounded into prices and so prices become efficient faster. Alternatively, if minimizing price variance is the goal, then the market maker system is dominated by a floor broker mechanism in which order flow information is not known by the price-setting agents.

There may be, however, other important aspects of price behavior to consider in designing market structure. For example, one aspect of price-contingent orders is their sequential nature. As prices fall, additional orders to sell become active as the book comes into play. In a market maker system, these price-contingent orders execute without affecting prices. In the broker system, however, floor brokers do not know which are stops and which are markets. If the price activates stops on the book, their execution causes prices to fall even lower. This, in turn, can activate more stop orders, and the market continues to fall *even though every stop order is not information-related.*

This sequence effect means that large episodic price volatility may arise in a floor broker system when it would not arise in a market maker system. Because floor brokers do not know which orders are stops, they have to consider the possibility that a sequence of sell orders is indicative of adverse information. This can cause large price movements unrelated to new information on the asset's true value, and that would seem an undesirable property for a trading mechanism. As we have already discussed, however, one-step price variance is actually higher in the market maker system, and so there are important trade-offs to consider. Under some circumstances, the uncertainty over order flow can actually improve the stability of the market. This divergence in price behavior can perhaps best be illustrated by an example.

An Example of Price Sequences and Price Stability. Suppose that any stops are orders to sell and that 10 percent of uninformed sellers use stops. Informed traders receive a signal, which is equally likely to be high or low, and 10 percent of all traders are informed. Let uninformed traders be equally likely to buy or sell. Prices are normalized to lie in the range [0, 1], with the true value given a low (high) signal set to 0 (1). To simplify the example, we focus on the sell side of the market.

In this simple framework, both the market maker and the floor broker set an opening bid of .445. The market maker clears the initial market order at .445, as well as any stop orders that have been triggered at .445 and above. The market maker then sets his new bid at .391. Where the floor broker sets his prices depends on his expectations of the structure of the book. Suppose, for example, that the floor broker believes that subsequent trades are equally likely to be market or stop orders. His price quote for the second trade is then .428.

Notice that if there were, in fact, no stop orders, then the floor broker's prices are "better" than the market maker's in that prices move less. If there are stop orders on the book, however, this need not be the case. For example, suppose the opening bid actually triggers eight stops on the book. The market maker clears them all at .445 and prices do not move. The floor broker clears the first stop at .428, the next at .41, and so on until the eighth clears at .31. Hence, his prices have fallen 20 percent from the opening bid.

Of course, the probability of receiving eight stop orders in a row is fairly remote given the market structure described above. It happens 0.8 percent of the time. Over a series of trading days, however, the probability of such a sequence arising, and hence of prices falling 20 percent, is quite high.

The latter fact suggests that how trading mechanisms are structured may have important effects not only on price stability but on trader welfare as well. These stability and welfare issues have been addressed by several researchers, particularly as they relate to issues stemming from the market crash. In the next section, we consider these market stability and design issues in more detail.

7.3 POLICY ISSUES IN MARKET STRUCTURE

The market crash in October 1987 posed an interesting conundrum for researchers interested in market performance. While it is an inescapable fact that security markets rise and fall, the magnitude and speed of the market decline seemed to many inconsistent with simple changes in underlying fundamental values of securities. If this were the case, however, what could cause the market to depart so dramatically from the efficiency-based paradigm held so dear to market observers (or at least to finance professors)?

One possible explanation was offered decades ago by Keynes [1936], who noted:

> There is the instability due to the characteristic of human nature that a large proportion of our positive activities depend on spontaneous optimism rather than on a mathematical expectation, whether moral or hedonistic or economic. Most probably, . . . the full consequences [of our decisions] . . . can only be taken as a result of animal spirits - of a spontaneous urge to action rather than inaction, and not as the outcome of a weighted average of quantitative benefits multiplied by quantitative probabilities.[17]

Such "animal spirits" explanations, however, leave a disquieting feeling that actual "nonspirit" explanations may simply hide beneath the cloak of such irrationality, leaving the true cause of the market's puzzling behavior unfound.[18]

If market behavior is to be ascribed to some rational cause, then, as discussed in the previous section, one explanation may lie in the design and structure of the trading mechanism. If trading mechanisms differ in how price setting occurs, then particular types of trades or trading strategies could result in very different market behavior, perhaps even leading to dramatic shifts in price. These issues are the focus of research by Gennotte and Leland [1990] and Jacklin, Kleidon, and Pfleiderer [1992] .

The focus in both papers involves the relationship between unexpected price-contingent hedging and market liquidity. The intuition is that unexpected hedging can exert "price pressure" on a market, causing

---

17. See Keynes [1936], p. 161.

18. An interesting line of research related to this reasoning are the "noise trader" papers of DeLong, Schleifer, Summers, and Waldman. In a series of papers, these authors investigate market performance when there can be a subset of traders whose trading introduces noise unrelated to the asset's performance into the security's price. If such price effects can exist, then other traders need to be compensated for the risk of trading with noise traders. The authors demonstrate that a number of market phenomena can be explained by this framework. See DeLong, Schleifer, Summers, and Waldman [1989, 1990, 1991].

providers of liquidity to depart. Their absence, in turn, means that prices can fall, possibly dramatically, because there is a large demand for liquidity, but little supply. This argument was first suggested by Grossman [1988] in his analysis of the effect of portfolio insurance on stock price volatility. Grossman argued that portfolio insurance could reduce the information available in the market because 'there is a crucial distinction between the [information provided by] a synthetic security and a real security." If traders employ dynamic hedging strategies that involve synthetic securities rather than actual securities, then risk averse providers of liquidity can be unable to forecast accurately future price volatilities.[19] This decreases their willingness to provide liquidity and allows prices to fall more than if hedging demands were readily observable.

Gennotte and Leland [1990] develop this "price pressure" argument in a two-period rational expectations model. In their framework, traders can be one of three types: uninformed, supply-informed, or price-informed traders. The uninformed traders are able to observe the equilibrium price p_0, but have no private information on the underlying asset being traded. Price-informed traders observe a private signal, $p_1{}^i$, of the asset's future value and also observe the equilibrium price p_0. Supply-informed traders observe a private common signal S related to the supply of the asset (but not related to its ultimate value) and also observe the equilibrium price p_0.

This distinction between price-informed and supply-informed agents is designed to capture the different types of information that influence security prices at any point in time. While the traded asset will have an eventual value of p, its price in period 1 may reflect unobservable supply factors affecting the market-clearing price. Hence, supply-informed traders might include market makers, who, because of access to the book, know more about the extent of liquidity demands than do other traders in the market.[20] The notion that information on order flow could be valuable apart from information on the value of the asset is also a feature of models examining block trading and dual trading. These are discussed in more detail in Chapters 8 and 9.

The actual supply of the asset is assumed to arise from three components: an exogenously given base amount, a liquidity-induced, exogenously determined net supply, and a component due to price-contingent hedging demands. Thus supply is given by

---

19. The effect of portfolio insurance strategies on market performance was also examined by Brennan and Schwartz [1989]. Using a representative investor model, they show that price volatility increases when portfolio insurance is employed in a market.

20. This idea of information on supply as opposed to information on underlying values has been generally investigated in a Kyle-type model by Lindsay [1990].

$$\overline{m} + L + S + \pi(p),\qquad(7.14)$$

where $\overline{m}$ is a fixed amount, L is an *unobservable*, random amount created by liquidity traders, S is a similar random liquidity shock that is *observable* by supply-informed traders, and $\pi(p)$ is a deterministic hedging demand, assumed decreasing in prices and potentially observable. L and S are assumed independently normally distributed as $N(0, \Sigma_L)$ and $N(0, \Sigma_S)$, respectively.

The model employs the familiar rational expectations example in which each trader in class j is assumed to maximize a negative exponential utility function of the form

$$-\exp\left(-W/a_j\right),\qquad(7.15)$$

where W is wealth, and a_j is trader j's risk aversion coefficient. The assumptions of normality of the random variables and exponential utility result in per capita demand for the asset by type j traders, denoted n_j, given by

$$n_j = a_j Z_j^{-1}\left(\overline{p}_j - p_0\right),\qquad(7.16)$$

where p_0 is the equilibrium price, Z_j is the conditional variance of the future price p, and $\overline{p_j}$ is the mean expected future price for investors in class j. Recall that since different types of investors receive different information, these means and variances need not be the same across the three investor types.

Equilibrium requires that supply equal demand, and so the equilibrium price must be such that

$$Z^{-1}p_0 + \pi\left(p_0\right) = \sum_j k_j Z_j^{-1}\overline{p}_j - m,\qquad(7.17)$$

where

$$k_j \equiv \frac{a_j w_j}{\sum_j a_j w_j},\qquad(7.18)$$

$$m = \overline{m} + L + S,\qquad(7.19)$$

and

$$Z^{-1} = \sum_j k_j Z_j^{-1}, \tag{7.20}$$

where the summation is taken over the three trader types in j. The exact form for the equilibrium price, however, depends on traders' expectations. Since this is a rational expectations framework, agents must form an expectation of the price, and in equilibrium this expectation must be correct.

If all traders are aware of the hedging demand $\pi(p_0)$, then Gennotte and Leland prove there is a rational expectations equilibrium of the form

$$P_0 \in f(p - \bar{p} - HL - IS), \tag{7.21}$$

where $f(\bullet)$ is a correspondence, p is the realized end-of-period price, $\bar{p}$ is the conditional expectation of the end-of-period price, and H and I are constants whose values depend on the risk aversion parameters and means and variances of the model's random variables.

Price stability clearly depends on the properties of this price correspondence. If $f(\bullet)$ can be discontinuous, then prices can exhibit "jumps," which Gennotte and Leland interpret as capturing the price behavior of crashes. Interestingly, they show that if there is no hedging demand, then such jumps cannot occur. Hence, prices in the absence of hedging demands are stable in the sense that they are continuous.[21] But prices can change dramatically (albeit continuously) because of uncertainty related to supply shocks. If market makers' information regarding supply movements is poor (either because they have none or it is of low precision), then their trading behavior does little to offset potential large shifts in supply.

If there are hedging demands, then the continuity of prices can break down. Whether it does depends on the observability of the hedging demand $\pi(p_0)$. If $\pi(p_0)$ is observable by all agents, then the magnitude of hedging required to introduce a discontinuity in $f(\bullet)$ is so large as to be unrealistic. If, however, $\pi(p_0)$ is unobservable or observable only to supply-informed investors, this need not be true. The amount of hedging needed to induce price jumps falls as the observability of the hedging demand decreases.

Gennotte and Leland argue that the less observable $\pi(p_0)$ is, the greater is the volatility of prices as measured by the variance of price changes.[22] In this

---

21. This continuity property is special to this example, as it arises due to the assumptions of negative exponential utility and normality of random variables. Generally, the correspondence can be very badly behaved. See Jordan and Radner [1982].

22. Note that since this is essentially a one-period model, the only characteristic of price movements that can be examined is the variance.

model, the greatest price volatility arises when traders are ignorant of hedging demands, and this same ignorance can induce jumps in the price process even at relatively small levels of hedging. Gennotte and Leland argue that this can cause a "meltdown" of prices consistent with the market's behavior on the day of the crash.

One important feature of the model that should be noted, however, is the critical role played by order observability. In this model, traders do not form expectations over the size of the hedging component $\pi(p_0)$, but rather they assume that if they do not explicitly see $\pi(p_0)$, then it simply does not exist. Consequently, if $\pi(p_0)$ is unobservable, traders seeing a large net supply believe it must be due to adverse information on the underlying asset. This can cause a discontinuity in $f(\bullet)$ as traders adjust their demands based on the information they extract from the equilibrium price. This information, however, is incorrect because traders are essentially using the "wrong" model to explain order flow. Indeed, in this model, it is even possible for prices to exhibit a "meltup" if demands are unusually positive. Traders thus no longer behave rationally in that they do not recognize that they are systematically using the wrong model.

Gennotte and Leland argue that it is this unobservable (and unexpected) hedging that explains the large price fall in the market crash. While it is certainly possible that traders do not recognize the existence of hedging activity in the market, it seems at least as (and perhaps, more) likely that if traders can form rational expectations with respect to prices, then they can also do so with respect to order form. Introducing such order expectations, however, requires a multiperiod rational expectations framework or at least some mechanism to permit learning on the part of traders. This latter approach is taken by Jacklin, Kleidon, and Pfleiderer [1992] (JKP).

The JKP model develops the same notion that hedging-based order flow could account for market behavior, but their analysis explicitly focuses on the inference problem market participants face in estimating the actual amount of such hedging. They employ a sequential trade model in which trades arrive probabilistically and the market maker attempts to infer from the trades the extent of hedging behavior. This framework is similar to the approach taken in the Easley and O'Hara paper discussed in the previous section.

In the JKP model, uncertainty over the hedging amount can result in market prices being biased upward or downward depending upon the extent to which the market maker under- or overestimates the actual hedging in the market. JKP argue that a scenario consistent with the 1987 crash is if the market maker underestimated portfolio insurance, causing prices before the crash to be too high. The subsequent revelation of the true hedging amount then caused market prices to fall to the correct, but dramatically lower, level.[23]

One conclusion common to these analyses is that uncertainty over order flows can have undesirable effects on prices. A similar conclusion led Grossman [1988] to suggest implementing 'sunshine" trading procedures in which uninformed price-contingent orders are revealed to the market prior to their execution. With sunshine trading, two possible benefits accrue. First, orders arising from price-contingent trading strategies are identified as such, thereby removing the possibility that those orders are actually information-based. This simplifies the inference problem of participants watching the market, potentially limiting unwanted instability in security prices. Second, if all market participants are risk averse, then preannouncing orders may increase the liquidity of the market by inducing more liquidity providers to enter.

These sunshine trading effects are the focus of research by Admati and Pfleiderer [1991]. They develop a two-period rational expectations model involving three types of traders: speculators, announcing liquidity traders, and nonannouncing liquidity traders. Speculators essentially absorb orders from liquidity traders and can be thought of as providing a market maker function. There is a continuum of speculators $\vartheta \in [0, 1]$ who can choose to enter the market. Liquidity traders trade an exogenous random amount, denoted by $\tilde{A}$ for announcers and $\tilde{N}$ for nonannouncers, with variances of a and n, respectively.

In this model, each speculator υ receives a private signal, $\tilde{Y}_\upsilon$, of the asset's value, where $\tilde{Y}_\upsilon = \tilde{F} + \tilde{\varepsilon}_\upsilon$ is the signal, $\tilde{F}$ is the true value, and $\tilde{\varepsilon}_\upsilon$ is an error term with variance s. Speculators are assumed to be risk averse with constant absolute risk aversion, and they maximize a negative exponential utility function. All random variables in the model are assumed to be independent and normally distributed with mean 0. The variance of $\tilde{F}$ is normalized to 1, and so the speculators' prior on $\tilde{F}$ is distributed as $N(0, 1)$.

Because speculators have private information, the equilibrium price may reflect that information, and traders must have expectations over the form of the equilibrium price function. Admati and Pfleiderer show that there is an equilibrium in which prices take the linear form

$$\tilde{p} = \gamma_F \tilde{F} + \gamma_A \tilde{A} + \gamma_N \tilde{N} \tag{7.22}$$

---

23. An interesting question is whether prices, given that they were too high before the crash, may have fallen too much. The subsequent partial recovery of the market in the week after the crash gives some support to this "overreaction" as does the fact that for 1987 as a whole, the market rose.

where the coefficients γ_F, γ_A, and γ_N are determined in the equilibrium.

In determining the equilibrium, it is easier to formulate the problem in the standard rational expectations framework. In particular, the assumptions of negative exponential utility functions and normality imply that each speculator υ's demand is given by

$$\frac{E\left[\tilde{F} \mid \tilde{P}, \tilde{Y}_\upsilon\right] - \tilde{P}}{\text{var}\left[\tilde{F} \mid \tilde{P}, \tilde{Y}_\upsilon\right].} \tag{7.23}$$

This is the standard demand function derived in the Appendix to Chapter 4. By now solving the demand under different information sets, the effects of preannouncement, or sunshine trading, can be determined.

If there is no sunshine trading, there is no preannouncement, and trades of both announcing and nonannouncing liquidity traders are unknown to speculators. Using Bayes Rule to calculate the conditional expectation and variance, each speculator's demand is then equal to

$$\tilde{Y}_\upsilon\left(\frac{1}{s}\right) + \left(\frac{\tilde{P}}{\gamma_F}\right)\left(\frac{1}{\gamma}\right) - \tilde{P}\left(1 + \frac{1}{s} + \frac{1}{\gamma}\right), \tag{7.24}$$

where $\gamma = \left(\frac{\gamma_A}{\gamma_F}\right)^2 a + \left(\frac{\gamma_N}{\gamma_F}\right)^2 n$. Total speculator demand is then found by integrating over the set of speculators, which yields

$$\tilde{F}\left(\frac{1}{s}\right) + \tilde{P}\left[\frac{1}{\gamma}\left(\frac{1}{\gamma_F} - 1\right) - \left(\frac{1}{s} + 1\right)\right]. \tag{7.25}$$

Speculators absorb the trades of liquidity traders, and so in equilibrium supply equals demand, or

$$\tilde{A} + \tilde{N} = \tilde{F}\left(\frac{1}{s}\right) + \tilde{P}\left[\frac{1}{\gamma}\left(\frac{1}{\gamma_F} - 1\right) - \left(\frac{1}{s} + 1\right)\right]. \tag{7.26}$$

Solving for the price yields the coefficient estimates

$$\gamma_F = \frac{s(a + n) + 1)}{(s^2 + s)(a + n) + 1} \tag{7.27}$$

and

$$\gamma_A = \gamma_N = \frac{s(s(a + n) + 1)}{(s^2 + s)(a + n) + 1} \tag{7.28}$$

Given these equilibrium prices, Admati and Pfleiderer calculate the expected cost of trading for the liquidity traders. This equals the difference between the asset's true value, F, and the price, P, times the number of shares traded. For nonannouncers, this is simply $\gamma_N n$, and for announcers it is $\gamma_A a$ (this follows because all random variables in the model have zero mean, and so the only surviving terms in the trading cost equation are variances).

If there is preannouncement, then A is known to speculators before trading and is thus no longer a random variable from their perspective. In equilibrium, the form of the price equation is unchanged, but the coefficients differ to reflect the lower variance of liquidity trading (since a is effectively zero). The equilibrium coefficients thus become

$$\gamma_F^* = \frac{sn + 1}{(s^2 + s)n + 1} , \tag{7.29}$$

$$\gamma_N^* = \frac{s(sn + 1)}{(s^2 + s)n + 1} , \tag{7.30}$$

$$\gamma_A^* = \frac{s^2 n}{(s^2 + s)n + 1} , \tag{7.31}$$

where * denotes the equilibrium values with preannouncement.

It is now straightforward for Admati and Pfleiderer to compare equilibria with and without preannouncement. They demonstrate that trading costs for announcers fall with sunshine trading, while those for nonannouncers rise. The overall effect is an improvement in liquidity traders' utility. For speculators, the opposite occurs. With preannouncement, prices become more informative, and this reduces speculators' ability to benefit from private information. This decreases speculators' expected *ex ante* utility, but by not as much as the increase in liquidity trader utility. Given a fixed number of speculators, the overall effect of sunshine trades is an improvement over the outcome when there is no preannouncement.

Because sunshine trades affect speculators' returns, the assumption of a fixed number of speculators may be problematic, particularly in ascribing welfare effects. If the number of speculators were endogenous, then sunshine trading could change the amount of liquidity by inducing speculators to enter or leave the market. Indeed, one argument given for sunshine trading is that it allows better coordination of the demand and supply of liquidity, and this seems consistent with changes in the number of such liquidity providers.

To address this issue, Admati and Pfleiderer endogenize the number of speculators by assuming that each speculator faces a positive cost $b > 0$ to enter the market. This cost is incurred after any preannouncement of orders. Admati and Pfleiderer, however, now introduce an important restriction into their analysis by assuming that speculators do not receive private signals, but function only to provide liquidity to the market. This changes the problem from one in which information affects trading decisions (and hence trader welfare) to one in which only liquidity effects matter. This dictates that the return to being a speculator depends only on the mean and variance of liquidity trading.

One reason this assumption is important is that it removes any information aggregation role from prices. Since no one has private information, prices do not convey information about the underlying asset value. Consequently, there is no longer any rational expectations equilibrium to solve, because the model's randomness arises solely from exogenously given liquidity demands. The demand for each speculator becomes simply $-p$, and the "supply" curve in this market is the 45-degree line through the origin.

How much each speculator actually takes, of course, depends on the number of speculators who enter, which depends in part on whether sunshine trading is permitted. When all orders are sunshine orders, Admati and Pfleiderer show that for every $b > 0$ the expected utility of speculators is strictly higher with preannouncement. This occurs because sunshine trading reduces variance, and since speculators are risk averse, this makes them better off. Note that this is the opposite of the result when speculators had private information; there, introducing sunshine trades reduced speculator welfare because it undermined the value of their private information.

The effect on liquidity traders is more interesting. If entry costs are low, sunshine trading has no effect on liquidity traders' expected trading costs because all speculators are already in the market. If, however, entry costs are high, the increased speculator welfare arising from sunshine trading induces more speculators to enter.[24] This, in turn, lowers the expected trading costs of liquidity traders because the greater number of speculators provides more liquidity. Admati and Pfleiderer argue that entry is positively related to the

---

24. While the characterization here is imprecise, Admati and Pfleiderer provide a more complete determination of the level of these costs in their analysis.

announcer's trade size, $|A|$, and so large sunshine traders benefit more when trades are revealed to the market than do small sunshine traders (since their trades induce less entry).

In this respect, Admati and Pfleiderer's analysis is related to Rock's argument that large traders benefit more from increased liquidity than do small traders. In both models, the increase in liquidity allows traders to rebalance portfolios at lower cost. In Rock's model, this liquidity arose from risk neutral limit order traders participating in the market, while here increased entry of risk averse speculators allows for better prices. Both papers suggest, however, that the liquidity available in the market is directly affected by the design of the market and the trading mechanism.

In the next chapter, we investigate these liquidity issues in more detail. Because liquidity provision is an issue both within and across markets, we consider the interrelationships among markets, and how the linkage of trading mechanisms affects security prices. In Chapter 9, we return to market design issues by looking at the effects of market structure on performance.

8

Liquidity and the Relationships Between Markets

In the previous chapter, price behavior and even market viability were seen to depend on the ability of the trading mechanism to match the trading desires of sellers and buyers. This matching process involves the provision of liquidity, and as we have seen, this liquidity arises not only from the market maker, but from other aspects of the trading mechanism as well. In this chapter, we consider the issue of liquidity in more detail. Because liquidity may differ both within and across markets, characterizing the effects of liquidity may give important insights into the behavior of markets and their interrelationships.

That our discussion should return to liquidity issues reflects the fundamental role liquidity plays in markets. As discussed in Chapter 2, the early work in market microstructure viewed providing liquidity as the primary role of the market maker. More recently, researchers have examined liquidity-related issues in myriad settings, and hence our discussion, of necessity, considers only a few of these many applications. Unlike the earlier work, much of this recent research has highlighted the linkages that liquidity introduces between markets, and it is this dimension of liquidity with which we will be most concerned.

Because liquidity, like pornography, is easily recognized but not so easily defined, we begin our analysis with a discussion of what liquidity means in an economic sense. We then consider the implications of liquidity for market structure, and in particular, we consider both how the fragmentation of trading across markets and the scale of trading affect market viability and performance. Because trading mechanisms may differ in their provision of liquidity, we next examine an alternative trading mechanism, the "upstairs market," and investigate how it provides liquidity for large block trades. Our focus here is on understanding why the market for blocks

215

differs from standard trading, and how it is that the block trader adds value for large trades.

We conclude this chapter by considering how the ability to trade in derivative instruments affects price behavior. The development of basket securities and stock index futures and options, as well as the extensive markets in equity options, allows traders to transact virtually identical instruments in multiple markets. We examine how this influences the liquidity of the respective markets, as well as the effects of market interrelations on market structure and performance.

8.1 THE NATURE OF LIQUIDITY

Liquidity has long been recognized as an important determinant of market behavior. While it is common today to ascribe only beneficial properties to liquidity, such a view was not always held. Keynes, for example, fulminated that:

> Of the maxims of orthodox finance, none, surely, is more anti-social than the fetish of liquidity, the doctrine that it is a positive virtue on the part of investment institutions to concentrate their resources on the holding of "liquid" securities.[1]

This view reflects the usually unseen "dark side" of liquidity. While liquidity, or the ability to trade essentially costlessly, may benefit the individual, it may impose costs on the market by allowing, or even encouraging, the flight of investors. As discussed in the previous chapter, this creates stability problems for established markets and introduces difficulties for beginning ones. We consider these market issues more fully later in this chapter.

Nonetheless, it is the case that individual investors benefit from liquidity. Liquid markets are generally viewed as those which accommodate trading with the least effect on price. What this means exactly in a formal sense, however, is less clear. For example, in the Kyle model, λ is a measure of liquidity, where λ measures the order flow needed to move prices one unit. Yet viewing aggregated order flow may provide a very different view of liquidity than faces any individual trader. From this perspective, perhaps a better measure of liquidity is the bid-ask spread, with markets having small spreads being the most liquid. As we discussed in Chapters 3 and 6, however, there may not be a single spread; if price varies with trade size,

---

1. See Keynes [1936], p. 155.

the spread for large trades may be significantly larger than the small trade spread. In this case, how does one compare the liquidity of markets?

Moreover, some might argue that spread effects are not the relevant measure of liquidity in any case. In liquid markets, it should be possible to trade, if not continuously, then at least with some frequency without unduly affecting prices. If prices move after trades, then these price revisions may provide a more accurate reflection of the "costs" of trading (or illiquidity) than do bid and ask prices.[2] This view of liquidity involves a time series dimension quite distinct from the cross-sectional properties normally associated with the spread.

This is the focus of Grossman and Miller's [1988] analysis of liquidity. Their focus is on the role of liquidity as the price of immediacy, or essentially the notion that a trader willing to delay transacting commands a "better" price than one who demands immediate execution. Hence, just as limit order traders could, by waiting, trade at more favorable prices, market order traders accept less favorable prices for the benefit of transacting now rather than later. This time dimension suggests that the intertemporal movement of price is the fundamental measure of liquidity.

To develop this concept of liquidity, Grossman and Miller consider a three-period model in which trade occurs in periods 1 and 2 and the asset liquidates in period 3. A crucial characteristic of this model is that there is no private information. What motivates trade is portfolio rebalancing induced by exogenously given liquidity shocks. Moreover, there is no formal specialist in their framework, but rather a group of speculators who are willing, for a price, to hold unbalanced inventory positions. Since it is this inventory imbalance that determines prices, this model is essentially a multiperiod inventory model much like those analyzed in Chapter 2.

In the model, there is a risk-free asset (cash) and a risky asset, whose terminal price in period 3 is given by the random variable $\tilde{P}_3$. There are two types of traders: outside customers and multiple market makers. Market makers function as speculators rather than specialists in that they take positions in the risky asset but do not quote bid and ask prices. Because there is no private information, the outside traders fill the role of liquidity (or noise) traders. There is assumed to be a liquidity shock, i, at time 1 and an equal, offsetting shock of $-i$ at time 2. This liquidity shock captures the notion that anyone desiring to trade at time 1 faces an imbalance of buys versus sales, but that waiting (in this case, one period) allows time for orders on the opposite side of the market to arrive.

---

2. Recall that in Chapter 6 we investigated whether there might be a trade-off between small spreads and the speed (and hence the size) of price adjustment. This dichotomy suggests that defining liquid markets is not so easily accomplished.

Grossman and Miller analyze the standard example in which all market participants maximize the same negative exponential utility function and all random variables are independent and normally distributed. They consider several variants of the model depending upon whether the setting analyzed is a futures market or an equity market. Rather than consider these specific applications, we consider a simplified version that captures the model's intuition.

Suppose there are two outside traders, one of whom receives an endowment or liquidity shock of i at time 1, and the other who receives an endowment shock of $-i$ at time 2. That such endowment, or liquidity, shocks should be perfectly negatively serially correlated is not an obvious (or potentially even a reasonable) assumption. Grossman and Miller, however, use this construction to capture the notion that at times order imbalances may arise that, while evening out across time, impose costs on the market when they occur. Consequently, if traders insist on trading rather than waiting, price effects may arise. Let x_t denote the number of units of the asset owned by a trader after trade at time t, and let B_t be that trader's holding of cash.

The problem for the outside trader who receives the endowment shock at time 1 is to maximize his expected terminal wealth, where this is given by

$$EU\left(W_3\right), \tag{8.1}$$

subject to

$$W_3 = B_2 + x_2\tilde{P}_3, \tag{8.2}$$

$$\tilde{P}_2 x_2 + B_2 = W_2 = B_1 + \tilde{P}_2 x_1 \tag{8.3}$$

$$\tilde{P}_1 x_1 + B_1 = W_1 = \tilde{P}_1 i + W_0 \tag{8.4}$$

In these equations, i represents the initial endowment of the asset and W_0 represents other wealth. The problem for the outside trader receiving the liquidity shock at time 2 is similar and is modified in the obvious way.

Because this is a multiperiod problem, the solution to (8.1) requires using dynamic programming. Thus, the problem is solved by working backward from the period 2 solution to the period 1 optimal decision. We first consider the time 2 decision problem of the outside trader. The outside trader's period 2 problem is to maximize his expected utility by selecting his optimal holding of the risky asset, denoted x_2^o. This problem is

$$\max_{x_2} E_2 U\left(W_2 + \tilde{P}_3 x_2 - P_2 x_2\right), \tag{8.5}$$

where E_2 is the expectations operator at time 2.

As we have seen before, the assumptions of exponential utility and normality of random variables result in the outside trader's gross demand for the risky asset, x_2^o, in period 2 having the standard form

$$x_2^o = \frac{E_2\tilde{P}_3 - P_2}{a \text{ var } E_2\tilde{P}_3},$$
(8.6)

where a represents the risk aversion coefficient common to all traders. Notice that the demand does not depend upon the trader's wealth; nor does it depend upon his endowment. Indeed, given the assumptions of negative exponential utility and normally distributed random variables, gross demands of the risky asset will always have this nondependence property.

In addition to the outside trader with the liquidity shock at time 1, there are also speculators, or market makers, who are identical to the outside customer. In period 2, each speculator maximizes his expected utility by selecting his demand for the risky asset, denoted x_2^m, and this results in the same demand function as in (8.6). As there are M speculators, their total demand is given by

$$Mx_2^m = M\frac{E_2\tilde{P}_3 - P_2}{a \text{ var } E_2\tilde{P}_3}.$$
(8.7)

Finally, there is also the outside customer who receives the offsetting liquidity shock at time 2. His demand for the asset is identical to that given in equation (8.6). Market clearing at time 2 must result in the demand from the outside customer arriving at time 1, the demand from the outside customer arriving at time 2, and the market makers' demands equaling the available supply, or

$$\frac{E_2\tilde{P}_3 - P_2}{a \text{ var } E_2\tilde{P}_3} + M\frac{E_2\tilde{P}_3 - P_2}{a \text{ var } E_2\tilde{P}_3} + \frac{E_2\tilde{P}_3 - P_2}{a \text{ var } E_2\tilde{P}_3} = i + -i = 0.$$
(8.8)

Since in equilibrium $E_2\tilde{P}_3 = P_2$, substituting this into (8.8) reveals that at time 2 the market maker's demand is zero.

Now consider the period 1 problem. The maximization problem for the outside trader arriving at time 1 is

$$\max_{x_1} E_1 U\left(W_1 + \tilde{P}_3 x_1 - P_1 x_1\right).$$
(8.9)

Again, outside customer demand is given by

$$x_1^o = \frac{E_1\left[\tilde{P}_2\right] - P_1}{a \, \text{var}_1\left(\tilde{P}_2\right)},$$

(8.10)

which can be reexpressed as

$$x_1^o = \frac{E_1\left[\tilde{P}_2\right] - P_1}{a \, \text{var}_1\left(\tilde{P}_2\right)} = \frac{E_1\left[E_2\left(\tilde{P}_3\right)\right] - P_1}{a \, \text{var}_1\left[E_2\left(\tilde{P}_3\right)\right]} = \frac{E_1\left[\tilde{P}_3\right] - P_1}{a \, \text{var}_1\left[E_2\left(\tilde{P}_3\right)\right]}.$$

(8.11)

The equilibrium at time 1 is simpler than at time 2 as there are only the time 1 outside customer and the market makers in the model. Market clearing requires that customer demand plus speculator demand equals the available supply, which at time 1 is simply i. In equilibrium, therefore,

$$\frac{E_1\tilde{P}_3 - P_1}{a \, \text{var}_1\left[E_2\left(\tilde{P}_3\right)\right]} + M\frac{E_1\tilde{P}_3 - P_1}{a \, \text{var}_1\left[E_2\left(\tilde{P}_3\right)\right]} = i,$$

(8.12)

or more simply,

$$\frac{E_1\tilde{P}_3 - P_1}{a \, \text{var}_1\left[E_2\left(\tilde{P}_3\right)\right]} = \frac{i}{1 + M}.$$

(8.13)

In this model, prices change between periods 1 and 2 solely because of the supply, or liquidity shocks, in each period. In period 1, customers demand liquidity, which is provided by speculators willing to buy at price p_1. In period 2, this imbalance is reversed, and so the change in price between periods can be thought of as the return to a speculator for providing liquidity. Let $r = p_2/p_1 - 1$ denote this return; equation (8.13) can be rewritten as

$$E(\tilde{r}) = \frac{ip_1}{1 + M}a \, \text{var}\,(\tilde{r}).$$

(8.14)

Thus, a speculator's return depends on the price movement, the total number of speculators, and the common risk aversion coefficient. This dependence on the risk aversion coefficient reveals an important feature of this model. If speculators were risk neutral, any role for liquidity-induced price changes disappears, as prices would be constant across periods. Moreover, notice that the first term $ip_1/(1 + M)$ in the return equation is simply each speculator's inventory position. Hence, as would be expected in a mean-variance world, the return to each speculator is just the value of the inventory times the variance.

In this model, therefore, liquidity arises because speculators absorb the excess demand in exchange for compensation given by the price change between periods. This captures the notion of liquidity as the "price of immediacy" in that traders wishing to trade now pay a cost relative to simply waiting to trade next period. How high this price of liquidity is depends on the factors noted earlier, as well as on the number of speculators. Since speculators earn positive returns, the equilibrium number of speculators is an important consideration. Grossman and Miller allow this to be determined endogenously by assuming there is a cost, c, to being a speculator. The equilibrium number of speculators then depends on the cost, the risk aversion coefficient, and the variances of prices and endowments.

The number of speculators, in turn, determines how much of the underlying liquidity shock is absorbed by speculators immediately in period 1, and how much is absorbed by traders simply waiting until period 2 to transact. In particular, it follows that

$$x_2^o - x_1^o = -\frac{i}{1 + M} \, , \tag{8.15}$$

and so the larger M is, the more liquidity is provided in period 1, and the larger the fraction of overall liquidity provided by the speculators is. As Grossman and Miller note, when M is large, more of desired trading can be accommodated in period 1, and the market is therefore liquid.

This view of liquidity is thus very basic. The greater the number of speculators willing to provide immediacy, the greater the liquidity of the market. Since the return to speculators increases in the price variance, markets with greater volatility will have more speculators, but they in turn require a higher return to compensate them for the greater risk. Liquidity can be enhanced in a market by improving the return to speculators (and thereby inducing more to enter) or by increasing their risk-bearing ability. Liquidity arises in this market simply because some traders are willing for a price to hold suboptimal portfolios, a view reminiscent of the approach in Stoll's [1980] model of the market maker.

There are, however, some important properties of this equilibrium to note.[3] First, in the absence of an assumed cost to being a speculator, there is no endogenous solution to the number of speculators. As c goes to zero, M goes to infinity, and the market becomes infinitely liquid. As M increases, however, the return to being a speculator falls, and so it is not clear that such an equilibrium could exist. With costs exogenous to the model, it is not entirely clear what determines the equilibrium provision of liquidity in a market.

If, as seems sensible, there are costs to being a market maker, then surely these should include the losses to traders with better information. This dimension of the problem is not captured here because there is no asymmetric information, and thus no real risk to providing liquidity today. If, however, the asset price tomorrow depended on more than just liquidity shocks, then the decision to provide liquidity becomes simply the counterpart of the "free option" problem discussed in the previous chapter. As we have seen, the solution in this case need not be straightforward.

A related difficulty is that since the number of speculators and their risk aversion affect price behavior, there would seem to be a natural advantage to a specialist incorporating and thereby spreading his risk. On some markets this may be accurate, but on others, for example the NYSE, such corporate market making is not observed, leading to doubts that a risk aversion explanation is a major factor of liquidity provision there. Finally, there are also the trading mechanism issues introduced in the previous chapter to consider. Since the form of the trading mechanism can affect both the composition of trades and the intertemporal behavior of prices, liquidity might also naturally depend on how the market is structured.

These structure issues have been developed by researchers in two different directions. Several researchers have investigated how liquidity arises endogenously in markets. This research, which we address in the next section, argues that since liquidity depends on the number of traders, and the number of traders depends on the liquidity, there is a circularity to the provision of liquidity that has important implications for the performance of markets. A second direction researchers have pursued is that liquidity concerns may dictate the emergence of entirely different trading structures. In many European markets (for example, Italy and Germany), trading takes place via "parallel" markets where banks and other participants directly intermediate trades though organized exchanges also exist. Large blocks of

---

3. A discussion of these issues is given by Whitcomb [1988].

stock also commonly trade in the "upstairs market," a trading mechanism employing the services of an intermediary known as a block trader. Since the block trader prearranges trades, this mechanism entails a very different structure than exchange trading, and how it functions has been investigated by several researchers. We discuss this research later in this chapter.

8.2 ENDOGENOUS LIQUIDITY AND MARKET PERFORMANCE

If liquidity is affected by the number of traders in a market, then the scale of trading may affect market performance. In particular, if prices are "better" in more liquid markets, there should be a natural incentive for traders to converge on one market rather than split their trades across markets. In actual markets, such convergence or consolidation of trades is often observed, but it is also true that multiple markets trading the same security exist (and thrive) as well. This duality suggests that how liquidity affects investor behavior, and market behavior, need not be straightforward.

In the previous section we considered the role of liquidity in an intertemporal setting where traders could choose to transact now or to wait for additional liquidity to arise in the future. An alternative view of liquidity is more "cross-sectional" in that traders can choose to trade in markets that have more traders or in ones that have fewer traders. In this interpretation, liquidity is not a measure of the cost of waiting, but rather is a function of the scale of trading, and liquidity arises endogenously as a result of individual traders' decisions where to trade.

Such a cross-sectional approach to liquidity is developed by Pagano [1989a]. Pagano considers whether multiple markets can exist given that liquidity is an increasing function of scale. As in Grossman and Miller, Pagano's model includes only liquidity trading and completely abstracts from asymmetric information considerations. What his model does focus on is the role of traders' expectations of other traders' actions in affecting market behavior.

Pagano considers a simple two-period model in which risk averse traders trade a risky asset in one or more markets. The asset is assumed to pay a random dividend $\tilde{d}$, where $\tilde{d}$ is distributed as $N(\mu, \sigma^2)$, and all traders have the same information regarding the asset's payoff. There are no market makers in this model, nor are there speculators who for a price are willing to provide liquidity. Instead, what motivates trading is that each trader receives a random endowment shock, k_{0i}, where $k_{0i} = k_0 + e_i$ and the e_i are independent and normally distributed as $N(0, \sigma_e^2)$. With some traders holding too much of the asset and others too little, trade arises to rebalance portfolios, and the market price is simply that which clears demands.

Each investor chooses his asset demand to maximize a mean-variance utility function of the form

$$E\left(U_i\right) = E\left(\tilde{w}_{1i}\right) - \left(b\big/2\right)\mathrm{var}\left(\tilde{w}_{1i}\right), \qquad (8.16)$$

where $\tilde{w}_{1i} = \dot{d}K_i + R\left[w_{0i} + p\left(K_{0i} - K_i\right)\right]$, b reflects the risk aversion coefficient, R is the risk-free rate, w_{0i} is i's initial wealth, and K_{0i} is the amount of the risky asset held by i. In this model, each trader recognizes that this demand affects the market price. In forming his demand, each trader must conjecture what other traders will demand and then choose his own trade to maximize his utility. This approach is similar to that of Kyle [1989] in that traders essentially maximize against the market's residual demand curve rather than simply take prices as given.

Pagano demonstrates that expected utility is affected by the number of traders in the market in two ways. First, as the number of traders N is increased, the volatility in the average endowment (σ_e^2/N) falls. This reduced variance lowers the volatility of the market price, which perhaps surprisingly, also lowers traders' expected utility.[4] What generates this lower utility is that, because traders take account of the effect of trades on market prices, they act as speculators rather than as inelastic noise traders. This speculative value of the market is increasing in variance, and its reduction lowers traders' expected utility.

Increasing the number of traders induces a second, positive, effect on traders' utilities through its effect on the mean price. As N increases, the elasticity of the market price with respect to the demand of trader i decreases, meaning that the trader gets a "better" price for his trade. This change in price with respect to order flow is similar to Kyle's λ and captures the liquidity value of being able to trade larger amounts without moving prices. The larger N is, the greater this liquidity value, and so the higher the trader's expected utility from trading in the market.

Suppose now that a trader can choose between alternative markets in which to transact. Since the number of traders in a market affects the trader's expected utility, where other traders are expected to trade becomes important. In an equilibrium, each trader's expectations regarding the location of other traders must be correct. Let N_A and N_B denote the number of agents expected to trade in markets A and B, respectively, and let the

---

4. This result also reflects the well-known property that indirect utility functions are concave in quantities but convex in prices. Thus agents in general seek out price risk, but avoid quantity risks.

endowment variances of traders in those markets be denoted σ_A^2 and σ_B^2. Pagano defines a *two-market conjectural equilibrium* (TMCE) to be one in which the conjectures of agents about the number of agents (N_A, N_B) and the variances (σ_A^2, σ_B^2) are correct.

Now the question becomes, where will traders choose to transact? Pagano argues that in the absence of transaction costs, there is trading in both markets in the knife-edge case that markets are identical. In this case, if traders conjecture that equal numbers of traders transact in A and B, then both markets behave identically, and traders are indifferent between trading in one or the other. If traders conjecture different numbers, then the larger market dominates, as all traders choose that market. Moreover, if markets are not identical to begin with, it is always the case that one market dominates. Thus Pagano argues that a two-market equilibrium is possible, but unlikely.

But can such an equilibrium actually exist? The answer depends, in part, on the equilibrium concept applied. If we consider Nash equilibrium and traders are constrained to follow pure strategies, then even the knife-edge case cannot be an equilibrium. The reason is that the trader takes account of how his trades affect the market, and this causes the two-market equilibrium to collapse. To see why, suppose that a trader expects equal numbers of traders in each market. In a Nash equilibrium the trader takes the actions of others as given in forming his decision. So, he will choose one market or the other, resulting in an uneven number in the two markets. If this is the case, however, then all traders will choose one market, and the two-market equilibrium cannot exist.

Suppose, instead, that the trader expects $N - 1$ traders in market A and N traders in market B. Now if the trader chooses market A, there will be an equal number of traders in the two markets. If, however, he chooses B, that market will have two more traders than A, resulting in a more liquid, and hence, better market in which to trade. Thus, the trader selects market B, and again the two-market equilibrium cannot exist.

If traders can use mixed strategies, however, then the two-market outcome is at least feasible. With mixed strategies, a trader has a probability of choosing one market or the other. For simplicity, let this probability be one-half, so that a trader is equally likely to trade in either market A or market B. Now if the expected number of traders is the same in both markets, then a trader deciding where to trade is also equally likely to go to either market, leaving the expected number of traders equal in each market. In this case, the two-market equilibrium could prevail. In general, however, a two-market equilibrium will not typically exist, and traders concentrate their trades in one market.

Suppose, however, that impediments to trade exist in the form of differential transaction costs. In this case, whether both markets exist depends on the underlying market endowment variance and transaction costs. In particular, for two markets to exist, the endowment variances of traders in each market must differ. If $N_A = N_B$ but $\sigma_A^2 \neq \sigma_B^2$, then the two markets differ only in their speculative value. If the transaction cost differential between the markets is sufficient to offset this, then both markets can exist. Alternatively, if both size and variance differ between markets, then two markets can exist for a range of transaction costs provided that the larger endowment variance market is also larger in size.

One way to interpret this latter result is that for some traders the ability to trade in a deeper but expensive market is dominated by the ability to trade in a less expensive but relatively illiquid market. For small trades, liquidity may be relatively unimportant, and so this divergence is most likely to arise with respect to large trades. In markets with low endowment variances, the amount of any individual trade may be small, resulting in the negative effects of transaction costs dominating the positive benefits of liquidity. Conversely, with large endowment variances, larger trades occur and the greater depth of a liquid market becomes more important. Such a dichotomy between markets for large and small trades is consistent with the structure found in actual markets, where large trades clear via a block-trading mechanism while small trades clear via a broker or specialist mechanism. We return to this issue in more detail in the next section.

If two markets do exist, Pagano demonstrates that their continued existence is not guaranteed. Since differences in liquidity across markets depend crucially upon the conjectures traders make about the location of other traders, any equilibrium with two markets similarly depends on such conjectures. As noted in Chapter 5, the equilibrium in such strategic models is not robust, in the sense that any variation in conjectures can result in a wide range of equilibrium outcomes. Not unexpectedly, in this setting any belief that traders will shift out of a market can cause all other traders to leave as well. This suggests that while multiple markets can exist at any point in time, the beneficial relation of scale on liquidity introduces incentives for markets to consolidate over time.

This welfare-improving liquidity effect raises the interesting specter that traders may be "better off" if trading were organized in a single setting rather than allowed to fragment across different markets. In the previous chapter we saw that a monopolistic price-setting mechanism could improve traders' utilities when asymmetric information problems were severe. Here there are no information considerations, but because trades are portfolio-based, the consolidation of trading may lead to more desirable trading prices. For all traders, the increased liquidity arising from scale is a benefit, but the consolidation of trading also increases or decreases the speculative value of a market, causing some traders to be disadvantaged by a single trading venue. Pagano demonstrates that, in general, the positive effects of liquidity are sufficient to offset any negative speculative effects. This suggest that liquidity considerations add another benefit to our previous discussion of the role of a monopolistic (or single) market-clearing structure. The issue of fragmentation versus consolidation is considered in more detail in Chapter 9.

In Pagano's analysis, therefore, liquidity differences between markets can arise and persist as a result of underlying differences in traders' transaction (or portfolio) needs and the existence of exogenous transactions costs. We stress, however, this model's assumed absence of any information-based reasons for trading. If traders possess such asymmetric information and can act strategically, then the differential effects of liquidity become problematic. Indeed, as Kyle [1985] demonstrated, an informed trader would be expected to choose his trade quantity based in part on the liquidity of the market. Consequently, if liquidity increased in a market, the informed trader would similarly increase his share of the expected trading volume to offset any beneficial effects on prices. This would result in no liquidity differences being able to persist across markets.

How liquidity affects market performance in the presence of asymmetric information is thus not apparent. If there are multiple informed traders, for example, then, as Kyle [1984] and Admati and Pfleiderer [1988] demonstrated, competition among informed traders in order quantities may cause prices (and, potentially, liquidity) to differ. Moreover, Admati and Pfleiderer's [1988] trade concentration results suggest that liquidity traders naturally clump together to escape the effects of informed traders. If this is the case across markets, then important liquidity differences could arise because of the number of traders and not merely their trading intensity.

This cross-sectional issue is the focus of research by Chowdhry and Nanda [1991] They consider a question similar to that originally posed by Admati and Pfleiderer [1988], namely, how does the ability to choose where to trade affect the functioning and liquidity of the market when some traders have superior information? Using a model closely related to that of Admati and Pfleiderer, Chowdhry and Nanda consider a market with informed traders, large discretionary liquidity traders, and small liquidity traders. Trade occurs simultaneously in multiple markets, and all traders except small liquidity traders are permitted to trade in more than one market. Because of differences in trader behavior, and trading rules and mechanisms, prices can differ between markets. This allows Chowdhry and Nanda to investigate some interesting issues related to the effects of insider trading on liquidity.

Their analysis employs a Kyle model in which informed traders learn the asset's value, a random variable $\tilde{v}$. Informed traders are assumed to trade in each of the N markets, and so their decision problem is to choose their order quantity in each market. The size of total liquidity trade is assumed exogenous in the model, with large traders assumed to trade a quantity $\tilde{d}$ and small traders to trade $\tilde{u}$. Small traders trade in an assigned market, but large traders can split their trades across multiple markets if they desire. All random variables are independently distributed with $\tilde{v}$ distributed as $N(0, \sigma_v^2)$, $\tilde{d}$ distributed as $N(0, \sigma_d^2)$ and $\tilde{u}$ distributed as $N(0, \sigma_u^2)$. Denote by x_i the informed traders' optimal order in market i and by d_i the large uninformed traders order in market i, where $\sum_{i=1}^{N} d_i \equiv d$.

In each market there are competitive, risk neutral market makers who earn zero expected profit on trades. The market makers are assumed to announce a price schedule based on the net order flow in that market. This order flow in market i is given by $x_i + d_i + u_i$. Chowdhry and Nanda first consider the case where there is only one trading period and neither traders nor market makers observe behavior in any other market. As in Kyle, traders conjecture that the market maker in each market i uses a linear pricing rule of the form

$$p_i = p_0 + \lambda(x_i + u_i + d_i), \tag{8.17}$$

where p_0 is the unconditional value of the asset before trading begins. This pricing rule results in market makers setting trading prices equal to conditional expected values given the order flow in that market. In an equilibrium, this will be the pricing rule used, and traders' conjectures will be correct. Note that, unlike in the Pagano model where the existence of multiple markets is a knife-edge result, the assumption that small traders exist in every market dictates that multiple markets always exist. Hence, since there will be order flow in every market, there will also be a price in every market, and by assumption, that price cannot depend upon the order flow in any other market.

Because large traders can choose to split their exogenously given trade quantity, their decision problem involves allocating their trades across markets. These traders are assumed to minimize the total cost of trading (measured by the price effects of trade, λ), and so the large uninformed trader solves the decision problem

$$\min_{\{d_i\}_{i=1}^{N}} \sum_{i=1}^{N} E\left[d_i \lambda_i \left(x_i^* + u_i + d_i\right)\right], \tag{8.18}$$

subject to

$$\sum_{i=1}^{N} d_i = d. \tag{8.19}$$

The large uninformed trader's decision depends on the informed trader's optimal order quantity because it affects the net order flow, which in turn affects the trading price.

Given these assumptions, the solution to the uninformed traders problem is given by

$$d_i^* = k_i d + \frac{1}{2}(k_i - 1) \sum_{j=1}^{N} E\left[x_j^*(v)\right], \tag{8.20}$$

where

$$k_i \equiv \frac{c_i}{\sum_{i=1}^{N} c_i}, \quad \forall i, \tag{8.21}$$

and

$$c_i \equiv \frac{1}{2\lambda_i}. \tag{8.22}$$

The solution to the uninformed traders' decision includes the expected trading behavior of the informed traders since this influences the expected price in each market. Consequently, to characterize the uninformed's solution, we need determine how informed traders choose to allocate their trades.

The informed trader solves a more complicated decision problem in that he selects both the size and location of his trades. This maximization problem is given by

$$\max_{\{x_i\}_{i=1}^{N}} \sum_{i=1}^{N} E\left[x_i\left\{v - \lambda_i\left(x_i^* + u_i + d_i\right)\right\}\right], \tag{8.23}$$

where the optimal solution is given by

$$x_i^* = c_i v, \quad \forall i. \tag{8.24}$$

Since $\tilde{v}$ is distributed as $N(0, \sigma_v^2)$, it follows that $E[x_j^*(v)] = 0 \, \forall i$, or that the expected informed trade quantity in any market is zero. This parsimonious solution to the informed traders' problem allows the uninformed's solution in equation (8.22) to simplify to $d_i^* = k_i d$, or the uninformed trader simply divides up his trades on the basis of the relative price effects his order induces in each market.

Because the informed traders' strategies are again linear in the value of the asset, the equilibrium pricing rule followed by the market maker is the conjectured linear rule, and agents' expectations are rational. An intriguing property of this equilibrium is that the informed trader's orders across markets are perfectly correlated and so, too, are the orders of the large uninformed traders. This can be seen by looking at the correlation coefficient, ρ, between the total order flow in any two markets:

$$\rho\left(x_i^* + u_i + k_i d, x_j^* + u_j + k_j d\right) = \frac{1}{2}\left[1 + \frac{\sigma_d^2}{\sigma^2}\right]. \qquad (8.25)$$

Since ρ depends only on the variance of the large uninformed trades to the total trading by uninformed traders, the trades of informed traders cannot differ between markets. This can only be true if the informed trades are identically correlated across markets. Large uninformed trades are also perfectly correlated, as the uninformed split their trades across markets to minimize their effect on order flow. If there are only large uninformed traders, the ratio of variances equals one and so, too, does the correlation coefficient; in this case markets become essentially identical, as both informed and uninformed traders submit the same orders (albeit different from each other) in every market.

Given this trading behavior, the price in each market reveals some of the informed trader's information. If traders can observe all prices, then they can infer the total order flow and can potentially impute the informed trader's information. Recall from Chapter 4 that in the single-period Kyle model, the informed trader's optimal trade resulted in the variance of the posterior distribution of the asset's value being half its original variance. In this sense, Kyle argued, half of the informed trader's information is revealed by trading. In this setting, a similar effect occurs, although the fall in the variance need not be one-half. Chowdhry and Nanda demonstrate that if traders can observe all trading prices, then the informativeness of prices is given by

$$\Psi = \frac{\text{var}\left[\tilde{v} \mid \left\{P_i - P_0\right\}_{i=1}^{N}\right]}{\sigma_{\tilde{v}}^2} = \frac{N}{(N+1) + \left(\sigma_d^2/\sigma^2\right)(N-1)}, \quad (8.26)$$

where informativeness is measured by the variance of the price change over the asset value's variance. If the number of markets $N = 1$, then, as expected, we get the Kyle solution, $\Psi = 1/2$. Notice also that if there are only large uninformed traders, then, regardless of N, Ψ also equals $1/2$. The more interesting case is when there are both multiple markets and small nondiscretionary traders. Then Ψ can exceed $1/2$, as the informed essentially trade to reveal more of their information. As the number of markets increases, informativeness also increases, and in the limit as N goes to infinity, all information is revealed.

What provides for this difference in information revelation across markets is the fixed behavior of small uninformed traders. Since they are unable to move, their trades across markets are not perfectly correlated, and this allows the informed to trade more aggressively in each market. If small traders could choose where to trade, however, then the behavior of markets could be very different than that predicted here. Chowdhry and Nanda do not allow this flexibility, but they do consider a simpler extension in which some small traders can select a market in which to trade. These traders are not allowed to split their trades across markets, and some small traders are assumed to remain in every market.[5] Since trading costs are decreasing in λ, the small discretionary traders select the lowest λ market in which to transact. Of course, if all small traders converge on a specific market, then it will indeed be possible to offer the lowest λ as that market now has the greatest liquidity.

Suppose, however, that *all* traders (small, large, and informed) could choose their trading venue. If their scale is large enough, then it is likely in this model that all trade collapses into a single locale, and the issue of where to trade becomes moot. This highlights the difficulties, noted also in Chapter 5, of analyzing discretionary behavior when traders choose strategically where to transact. If there are impediments to traders' mobility that favor certain market settings, then such markets would be likely remain active, and liquidity would be large. Without such impediments, the beneficial effects of liquidity may implode trading into a single setting.

---

5. Their argument is that since they trade small amounts, it does not make sense to split the order across markets. This assumption, however, is not innocuous. If such splitting did occur, then most of the results of the model similarly disappear.

An implication of both this and the Pagano papers is that increased liquidity benefits uninformed traders. Interestingly, this may not be the case for the informed traders, as their trading behavior may be less when orders are consolidated than when they are fragmented.[6] This suggests that factors favoring uninformed trading can increase not only the liquidity of a market but its viability as well.

Chowdhry and Nanda use such an argument to explain why curbs on insider trading or more complete order form information revelation by the market maker may be preferred in securities markets. Since order form in each market is correlated with the informed traders' information, knowing each market's trade price reveals information. They provide the nice result that a market maker who reveals his trading prices to the market can set better prices than a market maker who does not. This occurs because informed traders prefer not to trade in such a market since it reduces their informational advantage, and with fewer informed traders, prices can indeed be better. Of course, if one market maker sets better prices by revealing, then all market makers must similarly reveal price information to remain competitive. The effects of trader choice on market liquidity thus improve uninformed trader utility.

This has the intriguing implication that, because of liquidity concerns, markets naturally gravitate toward equilibria with "stricter" behavioral bounds. In particular, markets with stricter information revelation requirements or more stringent rules governing trading practices will prevail over markets with laxer requirements. This issue has been a subject of extensive policy interest, particularly with respect to listing requirements. Because the NYSE in particular, and US markets in general, require greater disclosure from listing companies, there has been concern that trading would gravitate to markets without such requirements. At least in the market structure considered by Chowdhry and Nanda, this is not a legitimate concern, suggesting that the benefits of liquidity endogenously enforce the efficient working of the market.

Our discussion of liquidity suggests that securities markets may have an inherent disposition toward being natural monopolies. Because scale increases liquidity, and liquidity benefits uninformed traders, one might expect markets to function best when trading is consolidated. The models of liquidity we have examined, however, all employ the abstraction of a call market clearing mechanism. In actual markets with continuous trading, the role of liquidity takes on greater complexity, in part because it entails both

---

6. This result, however, is heavily dependent on the restrictions of the model. A general result of this nature seems likely, but not certain.

cross-sectional and intertemporal dimensions. One area where this issue arises is with respect to block trades. While some large trades are cleared directly by the specialist, it is also common for large trades to involve the services of a different intermediary, a block trader. In the next section, we investigate why such an alternative trading mechanism exists, and how it affects the behavior of security prices and markets.

8.3 BLOCK TRADES AND ALTERNATIVE TRADING MECHANISMS

A surprising statistic to many market observers is that slightly more than 50 percent (50.7 percent, to be exact) of total volume on the New York Stock Exchange is accounted for by block trades.[7] These large transactions (defined as trades of 10,000 shares or more) have a number of features that have long intrigued researchers. For example, Kraus and Stoll [1972] noted that "blocks are sold not bought," recognizing an asymmetry in how block orders are actively submitted to the market. Dann, Mayers, and Raab [1977] and Holthausen, Leftwich, and Mayers [1987] showed that blocks tend to have predictable price effects in that blocks trade at "worse" prices. Moreover, prices following such trades only partially recover to their pre-trade level. This price behavior was examined theoretically by Easley and O'Hara [1987a] in their investigation of the price-trade size information linkage (see Chapter 3), and more recently in empirical work by Keim and Madhavan [1993].

An aspect of block trades germane for our discussion is that they often involve a different trading mechanism. Many block trades use the services of a block trader, or "upstairs market maker," who forms a syndicate of buyers to take the other side of the trade. In 1992, for example, this was the trading mechanism used for 27 percent of blocks. This syndication feature is a significant departure from the specialist mechanism considered thus far. Block trading also differs from more standard trades in that the identity of the seller is known to the block trader. Hence, the anonymity of trading characterizing exchange transactions is not typically found in block trades.

Why blocks trade through this alternative mechanism is an interesting question. One possible answer is that the large size of such transactions is beyond the risk-bearing capacity of the specialist. Since exchange rules prohibit the specialist from soliciting trades, a large block sale may require the market maker to hold a unbalanced position for the time it takes for offsetting orders to arrive. In markets in which the daily average volume is

---

7. Data are for 1992 and are taken from the *New York Stock Exchange Fact Book*, 1992, p. 15.

small, this could entail considerable inventory risk and would impel the specialist to set a low price. A related difficulty is the size of the specialist's capital, since taking a large position could reduce his ability to meet normal trading demands. Another possible explanation for a separate mechanism is the information problem inherent in large trades. If market participants interpret trade size as a signal of information, then a large seller may prefer some other trading approach than simply submitting a large order to the market maker. The lack of anonymity in upstairs transactions may be useful in this regard.

These issues have been the focus of research by Burdett and O'Hara [1987], Seppi [1990, 1992], and Grossman [1990]. Burdett and O'Hara consider the syndication strategy of the block trader, while Seppi focuses on the role played by the lack of anonymity in affecting a trader's dynamic trading strategy. Grossman considers the informational advantage an "upstairs market maker" has relative to an exchange specialist. As each of these papers examines different aspects of the block trading mechanism, it is useful to consider them in more detail.

Burdett and O'Hara analyze the syndication process in block trading and, in particular, analyze the problem of forming a syndicate of buyers when the syndication effort itself may affect the block price. This problem arises because block trades have predictable price effects in that block sales go through at 'worse" prices. Other traders, learning of an impending block, have an incentive to short the stock and simultaneously enter limit buy orders. This selling pressure can cause the stock price to fall in anticipation of the actual trade. Since blocks must be cleared on the floor of the exchange and any qualifying orders on the book must be included when the block is cleared, traders pursuing this strategy can cover their short positions with a profit. For the block trader, therefore, the challenge is to form a syndicate without inducing such "free-riding" price effects.

This strategic behavior on the part of other market participants introduces a new dimension into the trading behavior previously analyzed. Here, the uninformed act as quasi-arbitrageurs in that they take advantage of the predictable short-run divergence of price surrounding block trades.[8] What makes this particularly interesting is that their strategy, in turn, exacerbates the price drop surrounding the trade. For the block trader, this

---

8. In a true arbitrage, the position taken is risk-free. Here there is some risk because the trade may be withdrawn before execution or the block trader may buy the entire order for his own account. The expected profit on this strategy, however, is clearly positive and since this profit is not related to any information on the underlying value of the stock, it is best viewed as the return to arbitraging the two trading mechanisms.

dictates that knowledge of impending block trades is valuable information in itself, and hence her syndication effort must recognize this property.

Burdett and O'Hara employ a search model to analyze this syndication problem. While search models are extensively used in many areas of economics, their use in finance has been limited. One reason may be that the problems typically analyzed in finance are specific to a single setting (i.e., a firm or an exchange) rather than to the multiple venues implicit in a search. For a block trader needing to form a syndicate, however, the notion of search is fundamental. How she searches for participants and the rules she uses to determine the scope of the search are crucial to understanding how the block syndication process works.

One aspect of this syndication problem that is not standard in search problems is the endogenous effect of the search on the asset price. For example, in the standard labor economics application of a worker looking for a job, search is used to find the best of an existing set of wages. The worker faces exogenous costs of searching, but his search per se does not affect the wage he is offered. This, however, is essentially the difficulty faced by the block trader. The decision to continue the syndicate runs the risk of lowering the asset's market price, and so the search process itself affects the trading price. Burdett and O'Hara develop a search model with endogenous search costs to address this problem.

As is typical in search models, the block trader's optimal strategy involves a series of optimal stopping rules. These rules dictate when the trader ceases contacting new potential syndicate members and simply buys the remaining shares for her own account. Since these stopping rules reflect the payoffs the block trader gets from syndication, the form of the trader's compensation function as well as the risks in the process must be specified.

Although there are numerous variations on the contract between the seller and block trader, a typical agreement specifies a commission rate and a (usually implicit) commitment price. The commission is simply the fee the trader makes per share in placing the transaction, while the commitment price sets a lower bound on the proceeds to the seller. This latter parameter reflects the block trader's role as market maker, as she could always choose to forgo syndicating the stock and simply purchase the shares for her own account. This price also serves an insurance role, however, since the trader's actions may adversely affect the price of the stock.

The level of the commitment price must reflect the possibility that large trades can be information-related. In this model, the block trader is assumed to be risk neutral, so that the commitment price, denoted z, is equal to the conditional expected value of the stock given a trade of size N, or $z = Z(N)$ with $Z'(N) < 0$. This presumably is the same price that would be offered by a risk neutral exchange specialist, and so there would seem little advantage to trading with a block trader. The block trader, however, can also syndicate the stock. In a syndicate, the seller receives either the syndicate price or, if it is greater, the commitment price. The block trader's commitment price is a minimum return to the seller, therefore, while the specialist's price is a maximum return.

For this divergence to provide value to the block trading mechanism, individuals must be willing to enter a syndicate at a price greater than the conditional expected value. There are several reasons why this could occur. Bagehot [1971], for example, argues that there are "pseudo-informed" investors who either exaggerate the value of their own beliefs or assume that all other traders transact only for liquidity purpose. Their willingness to transact results in their always losing to informed traders, a strategy inconsistent with rational behavior in the long run. Another explanation is inventory. If the specialist is risk averse, his price for purchasing a large block will include a premium for bearing the inventory risk. By syndicating the stock before purchase, the block trader can divide this exposure among the participants, resulting in a smaller risk premium. A third explanation, and the one employed in this model, is that liquidity reasons may induce a trader to enter a syndicate. For many institutional investors, portfolio management costs preclude holding small positions. Entering a syndicate avoids either paying a premium in a block buy or the time lag (and larger per share commission) involved in purchasing the shares in round lots from the specialist.

Burdett and O'Hara model this by assuming that syndicate participants purchase the stock at some discount, denoted r, from the market price, p_m, at the time the trade is completed. This structure captures the stylized facts that syndicate participants in a block trade all pay the same price and that this is the price when the trade clears. The exact determination of r is exogenous, clearly the weak point of this model. This framework does permit the success of the syndication effort to depend on the state of the market, and hence it indirectly captures the effect of the block trader's syndication efforts on the final block trade price.

The block trader is assumed to contact potential syndicate members and offer them the opportunity to purchase one of N subblocks. Because of the aforementioned problem of traders short selling against the trade, there may be downward pressure on the price when traders learn of the trade. While this pressure could arise from the entire syndication effort, Burdett and O'Hara assume that uninterested buyers are more likely to short (since they are not now involved in any commitment to participate with the block trader). Let the amount the current stock price falls following an unsuccessful phone call be the random variable τ, with cumulative distribution function $F(\bullet)$, where F is assumed differentiable and $F(0) = 1$.

The probability that any person called will want to purchase a subblock depends on that person and on the state of the market. Let $\Pi(k, \Theta)$ denote the probability of success on the kth contact (or phone call) given that the market state is Θ. As the block trader will contact the most likely purchasers first, assume

$$\Pi(k, \Theta) = \alpha_k \Pi(k - 1, \Theta), \tag{8.27}$$

where $0 < \alpha_k < 1$. Because the block trader does not know the exact state of nature, she uses the information she learns from trading to update her beliefs. Suppose that the trader has $N - n$ successes in $k - 1$ contacts. Let $\lambda(N - n, k)$ denote the block trader's subjective probability that the kth contact will be successful, where

$$\lambda(N - n, k) = E_\Theta \left\{ \Pi(k, \Theta) \mid N - n \text{ successes in } k - 1 \text{ calls} \right\}. \tag{8.28}$$

Based on the outcome of the call, the block trader update her beliefs using a Bayesian adjustment process. Let

$$\hat{\lambda}_s(N - n, k) \geq \lambda(N - n, k) \text{ if the } k\text{th call was successful, and} \tag{8.29}$$

$$\hat{\lambda}_u(N - n, k) \leq \lambda(N - n, k) \text{ if the } k\text{th call was unsuccessful.} \tag{8.30}$$

So the block trader raises her probability of success if she has been successful, and lowers it if she has been unsuccessful.

This learning feature of the syndication process allows the block trader to adapt her strategy to the market condition. The syndication effort, however, provides information not only to the block trader but also to the traders who learn of the block. This increases the risk of traders gaming the syndication, and hence the block trader's strategy must weigh the relative costs and benefits of continuing the syndication effort.

Suppose the trader has made $k - 1$ contacts and has placed $N - n$ subblocks. The trader can make the kth call and hope to place the $(N - n + 1)$-th sub block, or she could elect to purchase the remaining subblocks. If she purchases the shares, then the trader now faces the problem of disposing of the shares for her own account. Burdett and O'Hara assume the trader can liquidate the shares at some discount from market price, where the discount, $\varepsilon(n)$, is a convex function of the number of shares to be sold. This assumption captures the notion that trading a small number of shares may require no loss, but for larger trades the need for greater liquidity reduces the share price. Let $\Phi(p, N - n)$ denote the expected return to the block trader from purchasing the remaining n subblocks when the current market price (less discount r) is p. Then, given a commission β, this is equal to

$$\Phi\left(p, N - n\right) = p\beta N - pn + n\left[p - \varepsilon\left(n\right)\right] = p\beta N - \varepsilon\left(n\right)n. \qquad (8.31)$$

The Φ function captures the value to the block trader of ending the syndicate and buying the remaining shares.

Alternatively, the block trader could syndicate the block further. Suppose the trader has made $k - 1$ calls and placed $N - n$ subblocks. If she continues, there are three possible outcomes following the next contact. First, the call is successful, and so the trader will have placed $N - n + 1$ subblocks and made k calls. Second, the call is unsuccessful and, while the discounted market price may move, it remains above the commitment price z. Third, the call is unsuccessful and the price falls below the commitment price. In this case, the syndicate collapses, and the trader buys the entire block at the price z.

These outcomes are captured by the block trader's value function. Let $V(p, N - n, k)$ denote the block trader's expected return from making the next contact in the situation described above. Then

$$V\left(p, N - n, k\right)$$

$$= \lambda(N - n, k)\Psi\left(p, N - (n - 1), k + 1\right)$$

$$+ \left[1 - \left(\lambda\left(N - n, k\right)\right)\right] \int_{\tau = z - p}^{0} \Psi\left(p, N - (n - 1), k + 1\right) dF(\tau) \qquad (8.32)$$

$$+ \left[1 - \left(\lambda\left(N - n, k\right)\right)\right] \int_{\tau = \tau_{\min}}^{z - p} \Psi\left(p + \tau - \varepsilon\left(N\right) - z\right) dF(\tau).$$

Given the value function, Burdett and O'Hara demonstrate that the trader's optimal strategy involves a series of stopping prices, denoted $x_n(k)$. They show that these stopping prices exist and are nondecreasing in the syndicate's success (i.e., n, the number of subblocks syndicated) and in customer contacts (the k's). Hence, as the syndicate progresses, optimal stopping prices rise. Once the market price falls below the relevant stopping price, syndication ceases and the block trader buys the remaining shares for her own account.

These optimal stopping rules dictate that the block trader does not typically call buyers until all N subblocks are placed. Indeed, the trader purchases some shares for her own account, even in the case when every contact has been successful. This reflects the endogenous search cost problem noted earlier, since even the most successful syndicates always run the risk that trading in anticipation of the trade will undermine the market price. Burdett and O'Hara also characterize how the stopping rules relate to the other parameters of the model such as the commission rate and the commitment price.

Of particular interest is how the stopping prices relate to the block trader's knowledge of the market (the λ's). In this model, a trader who has better information on market conditions can offer customers a better deal (i.e., lower commission or higher commitment) for syndicating stock than can a competitor without such information. Since greater trading activity makes, and keeps, a block trader informed, there is a natural tendency for consolidation of orders to a single trader. This suggests the potential for monopoly power amongst block traders. Previously, we noted several other explanations for the emergence of a single provider or market, but this explanation differs in that it arises from the block trader's ability to glean (and use) information from the trading process itself.

This informational role of the block trader is also the focus of research by Grossman [1990]. His analysis focuses on the ability of the upstairs market maker to have greater knowledge of the total order flow than does the downstairs market maker, the exchange specialist. What motivates the analysis is the problem that traders may be unable to continuously monitor markets, and hence they are unable to implement trading strategies optimally. One possible solution is to submit limit orders, but as we discussed in the last chapter, simple limit orders introduce a "free option" problem and hence can be too risky for some traders. If traders could submit detailed contingent orders, then this problem might be alleviated, but Grossman argues that this may be infeasible, largely due to the difficulty of determining, specifying, and expositing the effects of multiple states on the desired trading strategy.

If traders do not explicitly announce their trading intentions, then the unexpressed demand will be as, or perhaps even more, important as the expressed demand. In Grossman's analysis, it is this unexpressed demand that is known by the upstairs market maker, while the downstairs market maker may have superior knowledge of the expressed demand. In addition, Grossman assumes that the upstairs market maker has superior information about the state of the market. These upstairs advantages are offset by the disadvantage that upstairs trade involves search costs, and hence the traders' choice of trading venue depends on the relative advantages and costs of trading locales.

The analysis employs a variant of the Grossman-Miller [1988] model, and hence it does not allow for private information on the asset's true value. Instead, what motivates trade (and price movements) is an exogenous liquidity shock, and market prices depend only on these liquidity factors. Rather than discuss the specifics of the model (which is done in Section 8.1), it is perhaps more useful to consider the analysis's conclusions. In this model, if the expressed order flow is informative (meaning that unexpressed demand is either not large or provides little additional information about the underlying liquidity shock), then the downstairs market can dominate the upstairs market. This occurs because the batching of orders in the downstairs market allows prices to reflect the true state, and the absence of search costs lowers the cost of trading. Conversely, when the order flow is not sufficiently informative, the upstairs market can provide a better venue because the upstairs market maker can better match the trading desires of individual traders.

Because the order flow provides information to the market makers, where traders decide to submit orders becomes the crucial issue. If many traders decide to send orders to the upstairs market, then it is the upstairs market maker, rather than the downstairs market maker, who knows more about the expressed demand. This can result in the upstairs market prevailing, and in equilibrium the downstairs market disappears. Since the upstairs market involves search costs, Grossman shows that such an equilibrium may be suboptimal in the sense that traders would be better off if only the downstairs market prevailed. This conclusion may explain why some markets, such as futures, prohibit prearranged trades, while others, such as the NYSE, require such trades to be executed on the floor of the exchange.

An interesting issue raised in this analysis is the ability to arbitrage between market settings. Since the same security can transact in both venues, it seems natural to believe that some customers will trade to exploit price differences in the two markets. Grossman argues that it is the informational discrepancies between markets that provides for such potential price divergences, but that such discrepancies also inhibit the ability to arbitrage. The market maker in each market knows only his order flow and hence cannot instantaneously determine whether prices and trades are different in the two locales. Since this is essentially a one-period model (prices are assumed to reach true levels at time 2), long-run divergences in price cannot occur. This issue of arbitraging markets in addressed in more detail in the next section.

If traders do face different prices between markets, what determines the order strategy they pursue? This issue is addressed by Seppi [1990], who considers why large traders do not simply split orders into smaller amounts to avoid the adverse price-trade size relationship. Seppi develops a multiperiod framework in which a block trader or dealer can trade a block of shares at time 0 or the specialist can trade shares in round lots at times 1,

2, . . ., *T*. In the model, there is a single, risk neutral institution (or large trader), *N* small uninformed traders, several competitive specialists, and several competitive block traders, referred to as dealers. The small investors trade for exogenously given liquidity reasons, and at each time *t* each small trader submits an order for some random number of shares e_{it}. These orders are cleared by the risk neutral market makers.

The trade behavior of the large institution is more complex. In some states of the world, the institution must trade for liquidity reasons. In other states, the institution may be trading on the basis of private information. Seppi captures this duality by assuming that the institution faces five possible states of nature. In particular, the large trader may (1) sell for liquidity reasons, (2) buy for liquidity reasons, (3) learn bad news and want to sell, (4) learn no news and hence do nothing, and (5) learn good news and wish to buy. Combinations of the states can be incorporated by simply viewing the optimal state demand as the net value.

The institution learns the state of nature before the start of trading. The institution can trade a block of size *b* at time 0 with the dealer and/or round lots of size x_t at each time $t = 1, 2, . . ., T$ with the specialists. If the institution needs to trade for portfolio-rebalancing reasons, it may do so anytime up to and including period *T*. Similarly, if the institution is trading on private information, it is assumed that the information becomes public after time *T*. Orders submitted to the specialist are aggregated, and, as in Kyle, the market maker sets the risk neutral price based on the net order flow. Similarly, blocks submitted to the dealer are also assumed to clear at the risk neutral price.

This framework allows for the explicit characterization of dynamic trading strategies. As we have discussed in this and in previous chapters, analyses of large trades typically start from the existence of such orders and examine their impact. Why traders choose to trade large quantities in the first place, however, is not obvious since a viable alternative is simply to split the trade into multiple small orders. This question is important because the ability to trade dynamically allows traders to avoid the adverse price effects usually connected with block trades. If blocks are to exist, it must be because they are the optimal trading strategy for some investor.

Seppi considers this issue by analyzing how the "contract" between investor and block trader differs from that between investor and specialist. He argues that an important difference is the lack of anonymity in block trading. This allows the investor and the dealer to make side agreements that cannot be made in an anonymous market setting.[9] Of particular importance is what Seppi identifies as a "no bagging the street" constraint. This constraint imposes a penalty on any subsequent trades by the investor, and thus it compensates the block trader for investor actions that might adversely affect the dealer. The block-trading contract Seppi analyzes involves trading a large number of shares at time 0 and a simultaneous agreement not to trade any additional shares with the specialist.

Seppi demonstrates that there is an equilibrium in which the large trader uses blocks when rebalancing his portfolio and uses the specialist when he is trading on information. Since the "no-bagging" constraint is costless for a liquidity trader but is not for an informed trader, this equilibrium captures the benefits of using a block trader for liquidity trades. For this equilibrium to prevail, however, the profit to the informed trader of trading multiple times with the specialist must exceed the profit from trading a block. This will be the case if the block size is small relative to the amount the trader could trade in the specialist market. Recall that a similar relative size condition was used by Easley and O'Hara [1987a] in their determination of separating versus pooling equilibrium with multiple trade sizes. Here the game analyzed is much more complex, but the underlying intuition remains the same. If the market is in this separating equilibrium, block trades have no price effects because blocks are always used only by uninformed traders.

If the block size is not sufficient to result in a separating equilibrium, then the trader's strategy may involve a more complex mixed, or randomized, strategy. The equilibrium in this multiperiod model is quite sophisticated in that the pricing policy followed by the specialists and dealers must incorporate all possible trading strategies. Seppi demonstrates that there is a market parameterization in which the investor continues to trade blocks to rebalance, but now randomizes between blocks and round lots when he trades on information. This causes the price for blocks to be "worse," but since not all information-based trades involve blocks, this new block price still dominates trading sequences of orders for a rebalancing institution. The price for the block will be increasing (decreasing) in trade size, as the larger the trade the more dealer can lose on an information-based block.

The result that the institution does not randomize between blocks and round lots for rebalancing suggests that there is a natural role played by the block-trading mechanism in meeting traders' liquidity needs. Just as in the

---

9. This distinction is reminiscent of the traditional distinction between loans and securities. Specifically, a loan was defined as a contract negotiated between two specific parties, while a security involved an impersonal transaction between multiple parties. The advent of loan syndication and securitization has eroded that traditional contract form.

previous section liquidity enhancements favored uninformed traders, here the block-trading mechanism arises for the similar reason that it improves the ability of uninformed traders to trade large amounts. Whether this mechanism is the *optimal* way to provide such liquidity remains an unanswered question. In Seppi's analyses, block trading is clearly preferred by uninformed traders in some circumstances. There can be multiple equilibria in this model, however. These multiple equilibria limit characterizing the general role played by specific market intermediaries and similarly impede determining which is the 'best" mechanism for providing liquidity. The analysis does demonstrate, however, that assuming uninformed traders transact in large trade sizes need not be unrealistic; at least in this model, such an outcome is an equilibrium.

In Seppi's analysis, block trading does not occur simultaneously with specialist trading. The trader must choose to trade blocks before the specialist trading begins. Moreover, while the model demonstrates the role played by the two distinct trading mechanisms, a trader cannot opt to trade in both mechanisms. This may be accurate in block trading and, indeed, in many other markets, but it may also be that multiple trading venues exist simultaneously. In this case, a trader can both increase his scale of trading and arbitrage any differences in price behavior between the two settings. We consider this issue in the next section.

8.4   INFORMATION AND MULTIMARKET ACTIVITY

Our discussion has focused on the liquidity effects of trading the same security in multiple settings and via different trading mechanisms. The development of stock index futures introduces another possibility, that of trading both individual securities and a basket composed of those securities. This ability to trade a "derivative" security introduces a new, and potentially important, dimension to the notion of security market liquidity. With the scale of trading in index products often exceeding that of the underlying securities, index products are important components of many trading strategies. Of related importance is that information flows may differ in markets, leading to divergences in market prices and introducing the possibility of arbitrage between markets. This latter issue is particularly germane given the alleged role of index arbitrage in the 1987 market crash. If derivative markets affect security market liquidity, then it is important to determine how such effects arise and what they imply for price behavior.

The issue of market liquidity and index futures is addressed by Subrahmanyam [1991a]. His analysis employs a variant of the Kyle [1984] and Admati and Pfleiderer [1988] models to determine where traders choose to transact given the ability to trade both individual securities and a basket of securities. Because the model is one-period, the analysis is very similar to the multimarket liquidity analysis of Chowdhry and Nanda. One difference in the analyses is that private information need not be individual security-specific, raising the interesting issue of how different types of information affect market behavior.

In this one-period model, there are assumed to be N securities that trade at time 0 and liquidate at time 1. The value of any security i at time 1 is

$$S_i = \overline{S}_i + \beta_i \gamma + \varepsilon_i, \ i = 1, \ldots, N, \tag{8.33}$$

where γ is some systematic risk common to all securities, β_i is security i's sensitivity to the systematic risk, and ε_i is an idiosyncratic risk to security i. The $\varepsilon_i, \ i = i, \ldots, N$, and the γ are assumed to be independent, normally distributed random variables with mean zero. There is also a basket of securities that trades at time 0 and liquidates at time 1; its value at time 1 is

$$S_m = \sum_{i=1}^{N} w_i \overline{S}_i + \sum_{i=1}^{N} w_i \beta_i \gamma + \sum_{i=1}^{N} w_i \varepsilon_i, \tag{8.34}$$

where w_i is the weight of security i in the basket, and $\sum_{i=1}^{N} w_i = 1$.

As in Admati and Pfleiderer, there are three types of traders: informed traders, nondiscretionary liquidity traders, and discretionary liquidity traders. There are assumed to be k_i risk neutral informed traders, who observe the idiosyncratic element ε_i. Liquidity trade is exogenously determined, and liquidity traders are assumed to submit a random quantity z_i, where z_i is normally distributed with mean zero and is independent of γ and ε.

The equilibrium in the model is the same as in Kyle. Traders submit orders to the market maker, who observes the net order flow, denoted $\tilde{\phi}_i$. The market maker sets the market-clearing price equal to the conditional expected value of the asset given $\tilde{\phi}_i$. The market maker is conjectured to use the linear pricing rule

$$P_i = \overline{S}_i + \lambda_i \tilde{\phi}_i, \tag{8.35}$$

where λ_i has the standard definition of the sensitivity of prices to order flow.

Subrahmanyam shows that, for a trader j with private information about security i, the optimal order for security i is given by

$$x_{ji} = \frac{\varepsilon_i}{\left(k_i + 1\right)\lambda_i}, \tag{8.36}$$

and the equilibrium λ_i is then

$$\lambda_i = \frac{1}{(k_i + 1)} \sqrt{\frac{k_i \mathrm{var}\left(\varepsilon_i\right)}{\mathrm{var}\left(z_i\right)}}. \tag{8.37}$$

As was true in Admati and Pfleiderer, the optimal λ_i is decreasing in the number of informed traders, reflecting the effects of competition amongst informed traders in their orders as their numbers increase. Given this trading strategy for the informed traders and this pricing strategy for the market maker, uninformed traders in market i can expect to lose $\lambda_i \mathrm{var}(z_i)$.

Suppose now that there are p *discretionary* liquidity traders, who wish to trade all securities. They could do so by trading in each market $i = 1, \ldots,$ N, or they could simply trade the basket security, denoted M. Let the demand for security i by these traders be $w_i l$, where w_i is the optimal portfolio weight. The demand for the basket security is then simply l (since, by assumption, the demands perfectly replicate the composition of the basket). Suppose there are also *nondiscretionary* traders, who are assigned a particular stock (or the market basket) in which to trade. Let their demand in market i, $i = 1, \ldots, N$, be given by $y_i = r_i w_i$, where the r_i are mutually i.i.d. random variables with mean 0 and $\mathrm{var}(r_i) = \mathrm{var}(r)$. The total nondiscretionary trade in the basket security is denoted m, with *total liquidity trade* (both discretionary and nondiscretionary orders) in the basket denoted z_m.

These assumptions on the types and allocations of traders are clearly restrictive, but as discussed in Chapter 5, the nature of equilibrium in these models is sufficiently fragile to require a great deal of structure. Without at least some liquidity traders constrained to transact in every market, the familiar problem of trade collapsing to one market arises, and then discussion of the effects of trading in alternative markets becomes moot. Nonetheless, as is typical in these models, the presumed lack of flexibility of at least some market participants is crucial for the analysis to have any nontrivial solution.

The question of interest is, how does trading in the basket affect the liquidity of the individual securities? To address this, Subrahmanyam examines the informed traders' demands for the basket security, assuming a given level of liquidity trades in each security and that the market maker does not observe the order flow in the other markets. This restriction is needed to simplify the pricing problem of the market makers, since otherwise each market maker's pricing decision could not be made independently of order flows in other markets.[10]

Subrahmanyam shows that each informed trader submits an order to trade in the basket, x_{im}, given by

$$x_{im} = \frac{w_i \varepsilon_i}{\left(k_i + 1\right)\lambda_m},$$ (8.38)

where the equilibrium pricing rule λ_m is given by

$$\lambda_m = \sqrt{\frac{\sum w_i^2 \, \text{var}\left(\varepsilon_i\right)/K_i}{\text{var}\left(z_m\right)}}$$ (8.39)

and $K_i \equiv (k_i + 1)^2/k_i$.

Given this order and pricing strategy, where do the discretionary traders choose to transact? Since informed trading increases in the variance of the order flow, uninformed trading costs are minimized by trading in the lowest variance market. Moreover, adding discretionary order flow lowers the variance in a market so, *ceteris paribus*, all discretionary traders will select the same venue, either all trading in the basket or all transacting in the stocks. There are many factors affecting overall variance, however, and consequently the choice of trading venue need not be straightforward. A factor favoring trading in the basket is that the diversification of the portfolio of securities reduces the effects of private information. This lowers the basket security's variance, thereby improving its desirability to discretionary traders. One equilibrium, therefore, is that all discretionary traders transact in the basket. If, however, there is large nondiscretionary liquidity trade in the individual securities, then this greater liquidity may dominate the diversification effect, with the result that in equilibrium all discretionary traders transact in securities. Moreover, an equilibrium in which some discretionary traders transact in the basket while others trade individual securities also cannot be ruled out. Consequently, in this model, virtually any equilibrium can prevail.

Subrahmanyam argues that the more reasonable equilibria involve concentration, with either all discretionary traders transacting in the basket

---

10. This assumption also limits the market makers' ability to draw inferences on the underlying information, an ability particularly valuable to the market maker trading the basket security.

or in the individual securities. The reason is simply that, as was the case in Pagano's model, a mixed-market equilibrium is essentially a knife-edge result, and any small change in parameter values would lead to the dominance of trading either only in the basket or only in securities. If the diversification effect of the basket is large, then an equilibrium in which discretionary traders trade in the in the basket would be a likely outcome.

Of perhaps more interest is the equilibrium that prevails when informed traders know information relevant to all securities, and not just to individual securities. In particular, suppose there are now some traders who are informed of the systematic factor of security returns. These traders are assumed to see the same signal $\gamma + \tilde{v}$, where $\text{var}(\tilde{v}) = \kappa$. These factor-informed traders trade on the basis of this information in all securities, but the impact of this information on the basket depends upon how much the factor sensitivities differ among securities. Provided there are differences in factor sensitivities, the basket benefits from diversification of both the systematic and nonsystematic components, and thus it would be expected to be the trading venue chosen by discretionary traders.

For our focus in this chapter, what is of interest is how the introduction of the basket affects market liquidity. As we have seen in other applications, the movement of discretionary traders to the basket results in directly reducing the liquidity of the individual securities. If the number of informed traders is endogenous, then a secondary effect is to affect the numbers of factor-informed and security-specific informed traders. Subrahmanyam demonstrates that in general this change results in increasing the sensitivity of individual securities to systematic information and also increasing the informativeness of the basket securities price. From a liquidity perspective, the adverse selection component of the basket is lower than it is for the individual securities, and hence individual securities may have less liquidity (and greater risk of informed trading) than they would in the absence of the basket.

What is interesting in this analysis are the differences introduced by different types of information. In much of finance, the focus is on systematic factors, yet this is the first model (to my knowledge) to specifically address the differential effects of systematic and nonsystematic information in a microstructure setting. While this model specifically addresses the issue of trading in baskets of securities, the trading of derivatives such as options is clearly related. In options, the greater leverage available, as well as the ability to trade multiple contracts, introduces important dimensions to the analyses of both market efficiency and market liquidity.

One interesting parallel with the model developed here is that traders could potentially be informed of information affecting option values (such as volatility) that does not affect the stock value *per se*. If, however, volatility-based trading increases option liquidity, then traders informed of asset-specific information could also shift to options from stocks, affecting both price and market behavior. How derivative markets affect market liquidity is thus clearly an important issue for future research.[11]

If there are multiple trading venues, then the issue of arbitrage must also be considered. In Subrahmanyam's model, the information flows and the clienteles for the basket differ from the individual securities, and so it would seem that interesting divergences could arise in their trading prices. If those divergences lead to arbitrage, this should affect the informativeness and behavior of prices. In a Kyle-type model, it is not really possible to arbitrage the two markets as traders do not know the trading prices when they submit orders. The existence of price gaps between markets and their implications for market behavior has been considered in related work by Kumar and Seppi [1990].

Kumar and Seppi analyze a model of a security market and a futures market trading index futures on the securities. Information flows differ between markets, and there is a lag in observing the prices in the other market. This lag could arise from timing differences or frictions in transmitting information, but its assumed existence is important for the model. Information differences are introduced by assuming that floor traders in futures markets have information about the level of the index, while specialists have information about the value of the individual stocks in the index.

For simplicity, there are only two stocks in the securities market; the index is simply based on their total value. The specialist for each stock i observes a signal $\vartheta_{it} = x_i + e_{it}$, while the futures traders observe $\vartheta_{3t} = x_1 + x_2 + e_{3t}$. As is standard, all random variables in the model are assumed to be independent and identically normally distributed with zero mean. In this model, the specialists quote a price at which they will fill all orders at time 1. Similarly, futures brokers quote a similar price at which they are willing to go long and short at time t. Initially, the order flow is assumed to be non-information-based.

---

11. Indeed, another and perhaps even more important dimension of this area is the effects of asymmetric information on option pricing. Option-pricing models such as Black-Scholes [1973] assume that the option is a pure derivative of the stock, allowing them to examine how changes in the stock price determine the option price. What is not permitted is changes in the option price affecting the stock price. Yet, if information is asymmetric, and informed traders transact at least partially in option markets, then the unidirectional linkages in option-pricing models cannot be correct. These issues have been considered by Back [1993]. Models of option market microstructure have been developed by John, Koticha, and Subrahmanyam [1991], Biais and Hillion [1991], and Easley, O'Hara, and Srinivas [1993].

Specialists and futures traders are assumed to set risk neutral competitive prices. As has been the case in other multiperiod models, these price-setting agents are assumed to use Bayesian updating in calculating the conditional expected value for their respective securities. Their information sets include their own signal, the history of prices in their own market, and the history of prices in the other markets with a k-period lag. This lag dictates that market makers in the two markets do not have identical information, and this provides the basis for prices in the markets to differ.

The explicit calculation of trading prices is complex, but it will be the case that a gap can arise between the prices in the security market and that in the futures market. Kumar and Seppi show that the gap has some intriguing statistical properties. First, the gap is normally distributed. This follows from the normality assumptions made throughout the model, but it does allow tractable characterization of the price differences in the two markets. Of perhaps more interest is that the gap converges to zero as the number of time periods increases. This implies that long-run divergences from "efficiency" are not possible. More intriguing is that this convergence is not monotonic. Consequently, short-term price discrepancies can arise, leading to arbitrage possibilities in the two markets.

Kumar and Seppi show that the composition of the gap is influenced by the properties of the underlying markets. In particular, if stocks are "noisier" than futures and there is a positive covariance between stocks, then the variance of the gap in the first k periods is increasing in the stocks' covariance. Essentially, what occurs is that the correlation in the securities market means that information in the futures market on the aggregate value is more informative. With their signal more valuable, traders in futures markets act more aggressively, and futures markets respond more strongly to information than do the underlying stock markets. Interestingly, the gap may also exhibit mean reversion, a property that results from the convergence of information sets.

In this model, if an uninformed trader could acquire technology such that he learns prices in the two markets faster than do the other market participants, then he could clearly profit by arbitraging the markets. In this case, the market makers in both markets would always lose to traders who possess such technology and hence would need to be compensated for the risk of trading with arbitrageurs. Hence, while arbitrage would ultimately draw both markets together, its immediate impact is to increase the bid-ask spread in both markets, thus reducing the liquidity in each market.

These two analyses of market interaction suggest several important directions for future research. While it is interesting that arbitrage induces a spread, it would also be interesting to characterize more fully all the liquidity effects that arise. For example, Subrahmanyam suggests that price variability is not affected by the introduction of the second market, but it is not obvious that this variance result would hold in a more general model. Moreover, if arbitrage is allowed, would this affect the variance structure? One reason this is interesting is that it is often alleged that liquidity traders prefer less volatile markets, a proposition that has not been addressed in the microstructure literature.

What is also interesting to consider is the differential learning that divergent prices permit market participants. An emerging, and potentially very important, literature has considered the role of "price discovery" in securities markets. In this research (see, for example, Leach and Madhavan [1992, 1993]), agents may find prices in some market more informative about the true value of the asset than are prices in other markets. In the context addressed here, this relates to the question of whether futures prices can predict security prices, or conversely.[12] Subrahmanyam's paper suggests that if agents have symmetric access to both systematic and idiosyncratic information, then neither market can act as a dominant price discovery venue. Whether this holds in a more general framework is of obvious importance.

From a liquidity perspective, these analyses suggest that multimarket linkages introduce complex, and often conflicting, effects on market liquidity. While adding markets would seem to add liquidity, the resulting diversion or even fragmentation of orders can have the opposite effect. As we have seen in this chapter, in the simplest market setting, liquidity can be enhanced simply by adding more market participants willing to trade. As alternative trading venues and alternative contracts arise, however, the provision of liquidity becomes similarly more complex.

---

12. There is some evidence that price discovery occurs in option markets, and not just in equity markets. In particular, Easley, O'Hara, and Srinivas [1993] show that option volume leads equity prices, a result they interpret as evidence of informed trading in option markets.

9

Issues in Market Performance

What makes a market perform better? As our discussions in the previous chapters indicate, this is not an easy question to answer. Markets provide a wide range of services and functions, and factors that facilitate the performance of some functions may impede the delivery of others. Equally difficult to ascertain is what is meant by *better*. As we have seen throughout this book, there is often a tension between the gains and losses of various market participants. While informed traders gain at the expense of uninformed traders, those gains also provide the impetus for the incorporation of information into security prices. The efficiency of the market, which presumably benefits overall welfare, is thus purchased at the expense of at least some groups of traders. Determining the best, or even the better, market-clearing mechanism is thus problematic.

Despite this complexity, few issues are more topical, or of greater importance, than the issues of market performance and design. The proliferation of new exchanges and markets, as well as the development of sophisticated electronic-clearing mechanisms, provides the opportunity to create more desirable markets and trading venues. Yet, without guidance on the costs and benefits of various market features, the winners among these markets may be those possessing superior robustness, and not necessarily those markets which most improve social welfare.

In this final chapter, we turn our attention to some of the many issues in market performance. That our discussion will be incomplete is a certainty; there is little hope of discussing, or even listing, all of the many issues connected with market performance. Instead, our goal in this chapter is to show how the analytical approaches and techniques developed in previous chapters can be applied to evaluate a wide range of policy issues related to market design. These policy applications represent a growing dimension of microstructure research, and they reflect, in a sense, the payoff from our increased ability to model and analyze market behavior. As will be evident,

however, the complexity of many performance issues defies easy characterization, and the simplifications needed to ensure tractable analyses limit the
generality of the resulting policy recommendations.

We begin by analyzing how differences in information about the market
itself affect the performance of the market. How much information price-
setting agents, or even other traders, have on order flow, for example, can
influence both the behavior of prices and the allocation of trading gains and
losses. This general issue is known as market transparency, and its analysis
involves comparing how alternative market designs (for example, batch
systems or continuous auctions) affect the resulting equilibrium. A related,
but distinct, issue is the anonymity of trading. Here, the focus is on
information regarding the identity of traders submitting orders. This
anonymity issue is particularly relevant for such important regulatory issues
as front running and dual trading. From a market design perspective,
transparency and anonymity are also fundamental to understanding the
desirability of alternative market features. We conclude this chapter with a
brief discussion of the issues involved in the optimal design of trading
mechanisms.

9.1 MARKET TRANSPARENCY

Market transparency refers to the ability of market participants to observe
the information in the trading process. Despite the simplicity of this
definition, the issue of transparency is remarkably complex. One difficulty
relates to exactly what information is observable. For many purposes, a
market is said to be transparent if the order flow can be observed. Yet, order
flow information itself is complicated, including potentially the size and
direction of orders, their timing, and their form (for example, a limit or a
market order). Moreover, who submitted the order may also be useful
information in many settings. A second difficulty in defining transparency
is who can observe the information. Is the information observable only to
price-setting agents, to those on the floor of the exchange, to traders who
submit orders, or to potential traders at large?

These issues are important because the information available in the
trading process can affect the strategies of market participants. For example,
if only net order flow information is available to the market maker (as is
assumed in the Kyle [1985] model), then an informed trader will trade
more aggressively than if each individual order were observable. Similarly,
if the book of limit orders is known only to the market maker, then the
market maker, as well as the informed and uninformed traders, will behave
differently than if the book were common knowledge. With participants'

strategies dependent on the transparency of the market, it follows that the market equilibrium also depends on the degree of transparency.

How much transparency is optimal in a market is a question addressed by several researchers. Madhavan [1992] analyzes how transparency of orders affects market behavior and viability when order flow information is observable to both price setters and traders. Pagano and Roell [1993] consider how transparency of orders to price-setting agents affects the trading costs of informed and uninformed traders. Biais [1993] analyzes how the transparency of quotes affects spreads when there is no private information. Forster and George [1992] examine how information on traders' identities influences price behavior, and Roell [1990], Fishman and Longstaff [1992], and Pagano and Roell [1992] address the related issues of how dual trading and front running affect the gains and losses of traders in the market. While all of these papers deal with aspects of market transparency, these latter papers on trader identity are best viewed as analyzing the effects of anonymity on market behavior, and they are considered in more detail in the next section.

Perhaps the simplest transparency issue to consider is how the degree to which the size and direction of order flow is visible to market participants affects the viability of the market. This issue is addressed in Madhavan [1992].[1] Madhavan's analysis, which is also discussed in Chapter 7, views the crucial function of a trading mechanism as price discovery, or the process of finding market-clearing prices. This process depends at least partially on the transparency of the market, and so the question arises as to which market structure better aids the price discovery function.

To address this issue, Madhavan divides market-clearing mechanisms into quote-driven and order-driven. In the quote-driven market, dealers post prices before orders are submitted. Such a system is typified by NASDAQ, and it is, in effect, a continuous dealer market. In an order-driven market, orders are submitted and then trading prices determined. An order-driven system can be a continuous auction in which traders submit orders for immediate execution on the floor by a dealer (or against an existing limit order), or it can be structured as a call market or batch trading system in which orders accumulate and are cleared at periodic (prespecified) intervals. A difference between the various trading mechanisms is their degree of transparency, as traders in the quote-driven system (and in the continuous-auction order-driven system) essentially know more trade information than do traders in batch systems.

---

1. Madhavan [1991] also considers the issue of transparency by looking at the effects of knowing the volume of trade, an issue we do not consider here.

Madhavan examines how price setting occurs in the different market settings. The quote-driven market is essentially that analyzed by Glosten [1989], a model we discussed in Chapter 7. Madhavan analyzes the order-driven system in a rational expectations model similar to Kyle [1989] where traders form expectations of price and take account of other traders' strategies in forming their own trading strategies. Rather than analyze the mechanics of the model, we focus on the properties of the resulting equilibria in each market setting.

Madhavan shows that if the informational asymmetry in the market is not too great, then equilibrium will exist in the quote-driven system. In the equilibrium, security prices follow a Martingale and are semi-strong-form efficient, and market makers offer a schedule of prices for different trade sizes rather than quote a single trading price. If the information asymmetry is too large, however, it may not be possible to find such a price schedule, and as was also true in Glosten [1989], equilibrium may not exist.

Equilibrium in the order-driven system depends on the type of market. Madhavan shows that in general, the equilibrium in order-driven markets is more robust; if equilibrium exists in the quote-driven system, it will also exist in the order-driven system.[2] Of perhaps more importance, however, is that when equilibrium does not exist in the quote-driven or continuous-auction order-driven markets, it may still exist in a batch-trading system. This reflects the aggregation ability of batch markets, in that traders' information essentially becomes averaged over all trades, allowing market-clearing prices to work on average rather than for each individual trade.

This aggregation reduces the transparency of the market, and hence the viability of the batch market is purchased at the expense of market transparency. If the goal of a market-clearing mechanism is price discovery, then aggregation facilitates this when market conditions are adverse, but can limit this otherwise by limiting the information traders can draw from market prices. How this affects trader welfare is not apparent, as the batch market will exist when other markets will not, making overall comparisons misleading. Moreover, how the efficiency of the market is affected is also not apparent, as information gathering is now more expensive since the trading process reveals less information. What this analysis does show is that the design of the market affects the equilibrium outcome. Consequently, features of market design have real effects on both traders and the market.

---

2. With free entry of market makers, Madhavan shows the equilibrium in the continuous auction converges to that of the quote-driven system, so that in the limit both systems are the same. In this case there is no difference in robustness.

This allocative effect of market design is considered by Pagano and Roell [1993], who analyze how transparency affects the distribution of gains among traders. Their model examines how the ability of price-setting agents to observe order flow affects the expected transactions cost (or trading costs) of uninformed traders. Since the losses of uninformed traders provide the gains to informed traders, this analysis focuses on the distributional effects of market transparency. If, as is sometimes alleged, the goal of a trading system is to protect the uninformed (the Aunt Agathas of the market), then this allocative question must surely be considered.

While Madhavan focused on quote-driven and order-driven markets, Pagano and Roell divide markets into four general types: batch markets, dealer markets, continuous markets, and transparent markets. The batch market involves periodic clearing of aggregated orders, and the price setter in this market observes only the net order imbalance, not any individual trades. In the dealer market, the dealer sees only his own order flow, and prices thus depend only on the specific trade. The continuous market also allows observation of individual orders, but at any point in time the price-setting agents in the market know only the past orders in the market and not necessarily all current orders outstanding. Finally, in a transparent market orders are accumulated as in a batch setting, but market participants see every order when they clear at the common market price.

Such a transparent market is clearly an abstraction, as such an instantaneous clearing system in which both individual orders and their aggregation are visible does not actually exist in current markets. It does provide a basis for comparison, however, in that continuous markets are intermediate in degree of transparency (every order visible) and batch markets are the least transparent (only the net orders visible). Dealer markets have less transparency than continuous markets, but may have more or less transparency than batch markets depending upon the particular market structure.

Given these market settings, Pagano and Roell examine how transparency affects the losses of the uninformed traders. This issue is complex, as the order strategies of market participants may vary with the different market structures. They first consider the simplest case, in which an informed trader's strategy is assumed to be the same in both the dealer market and the transparent market, and the informed trader is permitted to submit only a single order, x. This essentially restricts the analysis to a single-period setting and hence ignores any dynamic effects of transparency on price adjustment and thus efficiency.

Pagano and Roell analyze a Kyle-based framework with one informed trader and many uninformed traders. The informed trader is assumed to know the final value of the security v, which is drawn from a distribution

$G(v)$, and G is assumed symmetric about the mean value $\bar{v}$. The m uninformed traders submit orders u_1, u_2, . . ., u_m, which are drawn independently from a distribution $F(u)$, and F is assumed symmetric around 0.

Given these assumptions, Pagano and Roell show that the expected trading costs of uninformed traders in the transparent market are always less than or equal to their expected trading cost in the dealer market. This occurs because the ability of the single informed trader to "hide" differs in the two market settings, and in general the greater trade information available in the transparent market reduces the informed trader's profit. In the case where the distributions of informed and uninformed trades are the same, this increased revelation of the informed trade does not occur, because the trades of informed and uninformed are indistinguishable. This results in the expected uninformed trading costs in the two markets being the same. More generally, however, the trade information available in the transparent market allows greater exposure of informed traders, and this results in the uninformed traders facing smaller expected losses.

Pagano and Roell argue that the expected trading costs in the continuous market will lie between those of the dealer and transparent markets. This implies that, in general, uninformed traders do at least as well trading in a continuous market as in a dealer market, and they can do even better trading in a transparent market. Interestingly, this improvement in uninformed trading costs need not arise if the transparent system is compared with a batch market. While it remains true that some uninformed traders will do better in the transparent setting, it is also the case that some will do worse, with the deciding factor being the trade size. Since the batch system aggregates trades, the resulting price can improve the expected trading costs of some traders and worsen those of others.

These results suggest that typically uninformed traders are better off in more transparent markets. These comparisons, however, are premised on the restrictive assumptions that the informed trader's (one-trade) strategy is the same in every market and that uninformed traders act purely as noise traders and so also trade the same in every setting. Since these conditions are unlikely to reflect optimal behavior, the robustness of this transparency conclusion is problematic.

To address this issue, Pagano and Roell extend the analysis to allow the informed trader's strategy to incorporate the type of market in which he is trading. Not surprisingly, this greatly complicates the link between transparency and expected trading costs. What becomes crucial now are the assumptions made on the distribution of uninformed trades. For the simple case where all noise traders submit the same size order, the result that expected trading costs are lower in the transparent setting than in the dealer market continues to hold. If, however, noise traders can submit different-sized orders, then this need not be the case. If, as in the Kyle model, the uninformed trades (and the informed trader's signal) are normally distributed, then transparency will have no effect on expected trading costs. This occurs because with normality the informed trader is completely able to hide in the distribution, making the informed trades indistinguishable from uninformed traders in either the dealer or transparent market setting. In a Kyle framework, therefore, transparency is irrelevant for traders' expected losses.

If the uninformed trades are not normally distributed, however, then transparency can raise the expected trading cost for some trade sizes and lower it for others. This occurs because of the equilibrium effects introduced by differing trade sizes. In particular, as we discussed in Chapter 3, if the informed trader is equally likely to trade large or small quantities (the pooling equilibrium), then the price for every trade must reflect at least some risk of informed trading. Conversely, if the informed trader only transacted large amounts (the separating equilibrium), then only large trade prices need reflect this risk, and small trade prices can be set at expected values.

Pagano and Roell show that in some market settings the optimal informeds' trade strategy may result in a separating equilibrium while in others it may result in a pooling equilibrium. Consequently, small uninformed traders can face lower trading costs in less transparent markets if those markets are in a separating equilibrium. Of course, given this separating equilibrium, large uninformed traders would be worse off, and so it is not immediately apparent how transparency affects aggregate trading costs. Pagano and Roell argue, however, that expected trading costs *averaged* over all trade quantities will be lower in more transparent markets.

The Pagano and Roell analysis shows that under a wide range of conditions, uninformed traders do better in more transparent markets. If a social planner wished to reduce expected trading costs, therefore, this would dictate designing markets with the maximum amount of transparency. This simple prescription, however, may not be advisable. One reason lies in the objective of the social planner. While reducing expected uninformed trading losses is certainly a potentially desirable objective, it can be most easily accomplished by having no trading occur at all. Moreover, the efficiency effects of market design may also be important, dictating a complexity beyond that considered here. We consider this design issue further in Section 3.

A second, and more immediate consideration, is that dynamic issues may subvert the beneficial effects of transparency. To understand why, recall our earlier discussions of liquidity and the free option problem. In Chapter 8 we saw that in general greater liquidity improved the terms of trade for the uninformed in much the same way that greater transparency does here. This liquidity, however, was assumed to arise at a point in time, so that uninformed traders benefitted by trading together. In transparent systems, however, each trade may be observable, and as we saw in Chapter 7, the free option that arises from exposing one's trading intentions may reduce an uninformed trader's welfare.

This raises the issue of whether uninformed traders would actually choose to trade in a transparent market.[3] For large orders (block trades), at least, this does not appear to be the case, as evidenced by the development of the upstairs trading mechanism in which trades can be hidden from the market until assembled. And in computerized trading systems, forcing traders to display their actual desired trade quantity rather than merely give an indication of their interest seems to greatly reduce the success of the mechanism. Indeed, the remarkable lack of success of the NYSE's crossing network for individual securities may reflect, in part, this concern. We consider this trader anonymity issue further in the next section. These concerns, however, suggest that the optimality of order flow transparency in markets may depend on the strategic decisions of uninformed traders, an issue not yet resolved in the microstructure literature.

Our discussion thus far has focused on the availability of pre-trade information. A further issue in the transparency debate is post-trade information. Post-trade information refers to the observability of a trade's price and quantity. In many markets, this information is available to all traders for small trades.[4] The post-trade treatment of large trades or blocks, however, can differ. For example, the New York Stock Exchange instantaneously reports a large trade's price and quantity, but on the London Stock Exchange such information may not be available for as long as seven days. This issue of last-trade reporting is a subject of extensive policy debate in Britain.

The rationale given for delaying last-trade reporting for large trades is to allow market makers to unwind their inventory positions at minimal cost.

---

3. Biais [1993] considers the price effects of transparency in a model with only uninformed traders. His analysis does not explicitly consider welfare effects, but instead considers how the ability to observe price setters' quotes in centralized markets results in different prices than in fragmented markets where such quotes are not observable. This analysis provides the intriguing result that spreads are equal in the two market settings due to an irrelevance result akin to that found in auction theory. Whether this result holds in a model with asymmetric information is clearly an important research question.

4. The Tokyo Stock Exchange treats post-trade information as proprietary, and as such makes it available only to members of the Exchange. In the US, the congressionally mandated Intermarket Trading System requires post-trade information for all exchanges, and hence it cannot be retained only for member use.

Historically, small trader participation on the London Stock Exchange has been low, and institutional trades, which are typically large, dominate trading. As discussed in the previous chapter, one mechanism for clearing large orders is to prearrange trades via the use of a block trader. While this is common in the New York markets, it is less so in London, and market makers instead tend to take the other side of blocks on their own account. Delaying trade publication facilitates the unwinding of these positions, but does so by restricting the market's access to trade information.

Proponents of delayed reporting argue that it lowers the cost of trading by reducing the risks a market maker faces, and thereby it improves the price the market maker is willing to offer to the trader. Offsetting this benefit, however, are several negative effects. For instance, until the trade is revealed, the market maker is essentially an information monopolist, enjoying exclusive access to trade information. As we have seen, if information is asymmetric, large trades tend to be more informative owing to their preferred use by informed traders. In this case, knowing the trade allows the market maker to update his beliefs before others can, and this provides an advantage in pricing future trades in the stock. This advantage may be at the expense of competing market makers, or it may come at the expense of other traders, who, with more complete information, might make different trading decisions.[5]

Delaying the reporting of trade information also necessarily results in stale prices, and this erodes the process of price discovery in a market. From a broader perspective, stale prices impose additional costs through their effect on the behavior of related markets such as derivatives. Without current stock prices, option prices are severely flawed, as are the prices of stock index futures. The dramatically lower volume of equity option trading in London as compared to US markets may reflect this difference in price informativeness.

The case for post-trade transparency thus involves determining who should benefit from trade information. Delays in reporting favor the market maker and potentially the large traders; transparency favors the other market participants and the operation of markets as a whole. If price discovery and efficiency are policy goals, then post-trade transparency would seem advisable, even though it comes at a cost to some market participants.

The debate over post-trade reporting highlights the benefits of knowing information related to the trading process. Another area where such

---

5. Gemmill [1993] provides interesting empirical evidence that the delay in publishing trade information has redistributed profits toward market makers and those involved in the trades.

information arises is with respect to the origin of orders. In the next section, we analyze how trader anonymity affects the behavior of prices and markets.

9.2 TRADER ANONYMITY

In most microstructure analyses, orders arrive from unspecified (and unidentifiable) traders, and prices are set by market makers who observe only the order flow. Such a framework certainly describes (or at least approximates) many trading venues, but it is also true that greater information on traders' identities or trading intentions is often known. Market makers may know something about future order flow based on information in the book. Futures traders may know the direction of trade particular traders need to enter in the near term. Brokers may know not only who submitted an order, but their future trading intentions as well. Each of these settings corresponds to at least a partial breakdown of the assumption of trader anonymity.

How the anonymity of trading affects market behavior is an important issue. From a regulatory perspective, issues such as dual trading and front running directly arise from the lack of anonymity. And as we saw in Chapter 7, allowing trading practices such as sunshine trading can result in very different equilibrium outcomes than occur if orders are anonymous. The proliferation of electronic trading systems also raises questions as to whether trading mechanisms work "better" with traders' identities revealed or concealed.

Issues relating to trader anonymity have been addressed by several authors. Forster and George [1992] and Lindsay [1990] analyze how information on the direction and magnitude of future trades affects trading costs and price informativeness. Roell [1990] and Fishman and Longstaff [1992] examine the effects of dual trading, while Pagano and Roell [1992] consider the impact of front running on market behavior. Each of these analyses demonstrates how knowledge of traders' identities or motivations can affect the market equilibrium.

Perhaps the most direct analysis of anonymity is pursued by Forster and George. They argue that the fiction of anonymous execution employed in much of the microstructure literature is unlikely to hold. Instead, due to the central position played by the specialist, it is likely that the market maker has information on the future direction or magnitude of trade. In addition, a subset of other traders, for example, brokers, may also have access to information on future trades. This information is assumed related to the uninformed, or liquidity trade, as information on future informed trading would surely affect the asset's conditional expected value and so would already be incorporated into prices.

In the framework of the Kyle [1985] model, Forster and George analyze the equilibrium outcome when a subset of traders (and possibly the market maker) has greater information on uninformed trade. Recall that in the standard Kyle framework, the amount of liquidity trade in any period is assumed drawn from a normal distribution given by $N(0, \sigma_\mu^2)$. If the distribution of liquidity trade did not have this form, however, then knowledge of particular parameters of the distribution could be useful information. Forster and George use this intuition to analyze how information on the direction and magnitude of liquidity trade each affect the market equilibrium.

Forster and George incorporate information on the direction of trade by assuming that the unconditional distribution of the net liquidity order, $\tilde{x}$, is given by

$$N\left(\mu_H, \sigma + \mu_H^2\right) \text{ with probability } 1/2, \text{ and}$$
$$N\left(\mu_L, \sigma + \mu_L^2\right) \text{ with probability } 1/2. \tag{9.1}$$

If trading is not anonymous, then a subset of agents is assumed to know the outcome μ_H^2 or μ_L^2 before trading begins. This allows greater ability to discern the direction of the uninformed orders and hence might be expected to affect equilibrium prices.

Similarly, information on the magnitude of liquidity trade is captured by assuming the unconditional distribution of the net liquidity order is given by

$$N\left(0, \sigma_H\right) \text{ with probability } 1/2, \text{ and}$$
$$N\left(0, \sigma_L\right) \text{ with probability } 1/2. \tag{9.2}$$

Again, if trading is not anonymous, then a subset of traders is assumed to know the outcome σ_L, σ_H. Note that (9.1) and (9.2) correspond to two different specifications. Hence, in the context of a Kyle model, the analysis is solved under various specifications of the uninformed order distribution and under various assumptions regarding who has access to that information.

In general, the analysis shows that revealing the *direction* of liquidity trade in advance decreases the expected trading costs of liquidity traders, does not affect the informativeness of prices, and reduces the incentives for information gathering for informed agents. This first conclusion is similar to that of Admati and Pfleiderer [1991] and Pagano and Roell [1993], and it suggests that in general greater transparency of orders benefits uninformed traders. Revealing the *magnitude* of trade decreases expected uninformed trading costs only if there is sufficient competition amongst informed traders, increases the sensitivity of prices to order flow, and does not affect the informativeness of prices. These results suggest that information on magnitude of trade is qualitatively different than information on direction, affecting the depth of the market as well as the gains and losses amongst traders. Since the depth of the market relates to its liquidity, the anonymity of trading can also influence the extent to which markets provide liquidity.

These results suggest that access to trade information can introduce real effects into the behavior of markets. From a regulatory perspective, this issue of access to trade information underlies the debate over dual capacity trading. Dual-capacity trading (or simply dual trading) refers to the practice of allowing brokers both to submit customer orders and to trade as dealers for their own account. Such a framework characterizes a number of trading venues including that of London equity markets and the Chicago futures markets. Because brokers potentially gain relevant information from their customers' orders, the ability to exploit such information for gain has prompted regulatory proposals to restrict such dual trading. At issue is how the ability to dual trade affects the behavior of prices and the welfare of customers.

These issues are addressed in theoretical research by Roell [1990] and Fishman and Longstaff [1992], as well as in empirical studies by Smith and Whaley [1991] and Chang and Locke [1992]. The Roell analysis employs a variant of the Kyle [1989] model to investigate the trading behavior of a dual-capacity broker who has better information about uninformed trading than does the market maker. This superior information allows the trader to, in effect, step in front of the market maker and provide liquidity directly to uninformed traders. The analysis demonstrates that this results in dual trading improving (i.e., reducing) the transaction costs normally faced by uninformed traders but increasing the costs faced by informed traders.

The model involves a one-period Kyle [1989] batch model with a single risk neutral informed trader, a risk neutral and competitive market maker, many uninformed traders, and N broker/dealers. These brokers are assumed able to identify particular uninformed liquidity trades, but have no information on others. This ability arises because brokers know the trading motivations of their specific customers and, hence, can discern information about the uninformed order flow. In particular, the aggregate uninformed demand, denoted u, is assumed to be distributed as $N(0, \sigma_\mu^2)$. Each of the N brokers can identify part of the uninformed demand, u_i, with variance σ_i^2, for $i = 1, \ldots, N$. Letting σ_0^2 denote the portion of uninformed demand unknown to any broker, it follows that $\sigma_u^2 = \sigma_o^2 + \sigma_1^2 + \cdots + \sigma_N^2$.

The brokers are assumed to submit net demand schedules of the form $Z_i(u, p)$, for $i = 1, \ldots, N$, where p denotes the price of the asset. This is a net demand because the brokers may choose to fill some orders themselves, thereby reducing the amount submitted to the market maker. There is one risk neutral informed trader, who knows the true asset value v. The other market participants (the uninformed traders, the brokers, and the market maker) share a common prior on v, which is distributed as $N(v_0, V)$. As in the Kyle model, the informed trader submits an order quantity, denoted $X(v, p)$. The market maker sees the aggregate net order flow, denoted y, where

$$y = \sum_{i=1}^{N} Z_i\left(u_i, p\right) + X\left(v, p\right) + \sum_{i=0}^{N} u_i. \tag{9.3}$$

Equilibrium in this model consists of strategies $Z_i(u_i, p)$ and $X(v, p)$ such that each agent maximizes profit, realizing his effect on p, and a price function satisfying the conditional expectation constraint resulting from competitive market makers. As this is a variant of the Kyle model, it should not be surprising that this equilibrium has the simple linear structure found in earlier applications. In particular, Roell demonstrates that the unique linear equilibrium is

$$P\left(y\right) = v_o + \lambda Y, \tag{9.4}$$

$$X\left(v, p\right) = \beta\left(v - p\right), \tag{9.5}$$

$$Z_i\left(u_i, p\right) = -\delta u_i - \gamma\left(p - v_o\right) \tag{9.6}$$

where δ is the unique real root of the equation

$$\left(1 - \delta\right)^3\left(2N - 1\right)\sigma^2 - \left(1 - \delta\right)^2\left(N - 1\right)\sigma^2 + 2\left(1 - \delta\right)\sigma_0^2 - \sigma_0^2 = 0, \tag{9.7}$$

and

$$\beta = \sqrt{\frac{\sigma_0^2 + N\left(1 - \delta\right)^2\sigma^2}{V}}, \tag{9.8}$$

$$\gamma = \frac{1 - 2\delta}{1 - \delta} \beta \,, \tag{9.9}$$

$$\lambda = \frac{1}{\beta} \frac{1 - \delta}{1 - \delta - N\left(1 - 2\delta\right)} \,. \tag{9.10}$$

The actual mechanics of finding the equilibrium solution are the same as in Kyle. What is important to note about the solution to this model is the sign and magnitude of the δ term, the brokers' response to the known order flow component. Roell shows that the solution of the real root requires that δ lie in the interval $[1/2, N/(2N - 1)]$. Hence, as N goes to infinity, δ goes to 1/2. Moreover, since in the broker's strategy δ enters negatively, this means that the broker essentially fills 1/2 of the uninformeds' order from the brokers' inventory. This behavior corresponds to the classic behavior of a monopolist: the broker trades only to the point of taking half of the "rents" and not to the point of driving the price to equal marginal cost. This equilibrium also reflects the notion that in markets the specialist need not be the only provider of liquidity. Here, as in actual markets, brokers may compete with the market maker in taking the order flow.

This equilibrium with dual trading can be contrasted with the equilibrium that arises with dual trading prohibited. Roell shows that such an equilibrium is essentially just that found in Kyle [1989]. In this case, $\delta = \gamma = 0$, and the equilibrium parameters of interest are

$$\beta^* = \sqrt{\frac{\sigma_0^2 + N\sigma^2}{V}} \tag{9.11}$$

and

$$\lambda^* = \frac{1}{\beta^*} = \sqrt{\frac{V}{\sigma_0^2 + N\sigma^2}} \,. \tag{9.12}$$

A comparison of the two equilibria reveals the interesting property that the insider trades more vigorously in the absence of dual trading. In particular, the β variable is greater without dual trading, reflecting that with no dual traders preempting order flow, all uninformed orders now go to the market. This provides more noise to hide the trade of the informed trader, and hence, he trades more aggressively.

In this model, therefore, dual-capacity trading removes uninformed order flow from the market and thereby changes the informativeness of the remaining order flow. This line of reasoning suggests that an important feature of a trading structure may be its ability to segment order flows into different streams. As these analyses demonstrate, this can affect not only the market maker's price-setting problem, but the stochastic process of prices as well.

Roell investigates these price effects by comparing the prices faced by various types of traders. She shows that with dual trading the unidentified uninformed traders are worse off, as their trading prices reflect the increased informativeness of the market order flow. For the same reason, the informed traders are also made worse off with dual trading. Conversely, the identified uniformed traders are better off because they receive the benefits of trading with the dual trader.

Perhaps more intriguing, Roell shows that dual traders make positive expected profits and that these profits are smaller than the decrease in informed traders' profits. Hence, on balance, transactions costs (as measured by the losses of the uninformed) fall with the inclusion of dual-capacity brokers in the market. In this one-period model, therefore, dual trading serves to reduce the asymmetric information costs borne by uninformed traders.

One implication of these results is that uninformed traders benefit from being known as uninformed. Indeed, to the extent that more than one broker knows the status of an individual trader, these benefits accrue even more. This provides an incentive for uninformed traders to preannounce their trades, or engage in "sunshine trading" similar to that analyzed in Admati and Pfleiderer [1991]. Roell also shows that in this model trading costs are minimized when all brokers know the same information, thereby rendering the unidentified order flow even more informative. From a policy perspective, this suggests that requiring brokers to announce their order flow would improve the performance of the market (in the sense of minimizing transaction costs).[6] Since this also reduces brokers' profits, however, it is not likely to be voluntarily adopted. Moreover, if the number of brokers is endogenously determined (depending in part on the profits available in the market), then this improvement might be vitiated by a fall in overall liquidity provision.

An alternative view of dual trading is espoused by Fishman and Longstaff [1992]. In their model, dual-capacity brokers do not provide liquidity but

---

6. This also assumes that informed traders are not able to mimic the trades of the uninformed, thereby leaving the overall order flow noninformative.

instead attempt to mimic the trades they believe come from informed traders. Thus, the advantage dual traders have in this market is superior information about the trades of informed traders, rather than the information on uninformed trades analyzed by Roell. Fishman and Longstaff consider a sequential trade model in which brokers receive orders from traders, who can be either informed (with probability q) or uninformed (with probability $1 - q$).

Traders submit their order to a broker, and the model assumes that the broker has only two customers, denoted A and B. An unusual (and restrictive) feature of this model is that the broker is also restricted from submitting more than two orders to the market. This dictates that if both the broker's customers submit orders, then the broker cannot trade. If only one customer wishes to trade, however, then the broker can submit the second order. In this one-period model, a customer can buy one unit of the asset, sell one unit, or not trade at all. If a trader is uninformed, she is assumed to buy with probability $h_i/2$, sell with probability $h_i/2$, and not trade with probability $1 - h_i$, where i denotes either trader A or B.

The market maker does not know the origin of orders (i.e., whether they are from customers or the broker), and it is this anonymity that allows brokers to profit on their information. In particular, the market maker knows the average probability that an uninformed trader will transact, denoted $\bar{h}$, but the broker knows the specific values h_A and h_B. This means that the market maker attaches probability $q/[q + \bar{h}(1 + q)]$ to any trade being informed, while the broker attaches $q/[q + h_i(1 + q)]$.

The broker's optimal trading strategy is then to not trade if neither A nor B trades, and, if either A or B trades, to submit the same trade if h_i is low enough. This condition corresponds to trading if the probability that the trade is information-based is high enough. Since the market maker knows only the average $\bar{h}$, this strategy allows the broker to trade when it is most likely to be profitable, and not to trade otherwise. Recall that if both A and B trade, the broker is precluded from trading.

In this model, it follows that banning dual trading improves prices because it reduces the probability that the second trade is related to information.[7] This allows the market maker to set "better" prices for the second trade and hence would reduce the expected trading costs the

---

7. This does not mean, however, that traders are necessarily better off, because this affects the commissions traders pay. In particular, Fishman and Longstaff assume that brokers face exogenous fixed costs and variable costs and that competition forces these to be passed on to customers. They show that the increased profits arising from dual trading allow these commission to be reduced, with the result that traders are actually better off with dual trading. This result depends heavily on the model's restrictive structure, and it is not clear that it would hold in a more general setting.

uninformed trader pays to the market maker. This result relies heavily, however, on the assumption of fixed trading behavior by the informed trader, as well as by the uninformed. If the optimal strategy of informed or uninformed differed depending upon whether dual trading is allowed, then the effects of dual trading could be very different.

Fishman and Longstaff also consider what comes to pass if the broker is permitted to trade before, rather than after, a customer order. Such a practice is generally known as front running. In this case, the critical value of h_i inducing the broker to trade rises, meaning that the broker is more likely to submit an order. This occurs because the broker faces better prices trading first and hence, can afford to trade more aggressively. Front running is generally prohibited, as the broker essentially free-rides on the trader's order information.

Pagano and Roell [1992] also consider the effects of front running in a model in which dual traders do not know customers' trading motivations but do know the size of their submitted orders prior to execution. In this model, dual-trading brokers can benefit from knowing customer order flow because they can exploit the information implicit in trading imbalances. Since informed traders will all be on one side of the market, a trade imbalance may signal future movements in stock prices, and front running allows dual traders to profit on this information. This notion of information in the order imbalance captures an important, and believable, aspect of the value of order information: Unlike trader motivations, trade imbalances are clearly observable to brokers.

An interesting finding in this research is that broker front running does not always negatively affect customer orders. Pagano and Roell use a variant of the Kyle model to show that while front running hurts noise traders in general, provided it is known to occur in the market, it does not necessarily affect the welfare of the brokers' customers. Of perhaps more importance is their result that traders in general would be better off if there were no front running. One might expect that a broker who promises not to trade on his own account could "out compete" the dual trader and thus achieve a competitive outcome without dual trading. Since, however, the profits of dual traders come from both their clients and the market as a whole, the brokers' gains exceed their clients' losses. Consequently, Pagano and Roell argue that a "no dual trading" outcome is unlikely to arise.

One way to characterize the research on dual capacity trading and front running is that allowing such trading behavior changes the underlying informativeness of the order flow. Indeed, this change in informativeness is fundamental to the larger issues of transparency and anonymity. As we have seen, changes in market structures and trading rules affect prices and trading profits because they affect the speed and ability of the market maker to discover private information. Given this, the question of what is the best trading mechanism naturally arises. We consider this issue in the next section.

9.3 HOW TO DESIGN A MARKET?

Perhaps the most striking development in asset markets over the past decade has been the proliferation of new markets. From the electronic networks of Globex and the Arizona Stock Exchange to the new exchanges now found in virtually every major European and Asian city, the growth of trading venues has been extensive. With this growth has come an array of market-clearing arrangements and a plethora of choices for the trading of assets. The long-envisioned global market for assets has virtually come to pass.

The economics of competition dictates, however, that not all these markets will survive. And the question of which market designs will, or even should, prevail is rarely asked, let alone resolved. Such a failing is perhaps not surprising given the complexity of the overall issue. Its omission may be costly, however, both in the losses suffered by traders in markets that ultimately fail, and in the costs borne by the economy at large from markets that operate suboptimally.

In this final section, we consider aspects of this market design issue. Our focus is on two simple issues: what should be the goal of market design, and how do the properties of markets contribute to these goals? Needless to say, there is little consensus on the answers to these question, but presumably the research in market microstructure provides some guidance for addressing these issues.

The goals of a market depend, of course, on whose perspective is considered. For an exchange or automated clearing system, the underlying goal may be as straightforward as the maximization of trading commissions. From a trader's perspective, the ideal market may be one in which orders are accommodated with the least effect on price, or one that has the lowest overall trading cost. For a regulator, the best market may be the one with the greatest stability. For society as a whole, however, it is clear that while each of these goals may be important, none captures all the ways in which markets affect welfare in the economy.

The notion of the "public interest" underlies much of the current regulation of existing markets. Domowitz [1990], in an interesting paper on the welfare effects of electronic clearing systems, notes that the Commodity Exchange Act of 1974 defines a market as meeting the public interest if it satisfies three requirements: reliable price discovery, broad-based price dissemination, and effective hedging against price risks. While clearly limited, this definition does provide a starting point for evaluating market designs.

What market features contribute to reliable price discovery? As our discussions have highlighted, this depends upon what is meant by the price. The simplest argument is that at any given time the price is simply that which clears the market. The best market, therefore, is the one in which a market-clearing price can always be found. From a reliability standpoint, this argues for a monopolistic system. Yet, as we have discussed, this reliability is purchased at the cost of all consumer surplus going to the market maker. Moreover, the trading price the market maker sets need have little relation to the underlying true asset value. Such distortions of the price suggest that the simple view of price discovery is not sufficient to capture the complexity of the price discovery process.

Abstracting from the rents a monopolist extracts, one feature that surely contributes to an ability to find a market price is simply scale. The aggregation of orders in a centralized market provides at least the potential for a market-clearing price to arise. And this argues against allowing the segmentation of trade into multiple venues. Here again, however, the issue of what price is desired is problematic. As we have seen, in the presence of asymmetric information, the market-clearing price must reflect the pooled risk of private information. Yet all trades need not carry the same risk, and thus aggregation imposes costs on some traders at the expense of others. The solution to this, of course, is to segment trading. And so we are back to the conundrum of which is better: a single setting providing a single market-clearing price, or multiple settings provide different market prices for different quantities?

From a welfare perspective, it may be that the latter prevails. Enforcing a single trading venue in a global market is a task worthy of King Canute, and its pursuit undoubtedly detracts from the ability of the market to meet all traders' needs. This suggests, for example, that the rules barring prearranged block trades in futures markets may impose needlessly high costs on traders. But it is also true that extensive fragmentation of markets cannot be optimal. The consequent lack of liquidity cannot foster price discovery, nor can it provide traders with the effective hedging of price risks.

The goal of broad-based price dissemination is more problematic. This second component of the public interest presumably is intended to make markets more transparent. And certainly, on some level, this is an important accomplishment. Yet there are several problems consequent to this. One difficulty is evidenced by the growth of third market traders who "free ride" off of the price discovery process elsewhere. To the extent that the dissemination of information allows others to capture rents, this undermines the goal of price discovery. Moreover, if price information is extended to include order information, then the greater availability of market information is not obviously better. As we have discussed, difficulties such as the free option problem and the strategic decisions of informed traders can inhibit the viability of transparent markets. It will, however, generally be true that the transparency of prices allows traders better ability to extract information from the market price, a process that surely abets the goal of equilibrium price discovery.

The third property of the public interest, the effective hedging of price risks, reflects the general role of markets in providing insurance to liquidity traders. This aim is implicit in the goal of minimizing expected trading costs for uninformed traders. There are several market features that foster this, including greater liquidity, the prohibition of dual trading and front running, and the reduction of anonymity in the market. Fundamental to attaining this goal, however, is the liquidity of the market. The greater this liquidity, the smaller will be the price effects that accompany orders, and thus the greater the ability of uninformed traders to hedge their consumption risk.

Underlying each of these three properties, however, is another, perhaps greater, function of the market that is not recognized in the working definition given above. This is the role of market efficiency. How well and how quickly a market aggregates and impounds information into the price must surely be a fundamental goal of market design. Yet its exclusion from the definition of public interest may not be an oversight. As we have discussed throughout this book, market efficiency is not an easy concept. While in principle the attainment of full-information prices is not contentious, its actual achievement is likely to be. And, indeed, the very process of doing so may abrogate some of the very goals espoused above for market design.

One difficulty is that the notion of dynamic efficiency, or the speed with which prices reflect full information, is not well defined. Is a market better or more efficient if prices reach the full-information level faster? The current usage of efficiency generally concentrates on prices in a trading mechanism reflecting full-information values eventually. At any point prior to that, however, prices are generally deemed at least semi-strong efficient if they reflect all publicly available information. Yet this latter requirement is not a stringent constraint. Two trading systems may both satisfy this condition, yet show very great differences in the speed with which prices move toward full-information levels.

If the speed of information incorporation is deemed important, then factors that facilitate this may lead to market behaviors that are not so obviously desirable. For example, markets that adjust rapidly to information will surely exhibit large price volatility. Certainly, much discussion has focused on market volatility, with most regulatory proposals attempting to *decrease* volatility. But is this truly optimal? One rationale given is that volatility inhibits the hedging ability (or at least the participation) of uninformed traders. Yet it is precisely because new information changes the value of assets in the economy that traders need to hedge.

Moreover, a second difficulty is that the speed of adjustment of prices depends on the extent of informed trading, with greater informed trading leading to the faster incorporation of information. The scale of information gathering and informed trading, however, surely depends on the returns to such activities, and these, in turn, translate into losses for uninformed traders. Thus, the goals of minimizing uninformed trading costs and increased price efficiency conflict.

One way to reconcile this conundrum is to consider how the efficiency of the market affects society in the long run. For a specific level of market efficiency, one can view the three goals discussed above as optimally allocating a given amount of surplus amongst various market players. Thus, society might prefer to give uninformed traders more rents and informed traders less, *ceteris paribus*. Or society might prefer less to more volatile markets, *ceteris paribus*. Once, however, the level of market efficiency is not fixed (and, since it depends on the returns to the informed traders, it really cannot be), then the total amount of surplus is also part of the equation. In effect, the question becomes, does greater efficiency increase the overall gain to be shared?

This link between the efficiency of the market and the overall gain to society is a crucial direction for future microstructure research. It would seem that market efficiency benefits society directly by reducing the cost of capital for firms. If market prices reflect true asset values more quickly and accurately, then presumably the allocation of capital can also better reflect its best uses. The calculus for achieving an optimal amount of market efficiency, however, is not clear, depending as we have seen on the critical balance between the losses to the uninformed and their participation in markets. And the general equilibrium linkage of markets to overall economic behavior is not yet well established in the microstructure literature. The issue of the optimal design of markets thus remains an open question for microstructure researchers.

References

Admati, A., and P. Pfleiderer, 1988, A Theory of Intraday Patterns: Volume and Price Variability, Review of Financial Studies 1, Spring, 3–40.

Admati, A., and P. Pfleiderer, 1989, Divide and Conquer: A Theory of Intraday and Day-of-the-Week Mean Effects, Review of Financial Studies 2, 189–224.

Admati, A., and P. Pfleiderer, 1991, Sunshine Trading and Financial Market Equilibrium, Review of Financial Studies, 4(3), 443–482.

Akerlof, G., 1970, The Market for Lemons: Qualitative Uncertainty and the Market Mechanism, Quarterly Journal of Economics 89, 488–500.

Allen, B., 1982, Approximate Equilibrium in Microeconomic Rational Expectations Models, Journal of Economic Theory 26, 244–260.

Amihud, Y., and H. Mendelson, 1980, Dealership Market: Market Making with Inventory, Journal of Financial Economics 8, 31–53.

Amihud, Y., and H. Mendelson, 1987, Trading Mechanisms and Stock Returns: An Empirical Investigations, Journal of Finance 42, 533–553.

Back, K., 1990, Continuous Insider Trading and the Distribution of Asset Prices, Working Paper, Olin School of Business, Washington University.

Back, K., 1992, Insider Trading in Continuous Time, Review of Financial Studies 5, 387–410.

Back, K., 1993, Asymmetric Information and Options, Review of Financial Studies 6, 435–472,

Bagehot, W., [pseud.] 1971, The Only Game in Town, Financial Analysts Journal 27, 12–14, 22.

Bhattacharya, U., and M. Spiegel, 1991, Insiders, Outsiders, and Market Breakdowns, Review of Financial Studies 4, 255–282.

Biais, B., 1993, Price Formation and Equilibrium Liquidity in Fragmented and Centralized Markets, Journal of Finance 48, 157–184.

Biais, B., and P. Hillion, 1991, Option Prices, Insider Trading, and Dealer Competition, Working Paper, INSEAD.

Black, F., 1989, Noise, Journal of Finance 43, 540–555.

Black, F., 1991, Trading in Equilibrium with Bluffing, Credits, and Debits, Working Paper, Goldman Sachs, New York.

273

Black, F., and Scholes, M., 1973, The Pricing of Options and Corporate Liabilities, Journal of Political Economy 81, 637–654.

Blume, L.E., M.M. Bray, and D. Easley, 1982, Introduction to the Stability of Rational Expectations Equilibria, Journal of Economic Theory 26, 313–317.

Blume, L.E., and D. Easley, 1990, Implications of Walrasian Expectations Equilibria, Journal of Economic Theory 51, 207–227.

Blume, L.E., and D. Easley, 1992, Evolution and Market Behavior, Journal of Economic Theory 58, 9–40.

Blume, L.E., D. Easley, and M. O'Hara, 1994, Market Statistics and Technical Analysis: The Role of Volume, Journal of Finance, 49, 153–182.

Bradfield, J., 1979, A Formal Dynamic Model of Market Making, Journal of Financial and Quantitative Analysis 14, 275–291.

Brennan, M.J., and E.S. Schwartz, 1989, Portfolio Insurance and Financial Market Equilibrium, Journal of Business 62, 455–472.

Brown, D.P., and R.H. Jennings, 1989, On Technical Analysis, Review of Financial Studies 2, 527–552.

Burdett, K., and M. O'Hara, 1987, Building Blocks: An Introduction to Block Trading, Journal of Banking and Finance 11, 193–212.

Campbell, J., S. J. Grossman, and J. Wang, 1991, Trading Volume and Serial Correlation in Stock Returns, Working Paper, Princeton University.

Chang, E.C., and P.R. Locke, 1992, The Performance and Market Impact of Dual Trading: Re CME Rule 552, Working Paper, CFTC.

Chowdhry, B., and V. Nanda, 1991, Multi-Market Trading and Market Liquidity, Review of Financial Studies 3, 483–511

Cohen, K., S. Maier, R. Schwartz, and D. Whitcomb, 1981, Transaction Costs, Order Placement Strategy, and Existence of the Bid–Ask Spread, Journal of Political Economy 89, 287–305.

Copeland, T., and D. Galai, 1983, Information Effects and the Bid–Ask Spread, Journal of Finance 38, 1457–1469.

Dann, L.Y., D. Mayers, and R.J. Raab, 1977, Trading Rules, Large Blocks and the Speed of Price Adjustment, Journal of Financial Economics 4, 3–22.

DeLong, J.B., A. Schleifer, L.H. Summers, and R.J. Waldman, 1989, The Size and Incidence of the Losses from Noise Trading, Journal of Finance 44, 681–696.

DeLong, J.B., A. Schleifer, L.H. Summers, and R.J. Waldman, 1990, Positive Feedback Investment Strategies and Destabilizing Rational Speculation, Journal of Finance 45, 379–396.

DeLong, J.B., A. Schleifer, L.H. Summers, and R.J. Waldman, 1991, The Survival of Noise Traders in Financial Markets, Journal of Business 64, 1–20.

Demsetz, H., 1968, The Cost of Transacting, Quarterly Journal of Economics 82, 33–53.

Diamond, D.W., and R.E. Verrecchia, 1981, Information Aggregation in a Noisy Rational Expectations Economy, Journal of Financial Economics 9, 221–235.

Diamond, D.W., and R.E. Verrecchia, 1987, Constraints on Short-selling and Asset Price Adjustments to Private Information, Journal of Financial Economics 18, 277–311.

Domowitz, I., 1990, The Mechanics of Automated Trade Execution, Journal of Financial Intermediation 1, 167–194.

Easley, D., and M. O'Hara, 1987a, Price, Trade Size, and Information in Securities Markets, Journal of Financial Economics 19, 69–90.

Easley, D., and M. O'Hara, 1987b, Large Trade Volume and Market Efficiency, Working Paper, Cornell University.

Easley, D., and M. O'Hara, 1991, Order Form and Information in Securities Markets, Journal of Finance 46, 905–927.

Easley, D., and M. O'Hara, 1992a, Time and the Process of Security Price Adjustment, Journal of Finance 47, 577–606.

Easley, D., and M. O'Hara, 1992b, Adverse Selection and Large Trade Volume: The Implications for Market Efficiency, Journal of Financial and Quantitative Analysis 27, 185–208.

Easley, D., M. O'Hara, and P.S. Srinivas, 1993, Option Volume and Stock Prices: Evidence on Where Informed Traders Trade, Working Paper, Cornell University.

Fama, E., 1976, Foundations of Finance (Basic Books, New York).

Finucane and Diz, 1993, The Time–Series Properties of Implied Volatilities of S & P 100 Index Options, Journal of Futures Markets, 14.

Fishman, M., and F. Longstaff, 1992, Dual Trading in Futures Markets, Journal of Finance 47, 643–672.

Forster, M., and T. George, 1992, Anonymity in Securities Markets, Journal of Financial Intermediation 2, 168–206.

Foster, F.D., and S. Viswanathan, 1990, A Theory of the Intraday Variations in Volume, Variance and Trading Costs in Securities Markets, Review of Financial Studies 3, 593–624.

Foster, F.D., and S. Viswanathan, 1993, Variations in Trading Volume, Return Volatility, and Trading Costs: Evidence on Recent Price Formation Models, Journal of Finance 48, 187–211.

French, K.R., and R. Roll, 1986, Stock Return Variances: The Arrival of Information and the Reaction of Traders, Journal of Financial Economics 17, 5–26.

Fudenberg, D., and J. Tirole, 1991, Game Theory (MIT Press, Cambridge, Mass., and London).

Gallant, A.R., P.E. Rossi, and G.Tauchen, 1992, Stock Prices and Volume, Review of Financial Studies 5, 199–242.

Gammill, J.F., 1989, Financial Market Design when Traders Have Private Information, Working Paper, Graduate School of Business, Columbia University.

Garman, M., 1976, Market Microstructure, Journal of Financial Economics 3, 257–275.

Gemmill, G., 1993, The Price Impact of Large Trades Under Different Publication Rules: Evidence from the London Stock Exchange, Working Paper, City University Business School, London.

Gennotte, G., and H. Leland, 1990, Market Liquidity, Hedges and Crashes, American Economic Review 80, 999–1021.

Glosten, L., 1989, Insider Trading, Liquidity, and the Role of the Monopolist Specialist, Journal of Business 62, 211–236.

Glosten, L., 1991a, Asymmetric Information, The Third Market and Investor Welfare, Working Paper, Graduate School of Business, Columbia University.

Glosten, L., 1991b, The Inevitability and Resilience of an Electronic Open Limit Order Book, Working Paper, Graduate School of Business, Columbia University.

Glosten, L., and L. Harris, 1988, Estimating the Components of the Bid–Ask Spread, Journal of Financial Economics 21, 123–142.

Glosten, L., and P. Milgrom, 1985, Bid, Ask, and Transaction Prices in a Specialist Market with Heterogeneously Informed Traders, Journal of Financial Economics 13, 71–100.

Grossman, S.J., 1988, An Analysis of the Implications for Stock and Futures: Price Volatility of Program Trading and Dynamic Hedging Strategies, Journal of Business 61, 275–298.

Grossman, S.J., 1990, The Information Role of Upstairs and Downstairs Trading, Working Paper, Wharton School, University of Pennsylvania.

Grossman, S.J., and M.H. Miller, 1988, Liquidity and Market Structure, Journal of Finance 43, 617–633.

Grossman, S.J., and J.E. Stiglitz, 1980, On the Impossibility of Informationally Efficient Markets, American Economic Review 70, 393–408.

Grundy, B.D., and M. McNichols, 1989, Trade and Revelation of Information Through Prices and Direct Disclosure, Review of Financial Studies 2, 495–526.

Hakansson, N.H., 1970, Optimal Investment and Consumption Strategies Under Risk for a Class of Utility Functions, Econometrica 38, 587–607.

Harris, L., 1986, A Transaction Data Study of Weekly and Intradaily Patterns in Stock Returns, Journal of Financial Economics 16, 99–117.

Harris, L., 1990, Estimation of Stock Price Variances and Serial Covariances from Discrete Observations, Journal of Financial and Quantitative Analysis 25, 291–306.

Harris, L., 1991, Stock Price Clustering and Discreteness, Review of Financial Studies 4, 389–416.

Harris, L., and J. Hasbrouck, 1993, Market vs. Limit Orders: The SuperDOT Evidence on Order Submission Strategy, Working Paper, New York University.

Harris, M., and A. Raviv, 1993, Differences of Opinion Make a Horse Race, Review of Financial Studies 6(3), 473–506.

Hasbrouck, J., 1988, Trades, Quotes, Inventories and Information, Journal of Financial Economics 22, 229–252.

Hasbrouck, J., 1991a, Measuring the Information Content of Stock Trades, Journal of Finance 46, 179–207.

Hasbrouck, J., 1991b, The Summary Informativeness of Stock Trades, Review of Financial Studies 4, 571–594.

Hasbrouck, J., and G. Sofianos, 1993, The Trades of Market Makers: An Empirical Analysis of NYSE Specialists, Journal of Finance 48, 1565–1594.

Hausman, J.A., A.W. Lo, and A.C. MacKinley, 1992, An Ordered Probit Analysis of Transaction Stock Prices, Journal of Financial Economics 31, 319–330.

Hellwig, M.F., 1980, On the Aggregation of Information in Complete Markets, Journal of Economic Theory 26, 279–312.

Hellwig, M.F., 1982, Rational Expectations Equilibrium with Conditioning on Past Prices: A Mean Variance Example, Journal of Economic Theory 26, 279–312.

Hicks, J.R., 1939, Value and Capital (Clarendon Press, Oxford).

Hinderer, 1970, Foundations of Non–Stationary Dynamic Programming with Discrete Time Parameter, (Berlin: Springer–Verlag).

Hindy, A., 1991, An Equilibrium Model of Futures Markets Dynamics, Working Paper, Sloan School of Management, Massachusetts Institute of Technology.

Ho, T., and H. Stoll, 1981, Optimal Dealer Pricing Under Transactions and Return Uncertainty, Journal of Financial Economics 9, 47–73.

Ho, T., and H. Stoll, 1983, The Dynamics of Dealer Markets Under Competition, Journal of Finance 38, 1053–1074.

Holden, C.W., and M. Bagnoli, 1992, Toward a General Theory of Market Making, Working Paper, Indiana University.

Holden, C.W., and A. Subrahmanyam, 1992, Long-Lived Private Information and Imperfect Competition, Journal of Finance 47, 247–270.

Holthausen, R., R. Leftwich, and D. Mayers, 1987, The Effect of Large Block Transactions on Security Prices, Journal of Financial Economics 19, 237–267.

Holthausen, R., R. Leftwich, and D. Mayers, 1990, Large-Block Transactions, the Speed of Response, and Temporary and Permanent Stock-Price Effects, Journal of Financial Economics 26, 71–95.

Houthakker, H.S., 1957, Can Speculators Forecast Prices? Review of Economic Studies 39, 143–151.

Jacklin, C.J., A.W. Kleidon, and P. Pfleiderer, 1992, Underestimation of Portfolio Insurance and the Crash of October 1987, Review of Financial Studies 5, 35–63.

Jain, P.C., and G.-H. Joh, 1988, The Dependence Between Hourly Prices and Trading Volume, Journal of Financial and Quantitative Analysis 23, 269–284.

Jackson, M., 1991, Equilibrium, Price Formation, and the Value of Private Information, Review of Financial Studies 4, 1–16.

Jennings, R., and L. Starks, 1985, Information Content and the Speed of Stock Price Adjustment, Journal of Accounting Research 23, 336–350.

John, K., A. Koticha, and M. Subrahmanyam, 1991, The Micro-Structure of Options Markets: Informed Trading, Liquidity, Volatility, and Efficiency, Working Paper, New York University.

Jordan, J., 1982, The Generic Existence of Rational Expectations Equilibria in the Higher Dimensional Case, Journal of Economic Theory 26, 224–243.

Jordan, J., and R. Radner, 1982, Rational Expectations in Microeconomic Models: An Overview, Journal of Economic Theory 26, 201–223.

Karpoff, J., 1987, The Relation Between Price Change and Trading Volume: A Survey, Journal of Financial and Quantitative Analysis, 22, March, 109–126.

Karpoff, J., 1988, Costly Short Sales and the Correlations of Returns with Volume, Journal of Financial Research 11, 178–188.

Keim, D., and A. Madhavan, 1993, The Upstairs Market for Large Block Transactions: Analysis and Measurement of Price Effects, Working Paper, Wharton School, University of Pennsylvania.

Keynes, J.M., 1936, The General Theory of Employment, Interest and Money (Harcourt, Brace and Co., New York).

Kim, O., and R.E. Verrecchia, 1991, Market Reactions to Anticipated Announcements, Journal of Financial Economics 30, 273–310.

Kraus, A., and Stoll, H., 1972, Price Impacts of Block Trading on the New York Stock Exchange, Journal of Finance 27, 569–588.

Kumar, P., and D. Seppi, 1990, Information and Index Arbitrage, Working Paper, University of Pennsylvania.

Kyle, A.S., 1984, Market Structure, Information, Futures Markets, and Price Formation, in International Agricultural Trade: Advanced Readings in Price Formation, Market Structure, and Price Instability, ed. by G. Story, A. Schmitz, and A. Sarris (Westview Press, Boulder and London).

Kyle, A.S., 1985, Continuous Auctions and Insider Trading, Econometrica 53, 1315–1336.

Kyle, A.S., 1989, Informed Speculation with Imperfect Competition, Review of Economic Studies 56, 317–355.

Laux, P.A., 1993, Intraday Price Formation in the Stock Index Futures Market, Working Paper, University of Texas at Austin.

Leach, J.C., and A.N. Madhavan, 1992, Intertemporal Price Discovery by Market Makers, Journal of Financial Intermediation 2, 207–235.

Leach, J.C., and A.N. Madhavan, 1993, Price Experimentation and Security Market Structure, Review of Financial Studies 6, 375–404.

Lee, C.M.C., 1991, Purchase of Order Flows and Favorable Executions: An Intermarket Comparison, Working Paper, University of Michigan.

Lee, C.M.C., B. Mucklow, and M.J. Ready, 1993, Spreads, Depths, and the Impact of Earnings Information: An Intraday Analysis, Review of Financial Studies 6, 345–374.

Lee, C.M.C., M.J. Ready, and P.J. Sequin, 1992, Volume, Volatility and NYSE Trading Halts, Working Paper, University of Michigan.

Leroy, 1976, Efficient Capital Markets: Comment, Journal of Finance 31, 139–41.

Lindsay, R., 1990, Market Makers, Asymmetric Information and Price Formation, Working Paper, Hass School of Management, University of California at Berkeley.

Lindsay, R., and U. Schaede, 1990, Specialist vs Saitori: Market Making in New York and Tokyo, Working Paper, University of California at Berkeley.

Lo, A.W., and A.C. MacKinley, 1988, Stock Market Prices Do Not Follow Random Walks: Evidence From a Simple Specification Test, Review of Financial Studies 1, 3–40.

Lyons, R., 1992, Equilibrium Microstructure in the Foreign Exchange Market, Working Paper, University of California at Berkeley.

Lyons, R., 1993, Tests of Microstructure Hypotheses Using Foreign Exchange Markets, Working Paper, University of California at Berkeley.

Madhavan, A., 1991, Security Prices and Market Transparency, Working Paper, The Wharton School, University of Pennsylvania.

Madhavan, A., 1992, Trading Mechanisms in Securities Markets, Journal of Finance 47, 607–642.

Madhavan, A., and S. Smidt, 1991, A Bayesian Model of Intraday Specialist Pricing, Journal of Financial Economics 30, 99–134.

Madhavan, A., and S. Smidt, 1993, An Analysis of Daily Changes in Specialists' Inventories and Quotations, Journal of Finance 48, 1595–1628.

Manaster, S., and S. C. Mann, 1992, Life in the Pits: Competitive Market Making and Inventory Control, Working Paper, University of Utah.

Mas-Colell, A., 1980, Noncooperative Approaches to the Theory of Perfect Competition: Presentation, Journal of Economic Theory 22, 1–15.

McInish, T.H., and R.A. Wood, 1991, An Analysis of Intraday Patterns in Bid/Ask Spreads for NYSE Stocks, Working Paper, Memphis State University.

McInish, T.H., and R.A. Wood, 1992, Price Discovery, Volume, and Regional/Third Market Trading, Working Paper, Memphis State University.

Mendelson, H., 1982, Market Behavior in a Clearing House, Econometrica 50, 1505–1524.

Merton, R.C., 1990, Continuous-Time Finance (Basil Blackwell, Cambridge, Mass.).

Milgrom, P., and N. Stokey, 1982, Information, Trade, and Common Knowledge, Journal of Economic Theory 26, 17–27.

Mulherin, J., J. Netter, and J. Overdahl, 1990, Who Owns the Quotes? A Case Study into the Definition and Enforcement of Property Rights at the Chicago Board of Trade, Working Paper, Securities and Exchange Commission, Washington, DC.

Muth, J., 1961, Rational Expectations and the Theory of Price Movements, Econometrica 29, 315–335.

New York Stock Exchange, 1992, New York Stock Exchange Fact Book, (New York Stock Exchange, New York).

O'Callaghan, 1993, The Structure of the World Gold Market, Occasional Paper No. 105, International Monetary Fund, Washington, D.C.

O'Hara, M., and G. Oldfield, 1986, The Microeconomics of Market Making, Journal of Financial and Quantitative Analysis 21, December, 361–376.

Pagano, M., 1989a, Trading Volume and Asset Liquidity, Quarterly Journal of Economics 104, 255–274.

Pagano, M., 1989b, Endogenous Market Thinness and Stock Price Volatility, Review of Economic Studies 56, 269–288.

Pagano, M., and A. Roell, 1992, Front Running and Stock Market Liquidity, in Financial Market Liberalization and the Role of Banks, ed. by V. Conti and R. Hamui, forthcoming (Cambridge University Press, Cambridge, England).

Pagano, M., and A. Roell, 1993, Transparency and Liquidity: A Comparison of Auction and Dealer Markets with Informed Trading, Working Paper, London School of Economics.

Pfleiderer, P., 1984, The Volume of Trade and the Variability of Prices: A Framework for Analysis in Noisy Rational Expectations Equilibria, Working Paper, Stanford University.

Radner, R., 1979, Rational Expectations Equilibrium: Generic Existence and the Information Revealed by Price, Econometrica 47, 655–678.

Radner, R., 1982, Equilibrium Under Uncertainty, in the Handbook of Mathematical Economics, Vol. 2, ed. by K. Arrow and M. Intrilligator (North-Holland, Amsterdam).

Richardson and Smith, 1991, Tests of Financial Models in the Presence of Overlapping Observations, Review of Financial Studies 4, 227-254.

Roberts, H., 1967, Statistical Versus Classical Prediction of the Stock Market, Unpublished Manuscript, Center for Research in Security Prices, University of Chicago, May.

Rochet, J.C., and J.L. Vila, 1994, Insider Trading and Market Manipulations: Existence and Uniqueness of Equilibrium, Review of Economic Studies, forthcoming.

Rock, K., 1991, The Specialist's Order Book, Working Paper, Harvard Business School.

Roell, A., 1990, Dual-Capacity Trading and the Quality of the Market, Journal of Financial Intermediation 1, 105–124.

Roll, R., 1984, A Simple Implicit Measure of the Effective Bid–Ask Spread in an Efficient Market, Journal of Finance 39, 1127–1139.

Seppi, D., 1990, Equilibrium Block Trading and Asymmetric Information, Journal of Finance 45, 73–94.

Seppi, D., 1992, Block Trading and Information Revelation Around Quarterly Earning Announcements, Review of Financial Studies 5, 281–306.

Smidt, S., 1971, The Road to an Efficient Stock Market, Financial Analysts Journal 27, 18–20, 64–69.

Smith, T., and R. E. Whaley, 1991, Assessing the Cost of Regulation: The Case of Dual Trading, Working Paper, Duke University, Durham, N.C.

Spiegel, M., and A.Subrahmanyam, 1992, Informed Speculation and Hedging in a Noncompetitive Securities Market, Review of Financial Studies 5, 307–330.

Stickel, S.E., and R.E. Verrecchia, 1993, Evidence that Volume Sustains Price Changes, Working Paper, The Wharton School.

Stoll, H., 1978, The Supply of Dealer Services in Securities Markets, Journal of Finance 33, 1133–1151.

Stoll, H., 1990, Principles of Trading Market Structure, Working Paper 90-31, Owen Graduate School of Management, Vanderbilt University.

Stoll, H., and R.E. Whaley, 1990, Stock Market Structure and Volatility, Review of Financial Studies 3, 37–71.

Subrahmanyam, A., 1991a, A Theory of Trading in Stock Index Futures, Review of Financial Studies 4(1), 17–52.

Subrahmanyam, A., 1991b, Risk Aversion, Market Liquidity, and Price Efficiency, Review of Financial Studies 4(3), 417–442.

Verrecchia, R.E., 1981, On the Relationship Between Volume Reaction and Consensus of Investors: Implications for Interpreting Tests of Information Content, Journal of Accounting Research 19, 271–283.

Wang, J., 1994, A Model of Competitive Stock Trading Volume, Journal of Political Economy 102, 127–168.

Whitcomb, D., 1988, Comments on Grossman–Miller, Journal of Finance 43, 634–637.

Wilson, C.A., 1977, A Model of Insurance Markets with Incomplete Information, Journal of Economic Theory 16, 167–207.

Working, H., 1953, Futures Trading and Hedging, American Economic Review 43, 314–343.

Zabel, E., 1981, Competitive Price Adjustment Without Market Clearing, Econometrica 49, 1201–1221.

Index

THE
OPPORTUNITY

Will Volley

myriad **m** ∞

For Grandad Roy.

IT ALL COMES DOWN TO THE
LAW OF AVERAGES.

THE HARDER YOU WORK,
THE LUCKIER YOU'LL GET.